Voter Turnout

This book develops and empirically tests a social theory of political participation. It overturns prior understandings of why some people (such as college-degree holders, churchgoers, and citizens in national rather than local elections) vote more often than others. The book shows that the standard demographic variables are not proxies for variation in the individual costs and benefits of participation, but for systematic variation in the patterns of social ties between potential voters. Potential voters who move in larger social circles, particularly those including politicians and other mobilizing political actors, have more access to the flurry of electoral activity prodding citizens to vote and increasing political discussion.

Treating voting as a socially defined practice instead of as an individual choice over personal payoffs, a social theory of participation is derived from a mathematical model with behavioral foundations. The model of turnout is empirically calibrated and tested using multiple methods and data sources.

Meredith Rolfe is a Fellow in the Management Department at the London School of Economics. Prior to joining LSE, she held a Postdoctoral Prize Research Fellowship at Nuffield College, Oxford, and was a Senior Research Fellow at Saïd Business School, Oxford. Dr. Rolfe holds a PhD in Political Science from the University of Chicago, and her dissertation was awarded the Mancur Olson Dissertation Prize by the APSA Political Economy organised section. Her research has been funded by the National Science Foundation, the British Academy, Oxford's John Fell Fund, the EU-sponsored EqualSOC Framework, and the Oxford University Centre of Corporation Reputation. Her work has appeared in *Public Opinion Quarterly* and *L'Année Sociologique*, and she was an invited contributor to the *Oxford Handbook of Analytical Sociology* and the *Oxford Handbook of Corporate Reputation*.

Political Economy of Institutions and Decisions

Series Editors

Stephen Ansolabehere, Harvard University
Jeffry Frieden, Harvard University

Founding Editors

James E. Alt, Harvard University
Douglass C. North, Washington University of St. Louis

Other Books in the Series

Alberto Alesina and Howard Rosenthal, *Partisan Politics, Divided Government and the Economy*

Lee J. Alston, Thrainn Eggertsson, and Douglass C. North, eds., *Empirical Studies in Institutional Change*

Lee J. Alston and Joseph P. Ferrie, *Southern Paternalism and the Rise of the American Welfare State: Economics, Politics, and Institutions, 1865–1965*

James E. Alt and Kenneth Shepsle, eds., *Perspectives on Positive Political Economy*

Josephine T. Andrews, *When Majorities Fail: The Russian Parliament, 1990–1993*

Jeffrey S. Banks and Eric A. Hanushek, eds., *Modern Political Economy: Old Topics, New Directions*

Yoram Barzel, *Economic Analysis of Property Rights, 2nd edition*

Yoram Barzel, *A Theory of the State: Economic Rights, Legal Rights, and the Scope of the State*

Robert Bates, *Beyond the Miracle of the Market: The Political Economy of Agrarian Development in Kenya, 2nd edition*

Jenna Bednar, *The Robust Federation: Principles of Design*

Charles M. Cameron, *Veto Bargaining: Presidents and the Politics of Negative Power*

Kelly H. Chang, *Appointing Central Bankers: The Politics of Monetary Policy in the United States and the European Monetary Union*

Peter Cowhey and Mathew McCubbins, eds., *Structure and Policy in Japan and the United States: An Institutionalist Approach*

(continued after Index)

Voter Turnout

A Social Theory of Political Participation

MEREDITH ROLFE
London School of Economics

CAMBRIDGE
UNIVERSITY PRESS

CAMBRIDGE UNIVERSITY PRESS
Cambridge, New York, Melbourne, Madrid, Cape Town,
Singapore, São Paulo, Delhi, Mexico City

Cambridge University Press
32 Avenue of the Americas, New York, NY 10013-2473, USA

www.cambridge.org
Information on this title: www.cambridge.org/9781107015418

First published 2012

Printed in the United States of America

A catalog record for this publication is available from the British Library.

Library of Congress Cataloging in Publication data
Rolfe, Meredith, 1971–
    Voter turnout : a social theory of political participation / Meredith Rolfe.
        p.   cm.
    Includes bibliographical references and index.
    ISBN 978-1-107-01541-8 (hardback)
    1. Voting – Social aspects.   2. Political participation – Social aspects.
    3. Voting – Social aspects – United States.   4. Political participation – Social
    aspects – United States.   I. Title.
    JF1001.R55   2012
    324.601–dc23   2011025902

ISBN 978-1-107-01541-8 Hardback

This book is dedicated to my grandfather, Curry, and to the memory of my grandparents, Audrey, Lalla, and Shelley. All four were (and are) politically active citizens who brought out the best in those around them, although only one had a college degree.

Why talk about social decision-making? Isn't it enough to talk about individual decision-making? Why do we need social decision making at all? Today there is abroad the land the libertarian delusion that individuals are some sort of Leibnizian monads ... each with a consistent independent utility function and each interacting with its fellows only through its knowledge of market prices. Not so. We are not monads because, among many other reasons, our values, the alternatives of action that we are aware of, our understanding of what consequences may flow from our actions – all this knowledge, all these preferences – derive from our interaction with our social environment. Some of our values and knowledge were sucked in with our mother's milk; others were taken, often quite uncritically, from our social environment. Still others, perhaps were acquired by reacting against that environment, but few indeed, surely, in complete independence of it.

– Herbert Simon, 1983 Reason

Contents

List of Figures   *page* xi

List of Tables   xii

Preface   xiii

1. Voting Together   1
   The social theory of voter turnout   3
   Conditional choice and conditional decision making   4
   The orthodox view: Voters making decisions   7
   Contextual explanations of voter turnout   10
   Overview of remaining chapters   18

2. Conditional Choice   21
   The evidence for conditional decision making   22
   Mathematical models of conditional decision making   28
   Engineering a model and mid-level theory   39

3. The Social Meaning of Voting   42
   Social meaning: People and relationships   43
   Data and methods   46
   Voting is the act of an American citizen   48
   Voters as Americans: Is there a consensus?   51
   American citizens: Formal equality, informal ambiguity   56
   Concluding thoughts   62

4. Conditional Cooperation   64
   Experimental decision situations similar to voting   64
   Distribution of decision rules   69

5. Conditional Voters: Dynamics and Networks   78
    Conditional cooperation: The basic dynamic   79
    Conditional cooperation in local social networks   84
    Conclusion   96

6. The Social Theory of Turnout   98
    *Strategic politicians and conditional decision
        makers: A theoretical synthesis*   99
    Cross-national variation: First movers and costs   101
    *Variation across elections: Campaign activity
        and political discussion*   106
    Individual variation in turnout   113

7. Education and High-Salience Elections   125
    Social theory: Implications of the model   126
    A new look at education   129
    Comparing social cooperation and civic voluntarism   141
    Discussion   148

8. Mobilization in Low-Salience Elections   151
    Turnout patterns in low-salience elections   152
    Data   156
    Candidates, campaigning, and social ties   162
    Mobilization and turnout at the precinct level   169

9. Paradox Lost   178
    *Conditional choice and the conditional
        decision-making model*   179
    *Empirical support for a new view of education
        and income*   182
    Making sense of existing research   183
    Further implications   185

*Appendix A   Simulations of the Conditional
    Cooperation Model*   191
    Validating the programmed model   193
    Model extensions: Network construction   194

*Appendix B   Methodological Notes on the
    General Social Survey*   197

References   201

Index   223

Figures

2.1. Three basic conditional decision rules   *page* 32
2.2. Example of weighted turnout decision rule   35
5.1. Expected turnout (cooperation) rate or adoption curve   80
5.2. Distribution of final-round turnout for each parameter
     combination   82
5.3. Average simulated turnout when voters have global
     networks   83
5.4. Effects of network size and density on simulated
     cooperation (turnout) rate   93
6.1. Average turnout when first movers are 12.5%
     of the population   103
6.2. Average turnout when first movers are 15%
     of the population   104
6.3. Histogram of voter turnout rates (national elections,
     1980–2000)   104
6.4. Turnout in lower-salience local and national American
     elections   111
6.5. Average turnout when first movers are 10% of the
     population   112
6.6. Frequency of political discussion by individual education   117
6.7. Personal network size and social network context   123
7.1. Educational diversity of discussion networks   133
7.2. Size and density of discussion networks in two social worlds   135
7.3. Voter turnout in two social worlds   143
8.1. County map with race and institutions highlighted   167
8.2. County map with education and income   173
8.3. Map of district with additional high-profile campaign   174
8.4. Map of turnout by precinct in 2004 primary election   175

Tables

2.1. Formal Mechanisms and Empirical Variables   *page* 40
3.1. Importance of Civic Obligations   51
3.2. Respondents Agreeing That Voting Is Not Necessary   54
4.1. Estimated Use of Basic Decision Rules   71
5.1. Estimates of Personal Network Size and Density   89
7.1. Average Turnout Rate in Simulations, by Network Size   128
7.2. Ties to a College-Educated Alter, by Individual Education   132
7.3. Political Discussion, by Individual Education and
Social World   142
7.4. Estimated Effects of Education and Social Network
Context on Voter Turnout   145
8.1. Predictions of the Social and Resource Theories
of Voter Turnout in Low-Salience Elections   153
8.2. Precinct-Level Turnout in the 2004 Primary   170
8.3. Predicting Turnout Rates at the Precinct Level   176
A.1. Simulation Parameters   192
A.2. Median Degree (and Density) of Simulated Networks   196

Preface

Although this book is a study of traditional political participation, it has intellectual roots in the study of collective action and social movements. As an undergraduate at Duke University, I delved deeply into the topic of collective action, with Ed Tiryakian and Tom Janoski serving as teachers and advisors. By the end of my time at Duke, I viewed the interaction between heterogeneous individual motives and social network structure as crucial to understanding social movements.

Early in my graduate career at the University of Chicago, I approached Jim Fearon to discuss whether it would be possible to write a dissertation expanding on these themes. He suggested I study voter turnout, a path that would allow me to explore the impact of heterogeneity and networks within political science. This book is based on the dissertation that resulted from that conversation.

This book owes much to the intellectual freedom cultivated at Chicago and to the strong support that was provided (and is still being provided) by my committee members and other current and former Chicago faculty. Mark Hansen's comments consistently inspired major improvements in the work, and our discussions pushed me to integrate politics and political mobilization into a theory grounded in social interaction. John Brehm served as both an intellectual and personal inspiration through the tough times of writing a dissertation and provided invaluable assistance when I had to grapple with the sticky issues involved with survey self-selection.

John Padgett introduced me to the technical study of networks, and I am still thankful for his insistence that I adopt a careful and mathematically rigorous approach to agent-based models. Jonathan Katz helped me get the project off the ground and ensured that I was able to pass on to candidacy only weeks before the birth of my first child. Jeff Grynaviski stepped in toward the end of the process, challenging me with comments that were always on my mind as I undertook the revisions required to turn a dissertation into a book. Long conversations with Michael Dawson and Lisa Weeden about the role of social meaning in decision making directly inspired the research behind Chapter 3 and helped me to fill a gaping logical hole in my original dissertation. I would also like to acknowledge my former MA advisor, the late Roger Gould, whose ideas are part of the intellectual basis for this work and whose presence is sorely missed.

Discussions with Mike Neblo pushed my thinking on social norms, while Anne Shiu spent hours discussing mathematics and probability. Matt Kocher read several chapters at various stages and always remained positive about the project while pushing me to deal with some of the vexing philosophical issues. Jason Plaks gave detailed comments from a social psychology perspective on an early draft of Chapter 2, although I doubt that the rewritten version has done his insights justice. Members of the American Politics and Political Economy Workshops at Chicago commented on multiple versions of this work in its early stages. Excerpts were also presented at the University of Pennsylvania Ashe Center, University of Manchester Sociology Seminar, Oxford University's Cabdyn group, Nuffield College Sociology and Social Networks Seminars, the annual Argonne-sponsored Agents conference, and the annual MPSA meeting.

The manuscript was largely completed while I was at Nuffield College, and I was lucky to have had personal and intellectual support from Peter Hedström, Diego Gambetta, Yvonne Åberg, and Des King as my family and I settled into a new country. Ray Duch and David Barron were (and are) supportive senior colleagues who added greatly to my time at Oxford. Adrienne LeBas' red pen left its stain on several chapters, but it is fair to say that she is a fantastic writing coach and a better friend. Elisabeth Ivarsflaten discussed various aspects of the work in depth and was a gracious host when I needed time away from home to focus on the manuscript. I was lucky to meet fellow intellectual traveller Quentin van Doosselaere, who also generously provided me with a space to work away from the chaos. My former student and ongoing collaborator Jason Bello read the entire manuscript closely, provided detailed and useful comments, and helped me maintain an interest in the topic long after I was ready to abandon it. Linn Normand provided able assistance in preparing the analysis for Chapter 3.

The models in the book were made possible by the terrific RePast team. Nick Collier spent hours coaching me up the steep Java and RePast learning curves, while Skye Bendor de Moll kindly designed a network creation package to my specification.

Last but not least, no mother of two can finish a PhD or a book without seemingly endless support from family, both literal and figurative. There are no words to convey my appreciation to Scott Blinder, as he knows, although more than a few of the words in this book are his. Both sets of grandparents, Vickie and Chris Rolfe and Madeline and Alan Blinder, were always ready and willing to help at a moment's notice. My mother took on the difficult task of proofreading early versions of chapters and was always available when I needed someone to listen. My mother-in-law made sure I had a quiet, well-provisioned place to write at several crucial junctures and has been a dedicated promoter of this project. This book grew up along with my children, and I was blessed with exceptional au-pairs, childcare providers and housekeepers throughout: Eva, Eric, Anousha, Gokçe, Devrim, Olga, Emilie, Gabor, Edja, Fabricio, and Leila. Malcolm and Levi Blinder may have slowed the whole process down, but they kept me going with their jokes and smiles as they got older. See Levi, there is a real book on the shelf now!

A very special thanks to series editor Steve Ansolabehere, and to Lew Bateman and Anne Lovering Rounds of Cambridge University Press for making the final steps of the process as painless as possible.

This material is based in part on work supported by the National Science Foundation under Dissertation Improvement Grant No. SBR-0453076. All faults and omissions remain my own.

I

Voting Together

If you were to ask most American citizens why they voted (or did not vote) in the last election, their explanations of their own choices would almost certainly take the form of a few familiar stories. One voter might speak of his deep and abiding interest in politics; another might speak passionately about her desire to see the right person win. A third might have little interest in the election yet still feel the pull of patriotism or civic duty, and yet another might worry that his family or coworkers would think less of him if he failed to make it to the polls. The stories of nonvoters would be similarly familiar stories. One would likely bemoan the fact that deadlines at work or long lines at the polling station had kept her from participating, another would rattle off a list of objectionable actions taken by politicians, and yet another might wistfully reply that people like him did not really matter anyway.

Surprisingly, such stories, writ large, form the basis of most scholarly explanations of variation in voter turnout. Voters, compared with nonvoters, are more likely to find politics interesting and less likely to find participation prohibitively costly. Strong partisans who care about election outcomes are more likely to vote than weak partisans or independents who care less about the results. Voters are more likely than nonvoters to have the education and skills needed to register and figure out how to get to the polls and cast a ballot. Finally, citizens are more likely to vote if their family, friends, and housemates are voting as well. Traditional theoretical explanations are cast in terms of individual desires, motives, beliefs, and utilities: People who want to vote and are able to vote are more likely to vote, whereas those lacking the desire or the ability will abstain.

This book argues that such explanations are at best partial and at worst biased explanations of variation in political participation because they fail to account for the impact of social context. Individual reasoning does not take place within a social vacuum, but depends in various ways on the actions and opinions of other people. When individual decisions are (even in part) conditional or interdependent, the structure of social ties has the power to shape social outcomes to a much larger degree than previously recognized. Therefore, to avoid bias, explanations of variation in political participation and other social phenomena must go beyond stories about isolated individuals to incorporate the potential impact of social interaction on social outcomes.

This is not an idle concern for researchers and policy makers, as the omission of social structure and social interaction limits our ability to understand the fundamental mechanisms through which the demographic correlates of American voter turnout drive participation. Over the years, political scientists have documented almost no change in the empirical predictors of turnout. Immigrants, minorities, young people, the uneducated, the poor, and the politically disinterested are systematically less likely to vote than those with higher social status (i.e., wealthy, white, and highly educated citizens), much as Merriam and Gosnell (1924) established close to a century ago. (Churchgoers and members of voluntary organizations have since been added to the list of turnout predictors.) Education, the most powerful predictor of turnout, is often described as enhancing benefits or reducing costs (see, e.g., Verba, Schlozman, and Brady 1995). However, recent work still acknowledges that the mechanism connecting education to voting is mysterious (Sondheimer and Green 2010), and some scholars even question whether education has a causal effect on turnout at all (Tenn 2007; see also Nie, Junn, and Stehlik-Barry 1996). The social theory of turnout offered in this book, on the other hand, argues that education is merely a proxy for belonging to a social world whose members have systematically different patterns of social relationships.

As a result of incomplete understandings of the causes of turnout, policies designed to increase participation have often failed to achieve their aims. Many recent voting reforms, including absentee voting and Motor Voter legislation, were explicitly designed to lower the costs of participating. Schemes that actively encourage voting at home by mail or the Internet have proven ineffective or even reduced turnout (Berinsky 2005), at least after the relaxation of efforts put into marketing such alternative modes of participation. Reducing registration requirements should raise turnout in the long run, although the impact may take some time to show up. Such cost-reduction policies may backfire, however, if the symbolic virtue of voting is reinforced by the requirement that one stand in lines and follow arcane procedures, or if citizens are less likely to behave in a public-spirited way if their neighbors are not at the polls to greet (and observe) them.

This book takes a fresh perspective on this long-standing area of research, one that explicitly accounts for how social and political context drives political participation, and provides new insight into the empirical correlates of voter turnout. The fundamental approach ties together existing strands drawn from scholarship on voting and other social phenomena. The ability of social interaction to alter social outcomes will not come as a surprise to game theorists, who have long been aware that most people condition their behavior on the expected choices of those around them. Behavioral economics, inspired by the groundbreaking work of Simon on bounded rationality and Kahneman and Tversky on heuristics, provides a firm foundation for the book's core conditional decision-making model. Key links in the social theory are pulled from long-standing research into the impact of social and political context on mass political behavior. None of these threads contain a full-fledged account of individual decision making and social dynamics akin to conditional choice, but they contain important elements that remain present in the social theory of turnout.

THE SOCIAL THEORY OF VOTER TURNOUT

So why do some people turn out to vote whereas others do not? This book proposes and argues for a social theory of voter turnout, grounded in the conditional choice approach. This theory places voters not only in a social context, but also assumes a less familiar logic of decision making. Conditional decision makers rely on conditional decision rules, sometimes termed heuristics or cognitive shortcuts, rather than optimizing payoffs in a forward-looking manner. Thus, it is possible to build a behavioral model of turnout based on a distribution of decision rules in situations like voting without solving the paradox of voter turnout. The social theory of participation may not speak to individual motives and reasoning, but it can provide a satisfying explanation of documented empirical variation in voter turnout, one in which variation in social network structures and citizens' social locations underlie the well-known demographic patterns.

Boiled down to its essence, my argument is that the turnout decision is best represented as a conditionally cooperative response to cooperative decisions made by friends, family, neighbors, and coworkers – members of the social network of the citizen in question. Sometimes a handful of people are willing to cooperate unconditionally, whereas some people will not cooperate under any circumstances. The bulk of the population is willing to cooperate if enough other people will do the same. Having more family members and friends who vote makes one more likely to vote as well.

But what of the long-standing empirical correlates of turnout? In the social theory of turnout, these individual-level correlates of voter turnout are reinterpreted as imperfect proxies for social structural variables: variation first in the size and structure of the social networks in which individuals are embedded, and, second, in individuals' social location within a given social network structure. These social structural properties have a primary and direct impact on whether a given individual is likely to vote or to abstain.

The general view of turnout as generated by political and social contexts has several important predecessors in scholarship on voting and other forms of mass political behavior.

CONDITIONAL CHOICE AND CONDITIONAL DECISION MAKING

This book provides a formal model of the decision to vote, but it is a model built within the theoretical framework of conditional choice (see Rolfe 2009). Put simply, conditional choice posits that individual choices are a function of the subjective social meaning of the situation and of the observed and/or expected choices of other people. The conditional choice view is compatible with an assumption of bounded rationality (Simon 1955). It is perhaps more persuasive, however, to simply note that most people make decisions that are responsive to the decisions of those around them, at least to some degree.

Thus, conditional choice is driven by the reality of observed individual decision making rather than a commitment to a set of assumptions about individual goals and desires. Few people make decisions like clear-headed, forward-looking, goal-directed economists (even if we often wish that we could). Real people continue to vote even when they are not fully informed about the candidates; they will lend their neighbors a cup of sugar, but will also mow the lawn before 8 A.M. on weekends; contribute to charities devoted to world peace, but also yell at their kids; and iron their shirt each morning for work, but forget to brush dog hair off their jacket. In other words, most people continue to act in ways that are entirely unpredictable if we assume that their behavior is the result a decision-making process that involves the rational, consistent pursuit of personal goals or that can be described by a consistent set of individual traits such as selfishness, altruism, aggression, kindness, laziness, or conscientiousness.

How can we understand individual action if individuals do not act consistently on the basis of economic rationality, or even predictably on the basis of personal motives, traits, or characteristics (Mischel 1968)? The answer is to direct attention away from individual decision makers to the social situations in which they find themselves, and to the social interactions that take place between them. Nothing of interest to social scientists takes place in a hypothetical social vacuum.[1] All individual action takes place within social situations, and individual action is only intelligible within the social context that gives rise to. it. Conditional choice puts social cognition and social interaction – not individual preferences – at the center of individual decision making.

How then do individuals make decisions if they are navigating social interactions rather than maximizing payoff functions or minimizing the risk of low payoffs? Conditional actors rely on conditional decision rules, sometimes termed heuristics (Kahneman 2002) or rules of thumb (Simon 1955).[2] People may purposefully condition their actions on those of others, as in a conscious desire to "do one's fair share." Alternatively, conditional responses may be automatic and unthinking, operating outside of the awareness of the individual decision maker.

Conditional responsiveness can vary from person to person. Some people can be largely or even entirely unresponsive to others ("unconditional" actors, whose behavior is a constant when expressed as a mathematical function of others' decisions). Most people, however, will respond at least somewhat to the actions of others. To account for social interaction, conditional decision rules are mathematically modeled as a function of (1) the social meaning of the decision situation, (2) the observed or expected actions of other people, and (3) individual heterogeneity. The

[1] Not even laboratory experiments take place in a social vacuum. Subjects enter the lab with a wealth of social knowledge that allows them to interpret all requests and respond accordingly, and leave the lab with that knowledge intact or perhaps even altered by the interactions in the experimental setting.
[2] Social interaction is not addressed by the decision rules proposed by the Kahneman and Tvesrsky project.

social dynamics of individual decision making in a particular social situation are modeled as a distribution of conditional decision rules – the basis of all conditional choice models. Evidence on the distribution of conditional cooperation comes from behavioral economics, a subfield within economics, which has documented that (seemingly) nonrational "anomalies" in individual decision making are the rule rather than the exception.[3]

Considerable empirical evidence supports the conditional interdependence of decision making. Conditional decisions are often consciously made in situations involving public goods or social dilemmas, when individual material benefits come into conflict with what is best for the group. (Voting may be such a social dilemma, or perceived as such by voters – this claim will be discussed in Chapter 3 in the analysis of the social meaning of voting). Conditional decision makers do not seek to maximize their own immediate benefit; rather, they behave in ways that involve cooperation with others but not complete capitulation to them. Cooperative acts, or contributions to the group, are conditional on the cooperation or contributions of others.

The conditional choice approach is neutral on the rationality of decision making, and indeed is silent on the matter of people's ends or goals; whether or not these ends conform to any external standard is beside the point, for the purposes of this book. What is essential is that people actually do make decisions that reflect social interaction with other people. Thus, a conditional decision model is strictly a mathematical representation of decision outcomes as conditional on the decisions of others, regardless of the rationale, motivation, or mental process of the decision maker (López-Pintado and Watts 2008; Young 2009). It may well be that the conditional cooperator believes his or her actions to be motivated by a desire to please, or to avoid social disapproval, or to gain the trust of a friend, or even to efficiently gather information in an uncertain world, but such possible motivations are all reducible to a conditional mathematical function. Regardless of the motivational story that might be told, the widespread use of conditional decision making has been demonstrated many times in both the real world and in researchers' artificially constructed lab situations and social dilemmas.

---

[3] Experimental outcomes may seem less anomalous after accounting for what Podolny (2001) terms the prismatic aspect of social networks: how social interaction, in particular asymmetries in power and influence in social relationships, shape individual decision making.

With conditional choice as a foundation, the social theory of turnout will remain silent on the immediate, conscious reasons people invoke to explain why they get out of bed on Election Day and plan a trip to the polls. A motivational story is probably a common expectation for a theory purporting to explain why people vote, but my focus is not on the inner mental states associated with voting, but rather on the mechanisms linking political mobilization and social structure to observed variation in turnout rates. I will not attempt to document "social pressure" to vote, or any other such carrier of interpersonal influence. In fact, I would expect that most conditional voters do not experience their decision as one motivated by social pressure, nor are they aware that their decision has been influenced by the choices of those around them. Rather, the level of explanation here focuses on the relationship between social structure and turnout rates.

Perhaps this will be a sufficient introduction to the perspective of this book; satisfied readers may wish to move on to the development of conditional choice in Chapter 2, or even to the second half of the book, in which conditional choice is translated into specific predictions about voter turnout that are then tested empirically against the predictions of the extant view. For others, the remainder of this chapter presents competing views on voter turnout in more detail.

THE ORTHODOX VIEW: VOTERS MAKING DECISIONS

As citizens in a democracy, Americans are by definition entitled to a voice in the affairs of their country, most commonly in the form of voting in elections. Indeed, Americans are called to the ballot box more often than citizens of most, if not all, other democratic nations, casting ballots in Presidential elections, midterm Congressional races, assorted state and local elections, referenda and initiatives, as well as primaries for the same. The right to vote is regarded with reverence in American civic culture. The extension of voting rights to women and African Americans constituted a crucial goal for two of the largest, most significant social movements of twentieth-century America. Why then do half or more of all eligible citizens fail to cast a ballot in most elections? This question inspired some of the most innovative and enduring political science research of the early twentieth century (cf. Merriam and Gosnell 1924; Gosnell 1927), with a book title summing up the basic research question: *Non-Voting*. Voting was seen as normatively desirable; nonvoters were described in undesirable and unfavorable terms. (As we will see in Chapter 3, nonvoting is still given quite harsh treatment in the contemporary media.) The question at the time was: Why would anyone not do the right thing?

Downs (1957) turned the conventional wisdom on its head, proposing that the turnout decision should be modeled as an economic decision, with individuals weighing the costs and benefits of voting before deciding whether to vote or abstain. In this view, an individual voter's decision would consider the relative benefits of having one party (versus the other) in office (B), multiplied by the probability of casting the deciding vote (p), and subtracting out the costs of voting (C) for the basic economic voting model:

$$pB - C.$$

Unfortunately, the probability of casting the deciding vote is quite small, and therefore abstention is always the choice of utility-maximizing citizens. Clearly, most citizens do not always abstain from voting, and thus the divergence between actual behavior and the predictions of the cost-benefit model became known as the paradox of voter turnout, sometimes jokingly described as "the paradox that ate rational choice."

Subsequent formal models have offered a number of solutions to the paradox. The most common solution, typically linked to Riker and Ordeshook (1968), involves including a D-term in the economic voting model:

$$pB - C + D.$$

The additional mathematical term (D) can be used to signify any additional benefits that an individual receives from the act of voting. These benefits might be linked to an internalized sense of civic duty (Riker and Ordeshook 1968), the expressive thrills of participation (Schuessler 2000), a sociotropic desire to support democracy or fellow partisans (Edlin, Gelman, and Kaplan 2007), and so on. Regardless of the motivational story, inclusion of a D-term reduces electoral participation to an unexplained taste, akin to a taste for chocolate (Tullock 1967; Morton 1991; Green and Shapiro 1994). If someone eats chocolate, we infer that they like it; if someone votes, we infer that they like it, intrinsically. Such modifications essentially reduce the economic voting model to a tautology that cannot be disproven: Voting is rational for people who vote and not rational for those who do not vote (Green and Shapiro 1994).

Most other formal attempts to solve the paradox of voter turnout also have been heavily criticized, either because they also produced high levels of abstention or relied on unrealistic assumptions. Early partisan team models that increased the probability of casting decisive votes (Palfrey and Rosenthal 1985) produced knife-edge results: models that could not sustain high turnout following minor changes of assumptions (Morton 1991). Minimax regret decision making (Ferejohn and Fiorina 1974) turns out to sound much less plausible when extended just slightly beyond the narrow decision of whether to vote or not once at the polling station. For example, scholars have argued that a potential voter using the minimax rule would not vote to avoid getting hit by a car en route to the polling place, or would only vote for themselves (Beck 1975; Stephens 1975; Tullock 1975; Aldrich 1993). Partisan mobilization models (Uhlaner 1989; Morton 1991; Bendor et al. 2003) fail to make sense of turnout among the huge number of independent and undecided voters in the American electorate, and suffer from second-order collective action problems (Olson 1965; Oliver 1980) as well as a lack of evidence (Green and Shapiro 1994). Thus, it remains difficult to adequately model voter turnout starting with a Downsian logic of costs and benefits.

The Rational Actor Takes a Survey

Despite these debates within the formal literature on voter turnout, the basic paradigm of individual costs and benefits was quickly adopted to explain established patterns in the demographic correlates of participation. A significant tradition of survey research into the causes of (non) voting was already well established (e.g., Merriam and Gosnell 1924; Lazarsfeld, Berelson, and Gaudet 1944; Campbell 1954), and was rapidly expanding with the creation of the American National Election Study (see Campbell, Converse, Stokes, and Miller 1960). Multiple attempts were made to incorporate a rational calculus of voting directly into the existing survey research literature, rather than relying on a reinterpretation of demographic variables, but these attempts did not meet with great success.

First, measurement of the three important elements of the utility model (costs, perceived difference between the candidates or benefits, and possible influence over the election outcome) proved difficult. Direct measures – for example, asking survey respondents how likely they were to cast the decisive vote – were usually found to be unrelated to individual-level

turnout (Ferejohn and Fiorina 1975). Although individual-level measure
of civic duty, the *D*-term, was found to be associated with higher turnout
(Campbell et al. 1960), this correlation stemmed from different patterns
of survey responses among African Americans, and therefore faded after
the passage of the 1965 Voting Rights Act (see Chapter 3).

Instead of rejecting the cost-benefit logic as a plausible individual
mechanism, however, the literature adapted the interpretations of previously established correlates of turnout to fit better with the compelling
new logic. Various measures of political interest, already linked to turnout by Lazarsfeld et al. (1944), were recast as measuring the benefit term
in the Downsian calculus of voting (Katosh and Traugott 1982). Sanders
(1980) argued that rural location depressed turnout because rural residents had to travel longer to get to polling places, thus increasing the
costs of turnout. Income and education, long known to predict turnout,
were linked to the calculus of voting through multiple pathways: impact-
ing the costs of turnout, the benefits of electoral outcomes, and the ability
to more cheaply acquire information needed to distinguish between the
candidates (cf. Frey 1971; Tollison and Willett 1973; Niemi 1976).

Indeed, the most prominent school of thought within survey-based
research on voter turnout is still built on the cost-benefit logic, imagining
that individual voters' chances of voting increase or decrease in response
to the personal costs and benefits of turnout, even though the cost-benefit
logic has such difficulty making sense of anyone voting at all. Earlier
mentions of nonrational considerations, including group consciousness
(Verba and Nie 1972) and socialization and social identity (Campbell,
Converse, Stokes, and Miller 1960), have been dropped from more recent
work in the same tradition (Verba, Schlozman, and Brady 1995). The
variables originally identified by Merriam and Gosnell are still the primary predictors of individual turnout, with a few additions. What has
changed is that demographic characteristics are now described as proxies
for civic resources (costs) and political interest (benefits).

CONTEXTUAL EXPLANATIONS OF VOTER TURNOUT

The social theory of voter turnout involves a different sort of explanation. Rather than asking what it is about individual voters that makes
them more or less likely to vote, the social view emphasizes the explanatory power of voters' social and political contexts. As noted earlier, this
book is not alone in emphasizing contextual rather than individual determinants of turnout. But, whereas the social theory belongs to the same

general family of explanation as these alternatives – and draws directly on some of them – this book explicitly pushes the limits of formal, contextual explanation further than previous research. The sections that follow review these various strands of research on turnout in more detail, and point out where the social theory picks up on their insights and where it departs from them.

Institutions

Beginning with the contextual factors least integral to the social theory of turnout, it is nonetheless important to acknowledge several institutional features that vary across elections and have been associated with variation in aggregate turnout rates. These include (1) institutionally imposed barriers to voter turnout, such as registration requirements, and 2) electoral systems (i.e., proportional representation or first-past-the-post, unicameralism or bicameralism, other features of polities that affect how votes are translated into representation). We might also regard closeness of elections as something that might vary with electoral institutions (Cox 1999), although more commonly it is seen as varying from election to election as candidates and circumstances change. Empirical research on each of these factors has shown a relationship to turnout rates, often conceptualized in cost-benefit terms.

Institutional Costs

A wealth of evidence confirms that turnout rates vary at the aggregate level across institutional settings. In American elections, turnout is higher in states that allow absentee registration, have no closing date for registration, and have registration offices regularly open during normal office hours and/or during the evenings and weekends (Wolfinger and Rosenstone 1980; Rosenstone and Hansen 1993). Prior to the passage of the Voting Rights Act, poll taxes, literacy tests, and periodic re-registration requirements were all effectively used to depress turnout among Blacks in the South (Key 1949; Kelley, Ayres and Bowen 1967). A significant degree of cross-national variation in voter turnout is also associated with institutional costs. Turnout is higher in countries where voters are automatically registered, voting is compulsory, or election day is a weekend or holiday (Powell 1986; Jackman 1987; Lijphart 1997; Franklin 2004).

All of the institutional features described earlier have been theoretically linked to individual turnout costs in the Downsian calculus of voting, with the removal of registration barriers or the introduction of

compulsory voting assumed to directly decrease the net costs of participation for an individual. Additionally, many of the studies have incorporated data from extremely large sample surveys, such as the Current
Population Study series run by the U.S. Census Bureau, with a sample size
of approximately 60,000. However, repeated attempts to show the impact
of institutional costs on a more traditional election study with a smaller
sample were largely unsuccessful (Campbell et al. 1960; Ashenfelter and
Kelley 1975; Katosh and Traugott 1982). Therefore, although it is clear
from the evidence that institutional "costs" can and do shift aggregate
turnout at the margins, the impact of such costs has only been reliably
established at the contextual – not individual – level.[4] As Blais (2006)
points out, political science still lacks "a compelling microfoundation"
for most cross-national findings on voter turnout.

   This pattern – a finding that institutional costs are related to marginal
shifts in aggregate level behavior turnout but have almost no perceptible
impact on individual-level behavior – fits nicely within the conditional-
choice approach. Conditional decision-making models have already been
shown to better fit empirical patterns of decision making in quite significant and costly decisions: the shift in patterns of retirement following
a change in the legal age of retirement (Axtell and Epstein 1999), and
adoption of a new form of hybrid corn among farmers (Young 2009).
I adopt a similar approach, arguing that institutionally imposed costs
of decision making are better understood as shifting the distribution of
decision rules (in particular the proportion of first movers), rather than as
having a direct and consistent impact at the individual level.

Electoral Institutions

Evidence on whether other aspects of the institutional context, particularly the electoral system, affect voting turnout is inconsistent. Turnout is
generally higher in countries with proportional representation (PR) voting systems (Powell 1986, Jackman 1987, Franklin 2004), as PR systems
are associated with competitive national election districts (Powell 1986,
Jackman 1987). Subsequent studies outside of Europe have largely failed
to replicate the finding that PR systems encourage turnout (Blais 2006,
for a review), however, and turnout can be depressed where PR voting

---

[4] Although no individual mechanism reliably links institutional costs to aggregate turnout,
   it is worth noting the low rate of agreement with the characterization of voting as a civic
   duty among African Americans prior to the passage of the Voting Rights Act, followed by
   an abrupt increase (up to the levels of white American respondents) afterward.

sustains large numbers of parties (Jackman 1987). Similarly, the division of power between various branches of the legislature may impact turnout (Jackman 1987), although once again subsequent findings on this institutional feature are mixed (Blais 2006). Party mobilization is most often mentioned as the individual-level mechanism through which electoral institutions affect turnout, an issue to which we will return shortly.

The probability of being decisive in an election, p in the calculus of voting, was recognized as important in early empirical work (Gosnell 1930; Key 1949) and was later explicitly linked to aggregate turnout variation (Barzel and Silberberg 1973; Settle and Abrams 1976). However, other scholars who found a relationship between closer elections (measured as the margin of victory for the winning candidate) and increased turnout continued to describe the margin of victory as a contextual, not individual, variable (Patterson and Caldeira 1983). As further confirmation of the contextual impact of electoral competition, Ashenfelter and Kelley (1975) found that subjective estimates of the closeness of the presidential race did not have a significant impact on individual turnout in the 1960 and 1972 U.S. presidential elections. However, it appeared that the perceived closeness of the race explained almost all of the marginal shift in aggregate turnout levels between the two elections, with 60% of 1972 respondents, but only 10% of 1960 respondents, stating that they believed the election outcome would not be close.

Mobilization and Strategic Politicians

The empirical evidence on whether institutions consistently affect voter turnout may be mixed, but one message from the previous section is clear: When institutions impact political participation, they do so only at the contextual (or aggregate) level. Even though some of the empirical results may be consistent with the individual calculus of voting, there is no empirical support for the calculus of voting acting as the mechanism through which institutional and electoral context might (with the sole exception of institutional costs) affect voter turnout.

Mobilization by strategic politicians (Morton 1991 Aldrich 1993; Rosenstone and Hansen 1993; Cox 1999) is the leading candidate to fill this void. Strategic politicians (and their supporters) have a strong incentive to invest in elections that they have a chance to win, and therefore strategically invest both time and energy into mobilizing voters in close races. Available evidence confirms that campaign expenditures do affect turnout (Patterson and Caldeira 1983), and reduces the impact of margin of victory to insignificance in properly specified models (Cox and Munger 1989). Political actors invest more in mobilization when elections are expected to be close (Rosenstone and Hansen 1993; Aldrich 1993). The rise in candidate-centered elections decreased the incentives for parties to invest in mobilization, leading to a subsequent decline in turnout in the United States (Rosenstone and Hansen 1993).

Cox (1997; 1999) extends the strategic politician's perspective to the puzzling impact of electoral institutions in a sophisticated formal theory linking voters, political parties, and electoral institutions. Cox argues that electoral rules affect voter turnout only indirectly, via the likely margin of victory and resulting mobilization efforts of strategic political elites. Political parties with an explicit goal of winning elections (and staying in power) put more or less effort into mobilizing voters depending on how various aspects of the electoral system translate "effort-to-votes, votes-to-seats, and seats-to-portfolios" (Cox 1999).

Although the strategic mobilization perspective makes sense of an impressive range of contextual-level political participation research, it does not focus on decisions of individual voters and thus does not speak directly to the individual-level survey research on turnout discussed earlier. The conventional wisdom holds that mobilization works by subsidizing the costs of participation (e.g., a bus to drive voters to the polls) or by offering additional incentives to vote (e.g., social events for union members), but strategic candidates invest far more money in various forms of advertising than they do in hiring buses to drive local residents to the polls. Moreover, empirical support for the direct impact of mobilization on turnout is based largely on personal contact by political elites and activists. I now turn to consider this rapidly growing body of evidence.

Mobilization and Canvassing

Citizens who are asked to vote are more likely to do so (Gosnell 1927; Rosenstone and Hansen 1993; Verba, Schlozman, and Brady 1995). Mobilization clearly influences turnout, but the individual-level mechanism is left largely unspecified in the current literature. Its impact does not fit readily with the dominant cost-benefit logic – why should a stranger knocking on my door and urging me to vote for a particular candidate (Gerber and Green 2000) change the cost-benefit calculus of my turnout decision? Yet voters who are contacted by parties report not only higher rates of voting, but that they are more likely to urge others to vote (Rosenstone and Hansen 1993) – an indirect mobilization effect also confirmed by recent field experiments (Nickerson 2008).

I argue that political mobilization does not effect marginal changes in the payoffs of voting, but increases the salience of the election for those exposed to it. As argued by Rosenstone and Hansen (1993), citizen participation takes place in a political environment with multiple actors competing for attention from citizens. Therefore, it is necessary to specify how activities undertaken by the political elite – candidates, organizations, activists, the media – are translated into changes in individual turnout probability. I conceive of political activity influencing individual decision making in three distinct ways: (1) providing information about the opportunity to vote in certain low information settings, (2) temporarily increasing the likelihood that someone will vote as a result of face-to-face contact, and (3) most importantly, increasing the salience of politics and the upcoming election among friends, family, neighbors, and coworkers.

It is the last of these three that underlies my claim that virtually all turnout is mobilized, either directly or indirectly, by campaigns and related activity. The entire political environment, the campaigns, personal contacting, and other forms of candidate and political activity play a role in the individual turnout decision by encouraging political discussion. Without a campaign, who would vote? Perhaps a few highly informed and highly motivated citizens; but most of us are, to one degree or another, drawn in by the discussion and activity that surrounds an election, whether scattered and highly localized as in a contested city council election or widespread and virtually inescapable as in a presidential race.

The theoretical approach of this book fits well with what is known about how canvassing, both face to face and via phone calls and other communication media, affect the probability that mobilized citizens will actually participate. Most strikingly, voters are more likely to vote when told that turnout in the previous election was high rather than low (Gerber and Rogers 2009), and when told about their neighbors' prior voting history (Gerber, Green, and Larimer 2008). The proposed conditional decision function is itself nonlinear (and likely to be so for most individuals), and evidence confirms that citizens with a moderate initial propensity to vote are most affected by mobilization (Niven 2004; Arceneaux and Nickerson 2009).

If mobilization also affects the (subjective) framing of the upcoming election among potential voters, we would expect the quality of the contact to affect the priming potential of the contact. Again, evidence is in line with this prediction, as volunteer college students making phone calls (Nickerson 2008) and local neighborhood residents knocking on doors (Sinclair, Michelson, and Bedolla 2007) are more effective at increasing turnout than professionals or volunteers from outside the neighborhood. Mobilization, in other words, is not a mechanical activity, but depends on the social interaction between those doing the mobilizing and potential voters they wish to mobilize. It is likely that strongly embedded citizens who mobilize endogenously, like precinct captains in the Chicago machine or organizational leaders, or, increasingly, ministers in black churches, will be more effective at stimulating both the situational frames and high levels of discussion that promote increased turnout.

Social Context and the Sociological Tradition

This book complements existing research documenting the influence of social context on political behavior, including older work from the Columbia School (Lazarsfeld, Berelson, and Gaudet 1948; Berelson, Lazarsfeld, and McPhee 1954) and more recent work by other researchers inspired by the Columbia School tradition (Huckfeldt 1979, 1980; Gimpel, Lay, and Schuknecht 2003; McClurg 2004; Zuckerman 2005; Campbell 2006; Klofstad 2007). Along with other scholars working inside the social context tradition, I assume that the decisions are not taken by isolated individuals, but individuals embedded in particular social contexts. The impact of social context cannot be reduced to individual experiences of "peer pressure" or conscious attempts to influence other people. Social context is often working in the background, through the "slow drip" of everyday life (Baybeck and McClurg 2005) that shapes social schemas, expectations of others, and understandings of the political world.

Traditionally, the impact of social context has been treated as interchangeable with a simple, linear flow of influence from one person to another. Thus, social context has been conceptualized (and formally expressed) as working at the individual level through alters, or friends, who (presumably consciously) shape the attitudes and behavior of the person whose ego-centered network is under consideration (called "ego"). The unavoidable stumbling block in this (somewhat reductionist) model of contextual effects on the individual is that people can change either their behavior or their friends (Heider 1944). Thus, observational studies of social influence on political behavior are (perhaps unfairly[5]) subject to the same basic criticism: How do we know whether the observed similarity between friends is a result of selection or influence (Achen and Shively 1995)?

However, the mathematical approach to social interaction taken in this book is more faithful to the broader understanding of social context that is present in the literature from Lazarsfeld through to the current day. Conditional choice provides a framework for thinking systematically about the impact of social context without reducing it to direct social influence via dyadic relationships. In particular, social structure and social location – not dyadic interaction – step to the forefront as explanations in any situation involving conditional decision making. Thus, empirical tests of the social theory of turnout, and research within the conditional choice approach more generally, are not subject to the criticisms commonly made of research in the social context tradition.

Whereas the underlying notion of conditional cooperation among friends remains indispensable to understanding turnout, it is the way in which these friendships fit into the larger structure of social interaction that offers the possibility of reinterpreting the effects of education and other empirical correlates of turnout. The key insight driving the social theory of voter turnout is that social networks are more than an accumulation of the characteristics of the individuals in them (Coleman, Katz, and Menzel 1957; Blau 1977; Cook and Whitmeyer 1992). The actual shape of the network itself can have important implications for the spread of a behavior in a society. In terms of turnout, if Jane the college graduate has more friends who vote than Joe the high school graduate, this may not indicate that Jane's friends are better able to understand politics, or have developed a stronger sense of civic duty, or possess more of some other characteristic or quality than Joe's friends. Rather, the difference in turnout rates may arise simply from the average size and shape of the larger set of personal networks in which these friendship groups are embedded. The importance of this insight cannot be overstated: Social network differences are not reducible to differences in the individuals in those networks.

This sociological perspective on the link between education and turnout bears a strong resemblance to the argument made by Nie, Junn, and Stehlik-Barry (1996). They resolve the "education puzzle" by claiming

---

[5] McClurg (2003) correctly points out the flip side of the issue: that any model of political participation that omits informal social interaction is undeniably misspecified.

that relative educational attainment, not years of education, is the important predictor of turnout probability. Relative education attainment is
assumed, although never conclusively shown, to be a proxy for social network status. Their results do not contradict my claims, and I also argue
that education is at best a proxy for something important about social
networks. However, I go beyond the claims in that book in two ways.
First, I provide a well-documented and empirically supported model of
decision making that includes a mechanism for exactly how social network structure impacts individual decisions. Furthermore, I examine in
depth their claim that social status is an indicator of access to political
power and find that this is only true some of the time. I analyze a large
community using both interviews with political candidates and individual and aggregate data to show that political history and institutionally
mediated social ties are more important than social status in determining
who has social access to political power.

OVERVIEW OF REMAINING CHAPTERS

The remainder of the book will unfold in three distinct steps. First, the
conditional choice framework and associated research strategy are introduced. The second step develops a decision model of conditional cooperation in situations similar to voting turnout. The third section expands
the decision model into a middle-range theory (Hedström 2005) of turnout and tests several implications of the theory.

Chapter 2 introduces conditional choice, a formal research framework for developing and testing positive propositions about the impact
of social context on social outcomes. I present evidence that our decisions
and actions are often conditional on the actions of others, even when
we are not consciously influenced or even aware of those other actions.
The chapter then moves to a mathematical model of conditional choice,
in which any individual action can be expressed as a function of others'
actions, more precisely as a weighted function of several basic decision
rules. From these basic decisions rules we can derive a limited number
of formal mechanisms that the conditional choice framework can use
account for social outcomes, including the "basic dynamics" of a decision
situation that make a behavior easy or difficult to diffuse, and aspects of
social network structures that further shape and direct this diffusion process. Although this may sound very mechanistic, subjective perceptions
are a keystone of the conditional choice framework: People's responses

to others' behavior depend on what sort of situation they think they are in, or the social meaning of the situation.

Chapter 3 uses a combination of existing evidence, newspaper articles and editorials, and survey data to establish that the shared social meaning of voting is consensually positive and widely shared throughout the citizenry. In other words, there is no socially acceptable justification for nonvoting, even among subgroups in the population. Substantively, voting is understood as the core act defining democratic citizenship in a community of equals. Thus, voting is a social dilemma in which voting is uniformly understood as doing one's fair share for the community, and American citizens are all equal in terms of citizenship status.

Chapter 4 identifies and reviews experimental scenarios with a similar social meaning to voter turnout: low-cost social dilemmas among equals. Evidence on the conditional (and unconditional) behavior of subjects in experimental social dilemmas is used to estimate a descriptively accurate model of the distribution of conditional decision rules in situations similar to voting.

Chapter 5 describes the general and more specific dynamics of the conditional cooperation model. Turnout is produced when the actions of "first movers," who are willing to cooperate unconditionally, encourage conditional cooperation among others. The expected level of cooperation (or turnout) responds to changes in two key parameters in the model: (1) the distribution of decision rules (based on empirical estimates from Chapter 4) and (2) the average size and density of personal networks within an individual's social circle (estimated using survey data on personal social networks.) The conditional cooperation model successfully produces a wide range of turnout levels within the parameter ranges set by external sources of data, and (as would be hoped) fails to do so outside those parameters.

Chapter 6 incorporates additional empirically based assumptions into the basic decision-making model to produce a complete, midrange social theory of voter turnout. Political mobilization, social location, institutional costs, and electoral salience are incorporated into the theory as working through mechanisms associated with either decision rule distributions or social structure. A relatively simple demonstration suggests that previously observed aggregate level variation in turnout is in line with predictions of the fully developed social theory.

Chapter 7 compares the predictions of the social theory to those of the civic resources view in high-salience presidential elections. Drawing on a relatively unique network component in the 1985 General Social Survey (GSS), I develop a suitable (although rather blunt) proxy for individual location in a larger social network structure. Although the proxy is not perfect, the test does provide support for the claim that social network structure and location provide a better explanation of individual variation in reported voter turnout than a civic resources framework.

Chapter 8 provides a more powerful crucial test of the two approaches, comparing the explanatory power of the two perspectives in low-salience elections. A combination of interviews, voter roll data, and geospatial analysis is used to describe the political and social geography of turnout in a large southern county across several elections. Social proximity to candidates is the single greatest driver of turnout in low-salience elections, whereas socioeconomic status has no impact beyond increasing social access to political candidates.

Chapter 9 concludes the book. I review the major findings, discuss the practical implications of the project for candidates and political activists, and offer suggestions for future research. I offer thoughts on how to extend the analysis to the individual level, and the applicability of the conditional choice framework to a range of other political behaviors.

2

Conditional Choice

Imagine a street musician performing on a bustling sidewalk, the hat in front of him placed to gather money from pedestrians who enjoy his performance. A man carrying a briefcase is walking down the street and notices the musician. The man with the briefcase reaches into his pocket to flip a few coins into the musician's donations hat.

A few steps later, a young woman intercepts the man with the brief-case on the sidewalk, asking for a few minutes of his time. She pulls out a clipboard, explaining that she is working on a research project. She asks the man why he decided to voluntarily make a contribution to the street musician. The man reports that he rather liked the song that the musician was playing, plus he had some extra money jingling around in his pocket that he did not need for the bus that afternoon because he had decided to walk to the office instead. When asked, the man could not remember anyone else donating money. The young woman thanks the man with the briefcase for his time and he continues on his way to work. A few minutes later, another pedestrian walks by the musician without dropping any money into the hat. Presumably, this pedestrian was not so fond of the song, or perhaps he simply did not have any change – at least this is what he reports to the woman with the clipboard.

While similar scenes occur everyday, albeit without the woman with the clipboard, the preceding case describes a field experiment designed by Robert Cialdini (2005) to look for evidence of conditional decision making. Cialdini's study featured a key experimental treatment: a confederate in the study who, at some randomly selected times, walked in front of passersby and dropped coins in the musician's hat. Cialdini found that eight times as many of pedestrians donated money when preceded by the contributing confederate than when not preceded by the confederate. Thus, the causal explanation of why the first man but not the second one tossed money to the musician had almost nothing to do with the reasons the pedestrians themselves cited – their individual preferences for particular songs or the relative availability of coins in their pockets, for example – but depended almost solely on whether or not someone else had dropped a few coins in the hat immediately beforehand. Amazingly enough, almost none of those who contributed recalled seeing anyone else make a contribution before them.

What does this study have to do with voter turnout? According to the social theory of voter turnout developed in this book, most people turn out to vote because other people are voting, just as the subjects in the street musician experiment donated money because someone else donated money. In other words, turnout results from conditional decision making, with people responding to the turnout decision the same way they respond to other social dilemmas. As in other social dilemmas, some people may vote unconditionally, and a few may refuse to vote under any circumstances. The bulk of the population will vote if and only if enough other people do the same. As in the case of the unwittingly cooperative pedestrians, the decisions of other citizens exert a powerful influence on potential voters even if these decisions are not visible to the voters themselves.

The assumption that individual decisions are fundamentally interdependent forms the basis of a new theoretical framework that I term conditional choice. Throughout this book, I develop that framework and use it to explain empirical variation in voter turnout. This chapter is devoted to detailing the conditional choice research framework. First up is a quick and focused review of the empirical support for the core assumption of conditional, interdependent decision-making. Conditional responses in both perception and action have been observed in a wide range of social situations. Next is a brief introduction to the formal mathematics and dynamics of conditional decision making. The chapter concludes with a pragmatic discussion of building a mid-level theory of voter turnout within the conditional choice framework.

THE EVIDENCE FOR CONDITIONAL DECISION MAKING

The conditional choice framework starts with the simple assumption that what people do depends on what the people around them do. In other words, human decision making is fundamentally interdependent. This is not to say that people ignore material incentives associated with different actions; later in the book, I argue that costs may affect the distribution of decision rules used by potential voters. Nor am I arguing that people follow the actions of others blindly. The central claim is straightforward: People respond conditionally to the actions of others in all sorts of situations, regardless of whether they are consciously attempting to impress other people, using the actions of others as information to reduce uncertainty, doing their fair share, or merely unconsciously mimicking or attending to those around them. In other words, conditional responses are found at all levels of social cognition, from relatively unconscious perception to more thoughtful actions. This section will briefly review evidence that people make conditional decisions in a variety of situations, including voting.

A famous – and startling – example of conditional decision making comes from the studies of conformity by Asch (1955). Asch's experimenters asked subjects to report several basic perceptual facts (most famously, identifying which of two lines was longer), in a group in which the experimenters' confederates gave deliberately incorrect answers. Many subjects followed the confederates and gave incorrect responses. Thus, even when asked a basic, factual question about line length, many subjects apparently used a conditional decision rule (go along with the majority) rather than relying on an independent, individual evaluation. A recent meta-analysis of Asch-like experiments, covering more than a hundred studies conducted in several countries over a thirty-year period, confirms the pervasiveness of social influence on individual judgments (Bond and Smith 1996), as experimental subjects frequently make perceptual "mistakes" that align their views with those of others in the room. Not surprisingly, subjects relied on their own judgments less and were more likely to go along with the majority when perceptual evidence was less clear or dramatic, as in the case of two lines that are very close in length.

It would be a mistake, however, to assume that the subjects were merely motivated by consciousness of social pressure or a fear of not conforming. Observation of other people can even shape privately held judgments (Wood 2000). In another line length experiment cited by Bond and Smith's (1996) review, the authors report that subjects continue to make mistakes and go along with the majority even when they are asked to identify the longest line privately. Subjects who conformed merely out of social pressure would presumably not experience the same pressure to conform when responding privately and anonymously. Thus, conditional responsiveness does not depend solely on intentional conformity to social pressure and majority opinion.

Indeed, experimental subjects may respond conditionally to the judgments of others even when the conditional response takes place outside of conscious awareness. In a series of studies exploring the power of minority influence (Moscovici and Zavalloni 1969; Moscovici and Personnaz 1980), some subjects claimed that a blue square that they were shown was really green. As in the line length experiment, subjects continued to report seeing a green square even when allowed to report their answers in private, thus removing the impact of any direct social pressure. Even more strikingly, some subjects reported an afterimage color that was consistent with their eyes having seen a green (and not a blue) square. These subjects were not even aware that they had been influenced by the others around them, as their brains told them that they had really "seen" a green square – not a blue one that other people described as green.

Conditional responsiveness to others has been found not just in perception, but also in observable action. In the street musician study described earlier, as well as numerous other experiments, Cialdini and colleagues (Cialdini, Reno and Kallgren 1990; Reno, Cialdini and Kallgren 1993; Cialdini and Trost 1998; Cialdini 2001; Cialdini 2007) show that the likelihood of subject compliance with social norms or injunctions is strongly conditional on the behavior of others, which they term "descriptive norms." Another series of studies by Cialdini and colleagues focused on the norm against littering. They find that many people respond to the amount of litter in the environment and other reminders of the behavior of others with respect to the norm against littering. More than half of subjects will drop trash on the ground in a heavily littered area, whereas less than one in ten will do so after observing someone else pick up litter, and almost no one will litter in a clean environment.

Similarly, subjects in public goods experiments are very responsive to the contributions of other subjects. In public goods experiments, subjects decide how much of a set amount (usually around \$10–\$20) to allocate to themselves and how much to allocate to a public good that offers a lower rate of return unless others also contribute to the public good. In groups where average contribution to the public good is already relatively high, subjects will contribute more to the public good in subsequent allocation decisions (Falk, Fischbacher, and Gächter 2011). Public goods and bargaining experiments will be discussed in more detail in Chapter 4, as subject behavior in these situations will be used to estimate the distribution of conditional decision rules used by American citizens deciding whether or not to vote.

It is tempting to assume that people who mimic or conform to the decisions of other people are motivated by a desire to please or to gain social approval, or in some cases to reciprocally cooperate or to do their fair share. However, the subjects in the musician experiment were not aware of the "real" reason that they donated money (i.e., that they saw someone else do the same.) They were interviewed and debriefed by a researcher shortly after walking past the musician and were asked why they had contributed. They tended to give plausible but misleading stories that explained their donation ("I just had some extra money in my pocket"; "I really liked the song"). None of subjects recalled seeing someone else put money into the hat, or reported that they felt pressured into making a donation. Their responses are similar in this respect to the self-reports of participants in Asch studies, many of whom were not consciously aware that their choice of line was conditional on the judgments of others (Asch 1955).

This obvious discontinuity between the motivational stories provided by experimental subjects (often given in terms of costs and benefits) and the experimental treatments that caused subject behavior to vary is at the heart of this chapter. Clearly, differences in behavior across experimental conditions are attributable to observations of someone else donating money or reporting lines lengths or square color. However, subjects in these studies are typically unable to provide reliable self-reports as to what factors influenced their actions (see Nisbett and Wilson 1977; Dunning, Heath, and Sulls 2004) – they are simply unaware of how affected they are by the people around them. Their self-reports are not meaningless, in that the answers undoubtedly tell us much about how the subject see themselves and the social world around them.[1] Such interpretations of an action are of vital importance to conditional choice research, as the model of decision making applicable to any particular situation will depend on participants' subjective perceptions of the social meaning of the situation. On the other hand, self-reports are simply not suitable as scientific explanations of variation in subject behavior in cases like donating to street musicians, judging line lengths, or, as I argue, turning out to vote.

In the previous examples, subjects responded conditionally to other people who were physically present or at least physically observable. But

---

[1] Self-reports may even hold clues as to which conditional decision rules subjects (or survey respondents) are most likely to use.

voting is often depicted as a solitary activity, carried out in the private confines of a voting booth. Presumably, not all voters are directly inspired to vote by seeing neighbors walking toward a polling place or coworkers wearing an "I Voted" button (even if these and similar scenarios occur more often than many people might think). Can the turnout decision be influenced by others, even when the relevant others are not physically present for the citizen on the day of the election?

Evidence from analogous experiments suggests that individual voting behavior can be conditionally responsive to others, even when the relevant others are not physically present and have not directly stated their turnout intentions in advance. In fact, conditional responsiveness is not limited to situations involving direct observation of others. Experimental subjects often respond conditionally even when they are not directly exposed to the person to whom they are responding. Simply thinking about another person automatically activates the social knowledge, valuation, and affect involved in social interaction (Zajonc 1980; Abelson, Kinder, Peters, and Fiske 1982; Fiske and Taylor 1991), and subsequent actions exhibit conditional responses characteristic of social interaction. For example, subjects primed to think about an elderly person will often walk more slowly (Bargh, Chen, and Burrows 1996). Subjects primed with the name of someone who wishes them to succeed perform better on subsequent tests (Bargh and Fitzsimons 2003). Similarly, subjects asked to call to mind two older women in their lives report more conservative attitudes toward sex on a subsequent survey (Baldwin and Holmes 1987). Thus, conditional decision making occurs even when the actor is not in the presence of other people or was not recently exposed to them.

Conditional decision making is not comprised solely of simple mimicry rules. It also incorporates more complex heuristics that are sensitive to the goals, values, and beliefs of the decision maker. A conditional response to the mere thought of another person may be mediated by the attitude of the subject to the person in question. For example, subjects primed with the social category "the elderly" will walk slower if they have positive attitudes toward the elderly, but those with negative attitudes will walk fast following the prime (Cesario, Plaks, and Higgins 2006). In a similar result, subjects primed to think of a person who wishes them to succeed may actually perform worse than control groups if they have the negative belief that the person who wishes them to succeed is overly controlling (Chartrand, Dalton, and Fitzsimons 2007).

Conditional decision making also has been found in a wide range of settings involving cooperation toward group objectives at the expense of individual benefit; these settings include conventional social dilemmas involving public goods (Marwell and Ames 1979; Marwell and Ames 1980; Dawes, van de Kragt, and Orbell 1990; Ledyard 1995), conflictual situations such as price or wage determinations (Akerlof 1980; Akerlof 1982; Kahneman, Knetch, and Thaler 1986), bargaining (Roth 1995 for review), tax compliance (Levi 1988; Scholz and Lubell 1998a, 1998b; Scholz and Pinney 1995), and tipping of service providers (Lynn and Grassman 1990).

Even though much of the evidence presented earlier is not specifically related to politics, conditional judgments have also been reported in wide range of topic areas relevant to politics, including attitudes toward abortion, the death penalty, pollution, military service, policies requiring standardized tests, gay rights, European currency policy, animal research, and voluntary euthanasia (Maass, Clark, and Haberkorn 1982; Mugny and Papastamou 1982; Clark and Maass 1988; Martin and Hewstone 2003). Political research outside the lab is also consistent with the existence of social influence in partisanship and vote choice (Berelson, Lazarsfeld, and McPhee 1954; Campbell et al. 1960; Huckfeldt, Johnson and Sprague 2004; Johnston and Pattie 2006) and voter turnout (Huckfeldt 1979; Pattie and Johnston 1998). In a field experiment, Gerber and Rogers (2009) even find that mention of a descriptive norm in favor of voting mobilizes actual voters, whereas voting is suppressed by suggesting a descriptive norm against voting. Further afield, adoption of policy reforms (Mintrom 1997), planting of hybrid corn (Young 2009), and drug prescriptions (Coleman, Katz, and Menzel 1966) are also characterized by conditional decision making. States, farmers, and doctors are all more likely to adopt a new innovation when those around them do so as well.

In summary, individual action, in general and in the context of voting, can usually be expressed as a conditional function of the actions of others. Individual judgments reflect the perceptions and/or actions of other people even when: (1) the individual making the choice is unaware that his or her decision has shifted as a result of influence; (2) decisions are made in completely anonymous, private situations with no possibility for group punishment, censure, or rewards; and (3) other people are merely thought about, not observed directly. Although interdependent decision making is widespread, individuals respond to others in different ways and to different degrees, and different situations may promote different levels of conditional responsiveness as well. Thus, the mathematical model of conditional decision making described in the following section builds on the notion that interdependence must be considered as a part of any social decision-making phenomenon, but, further, incorporates individual and situational heterogeneity in type and degree of conditional responsiveness to others.

MATHEMATICAL MODELS OF CONDITIONAL DECISION MAKING

The evidence is clear: In a wide variety of situations, individual decisions often depend on others' behavior. This responsiveness, I will argue, turns out to be the key driver of voter turnout in U.S. elections. Moreover, this conditional responsiveness cannot be reduced to any single motivation or selective incentive such as social pressure, desire for social approval, or fear of punishment, although such motives may come into play in particular cases. Instead of focusing on motivations, I will focus on a more straightforward formal (or mathematical) representation of conditional responsiveness as simply a distribution of conditional decision rules.[2] For readers unfamiliar with the conditional decision-making approach, this section presents a brief overview of the mathematical framework and dynamics of conditional decision models.[3]

Conditional Decision Rules

Conditional decision makers do not calculate or maximize preference functions; instead, they follow rules that tell them how to alter their behavior in response to the actions of others. What exactly is a conditional decision rule? A conditional decision rule is simply a mapping of others' actions onto a given individuals' choices, or probabilities of choosing one course of action over another. When I say that voters follow a conditional decision rule (or weighted combination of rules), I mean only that their choices can be accurately represented as a function of others' choices. It does not mean that they observe others' choices and consciously follow the crowd or try to do their fair share, or that their actions are fully determined by what other people do, or even that potential voters are consciously aware of following a conditional rule.

A simple example of conditional responsiveness is the standing ovation. A basic conditional decision rule might guide audience members at the end of a performance: stand and clap so long as the majority of

---

[2] Mathematical models of conditional decision making are built on the assumption that people are satisficing rule followers (Simon 1955), not bundles of preferences.
[3] For a longer treatment, see Rolfe (2009).

those seated nearby are already on their feet clapping (c.f. Miller and Page 2004). To explain a more complex behavior, Schelling(1973) used conditional decision rules as the basis of his model of residential racial segregation. Neighborhood residents in his model prefer to live near others of the same race and use a threshold conditional decision rule: stay in your current home if at least 30% of your neighbors are of the same race, otherwise move.[4]

Granovetter (1978) provides another well-known example of a mathematical model incorporating conditional decision rules that comes closer to the model I use for voting. Citizens in Granovetter's model of collective action decide whether or not to join in a collective protest based on what others around them were doing. The Granovetter model introduces the crucial notion of individual heterogeneity in the form of a distribution of threshold rules, allowing conditional responsiveness to vary across members of a population. In the model, some citizens would protest if only a few others were participating, whereas others with higher thresholds would only participate if a large crowd was already involved.[5] Although all of the crowd members in the model use conditional decision rules when deciding whether or not to participate, there was a high degree of individual variation in conditional responsiveness to the actions of others.

As seen from the preceding examples, a conditional decision rule is simply a mathematical function that links the decision ($d_{i,s}$) of an individual actor (i) to the decisions of other actors ($d_{j,s}$) and the decision situation (s).[6] Generically, a conditional decision rule takes the following form:

$$\Pr(d_{i,s} = 1) = f(d_{1,s}, d_{2,s} \ldots d_{j,s}), \quad \forall j \neq i. \tag{2.1}$$

A conditional decision model of a social situation includes all of the individuals involved in the situation, and is therefore characterized by

---

[4] Bruch and Mare (2006) update the Schelling model with an impressive empirical basis for conditional decision rules. See also Bruch and Mare's (2009) review of literature built from Schelling's segregation model.

[5] More precisely, Granovetter's model has 100 actors with thresholds drawn from a uniform distribution over the interval from 0 to 99, inclusive. Thus, each actor has a threshold from 0 to 99, with an equal probability of any number in that range.

[6] For more on the link between individual decision rules and aggregate dynamics, see works by Young (2009) and by Watts and collaborators (Dodds and Watts 2004; Lopez-Pintado and Watts 2006; Watts and Dodds 2009). For a less mathematical treatment of the dynamics of conditional decision models, see Rolfe (2009).

a distribution of such conditional rules. In short, a conditional decision model is a mathematical expression of the claim that individual decisions are better represented as conditional functions of the social situation and the actions of others involved in it, rather than as functions of individual intentions or motivations.

Applying this rule to the situation (s) of voting turnout ($s = vote$) would proceed as follows. If actor i decides to vote, her decision would be indicated as $d_{i,vote} = 1$, while $d_{i,vote} = 0$ indicates nonvoting. The left-hand side of the generic conditional decision rule, Equation 2.1 gives the probability that an actor decides to vote ($Pr(d_{i,vote} = 1)$). The probability that the actor votes is the range of the function, which varies between 0% and 100% (or 0 and 1.) Whereas the turnout decision is technically a binary one – vote or do not vote – in any given election, it is continuous across multiple elections and is easily (and perhaps best) represented as a probabilistic decision in any given election.

Actor i has a group of friends and family who influence his or her decision to vote. The turnout decisions of these other actors appear on the right-hand side of the equation ($d_{j,vote}$). The total number of actor i's friends and family members is given by the network degree (k_i). Therefore, a complete strategy (or conditional response) for any actor includes a response to all possible decisions by other actors. In the case of voting, this would be a conditional rule that calculates an actor's probability of voting from the proportion of his or her friends who vote, ranging between 0% to 100% turnout among friends and family. In other words, a conditional decision rule for voting is simply a function that maps from all possible turnout decisions ($d_{j,vote}$) of all k_i actors in actor i's social network (i.e., the domain of the function or decision rule is 0% to 100% turnout among all friends) to the probability that actor i will vote ($Pr(d_{i,vote} = 1)$) (i.e., the range of the function may vary between 0% and 100%.)

The Three Basic Rules

I propose that any individual's decision to vote (as well as engage in most other activities) can be expressed as a weighted combination of three basic decision rules.[7] Each rule is simply a mapping from others'

---

[7] More complex or socially contested decision situations could potentially still be characterized by these three rules, taking into account variation in the valence (positive or negative) applied to decision rules and reference groups, both of which are related in a straightforward way to conflict over the social meaning of an action.

decisions to one's own decision, or, equivalently, an expression of an individual decision as a function of the decisions of others. The three decision rules are: (1) unconditional decision making, (2) linear conditional decision making or mean matching, and (3) nonlinear conditional decision making or focal point/median matching. Each of these three basic rules is described in more detail below. Graphical examples of each rule appear in Figure 2.1, showing the probability of individual action (or turnout) as a function of the activity (or turnout rate) among one's friends.

Actors who rely wholly on *unconditional* decision rules are not affected by others in a given decision situation. For example, in the context of voting, an unconditional cooperation rule (see Figure 2.1[a]) dictates that the decision maker vote regardless of how many other voters go to the polls. Unconditional decision rules may reflect internalization of a moral imperative (Riker and Ordeshook 1968; Elster 1989; Finkel, Muller and Opp 1989; Coleman 1990), automatically activated impression management goals (e.g., internalized motivation to avoid prejudice [Plant and Devine 1998], or "chronic" egalitarianism [Moskowitz et al. 1999]), unconditional commitments (Sen 1977; Sugden 1984), emotionally driven commitments (Hirschleifer 1987; Frank 1988), or unilateral cooperation (Chong 1991). Altruism – a large value placed on the welfare of others – is another potential source of unconditional cooperation, whether altruistic orientations are produced by biology or the "warm glow" people get from cooperation (Margolis 1982; Frohlich et al. 1984, Oliner and Oliner 1988; Cronin 1991; Barkow, Cosmides, and Tooby 1992; Andreoni 1995).[8] Alternatively, unconditional cooperation may reflect a strong value placed on future selves (i.e., discount rate) in conjunction with consequentialist beliefs about the positive impact of one's own cooperation, an alternative that Elster (1989) dismisses, perhaps prematurely, as magical thinking. A desire for status in a gift economy may also promote unconditional cooperation (Mauss 1954; Posner 1998).

Figure 2.1(b) depicts the linear, mean-matching rule at the line $y = x$. A pure follower of mean matching would cooperate in a social dilemma precisely to the degree that relevant others cooperate. For example, Gould (1993) modeled the decision to volunteer to pick up litter in a residential neighborhood using a *linear or mean-matching conditional decision rule*. If a neighborhood was made up of ten residents using the mean-matching rule, then one resident picking up litter would make all of the

---

[8] Although see Monroe (1994) for a compelling argument in favor of a more stringent definition of altruism than is commonly used in the literature.

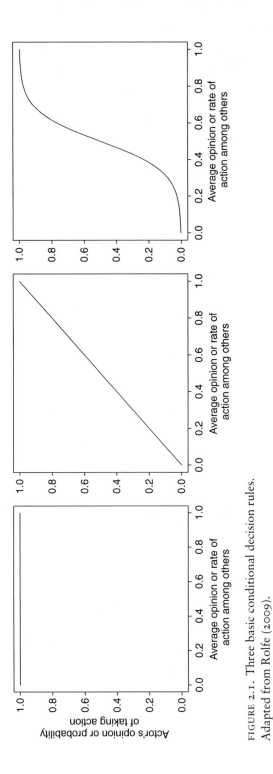

FIGURE 2.1. Three basic conditional decision rules. Adapted from Rolfe (2009).

other residents 10% more likely to pick up litter themselves.[9] Decision makers choosing among continuous actions, not merely binary ones, can use the linear matching rule. Instead of either protesting or not protesting, as in Granovetter's example, Gould's neighbors could conditionally cooperate to a greater or lesser degree, by dedicating more or less time to the litter cleanup effort based on the contributions of the other neighbors. Any given individual would respond to an hour worth of additional volunteering among all their neighbors with a proportional contribution of their own – say, 10 minutes.[10]

In game theoretic terms, linear matching is an analogue to the tit-for-tat strategy that proves successful in repeated social dilemmas (Axelrod 1984), even those among strangers (Macy and Skvoretz 1998). Doing one's fair share is a common concern in social dilemmas (Margolis 1982; Elster 1989; Rabin 1993; Bolton and Ockenfels 2000) and may serve as an internal motivation for use of the mean-matching rule. However, actors using the linear matching rule may also be externally motivated by a desire to avoid punishment (which is typically based on deviation from the mean of the group) or to seek social status by "keeping up with the Joneses." Again, the motivations experienced by the decision maker are less important to conditional choice than is the empirical responsiveness to others' decisions.

The next rule, median matching, offers a second representation of conditional responsiveness. Here, cooperation rises rapidly when cooperation approaches a focal point or "critical mass" level of cooperation. Although the focal-point concept might also be represented as an all-or-nothing threshold or tipping point for each individual, as in the earlier examples from Schelling and Granovetter, a more realistic representation of an individual decision rule is a probabilistic nonlinear decision function, such as the logistic cumulative density function pictured in Figure 2.1(c).[11] Any of the reasons given previously for selecting a linear

---

[9] Gould (1993) proposed that "fairness" has a self-regarding bias and that matching would therefore take place at a reduced level, $y = \alpha x$, $\alpha \in (0, 1)$. I do not consider this possibility in voting simulations, but it is an interesting proposition worthy of further research.

[10] Technically, the neighbors used the rule $0.9(\Sigma x_j)/k$, with k as number of neighbors.

[11] This function can be fine-tuned as needed. When $b = 2a$, then the function is centered at 50% participation. Variations in a simply increase or decrease the steepness of the increase at 50%. (That is to say, it affects the standard deviation of the underlying individual distribution.) Similarly, it is possible to shift the focal point or point of inflection for nonlinear increases in participation up or down by setting $b < 2a$ or $b > 2a$, respectively. In the simulations later in this book, I use $a = 6$, $b = 12$, corresponding to an underlying probability distribution with $[\mu = .5, \sigma = .15]$.

matching strategy may also apply to a median-matching strategy; it is not clear how concerns with fairness, status, or a tit-for-tat strategy would generalize to a multi-actor context. The intrinsic benefits of participation, such as a chance to see one's friends or be a part of an important public event, may play a special role in encouraging cooperation once a large number of people are involved as well.

Whereas we have already seen that different people may use different rules in the same situation, it is also possible (and perhaps even likely) that a single individual will rely on a mixture of rules in a given situation. Therefore, the three rules can be combined into a single rule by use of weights that can then vary for different individuals. Formally, in the model, each individual has a weighting vector with three scalar weights, designated as α, β, and γ. The model assigns these weights to the unconditional cooperation, linear or uniform matching, and nonlinear or focal-point-matching rules, respectively, and imposes the condition that the weight each range from 0 to 1 and sum to 1 for any given individual ($\alpha + \beta + \gamma = 1$; α, β, $\gamma \in [0, 1]$). Building on Equation 2.1, the single weighted decision rule can be represented as:

$$\Pr(d_{i,s} = 1) = \alpha_{i,s} 1 + \beta_{i,s} \frac{w_{i,j} d_j}{k_i} + \gamma \frac{1}{1 + e^{a - b \frac{w_{i,j} d_j}{k-1}}} \tag{2.2}$$

where $d_{i,s}$ is the decision made by person i in situation s, and cooperation or voting is signified by $d_{i,s} = 1$. Figure 2.2 gives an example of how the complete decision rule would appear if $\alpha = .1$ and $\beta = \gamma = .45$ (with a reference to the $45°$ line for comparison, see Dodds and Watts 2004).

Different weighting combinations capture individual heterogeneity in a more flexible way than, for example, Granovetter's varying thresholds. This variation may result from a number of different mechanisms; for example, it may be the innate result of different value orientations toward cooperation ranging from altruism to aggression (Frohlich et al. 1984; Liebrand 1984; Offerman, Sonnemans, and Schram 1996), or merely from different past experiences in social dilemmas or emotional commitments. Regardless of the motivation, a large weight on the conditional cooperation elements represents an individual whose decisions depend heavily on his or her friends or relevant others; someone who depends less on what their friends are doing would have larger weights placed on the unconditional rule. Some individuals might be "pure" types who always cooperate or always match others' behavior, but many are

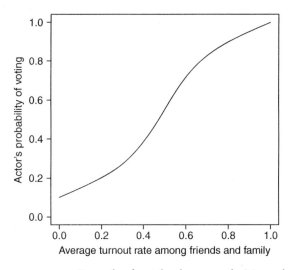

FIGURE 2.2. Example of weighted turnout decision rule.

likely to mix and match, behaving, for example, with one eye toward others' choices and one eye toward personal preferences for cooperation or noncooperation.

By extension, a distribution of weights on the three elements of individual decision rules can be used to describe decision making in a particular situation. In a given situation, the weights on each rule for any person in the group are drawn from the population distribution of weights (e.g., $\alpha_{i,s} \sim N(\mu_{a,s}, \sigma_{a,s})$). If people have strong value orientations that hold across situations, we would expect that the weights of person i relative to the rest of the population would be highly correlated across any two similar situations (Oliner and Oliner 1988; Monroe 1994; Offerman, Sonnemans and Schram 1996). In other words, small changes in situational context may not affect a rank ordering of people based on a tendency to cooperate, but may shift average cooperative tendencies.

In this and subsequent discussions of conditional decision models, I refer to distributions of rules and not distributions of actors. I also use mathematical descriptions of the rules (unconditional, mean-matching, median-matching) as opposed to more prosaic terms (civic duty, fair share, and bandwagon are a few that have been suggested in the past). This usage departs from existing research on diffusion models, but I have chosen this language as a better representation of what we know (and do not know) about conditional decision making.

For example, it is possible that innovators, early adopters, and laggards might use different decision rules (Rogers 2003). However, it is equally possible that an early adopter and a laggard are using the same conditional decision rule in a probabilistic or stochastic manner. Suppose that both the early adopter and laggard are willing to adopt an innovation with a probability equal to the proportion of those around them adopting it (i.e., both use a linear mean-matching rule.) Thus, both plant hybrid corn with a 20% probability if 20% of their friends do the same, and 80% probability if 80% of their friends do the same. We would then call the portion of the population that adopted at 20% early adopters and those at 80% laggards, even though both types of decision makers were using the same conditional decision rule. It is essentially impossible to make inferences about types of actors from observed behavior, or about the motivations of actors even if we observe their preferred conditional decision rule directly. Therefore, I argue that it is more accurate to model a social situation as a distribution of decision rules (not actors) and to refer to the decision rules by their mathematical properties (not the assumed motivations of the decision makers).

In summary, a conditional rule can take on many forms. Conditional rules may be represented as static thresholds, or continuous functions dictating a smoother or more probabilistic response to others. All individuals facing the same decision may use the same rule, or there can be a distribution of different rules used throughout the population. Regardless of the functional form, conditional decision rules are all built from an assumption that interdependence is an unavoidable part of social action. However, the fundamental assumption of interdependence is not grounded in any more basic beliefs about basic human nature or motivation. There is no reason to think that conditional decision makers care more about themselves or others, or that they place a higher value on social or economic costs and benefits when making decisions.

Dynamics of Conditional Decision Models

Conditional decision making is inherently a dynamic process, because a change in one person's behavior can set off a wave of changes in the decisions of those around her. The dynamics of a particular conditional decision-making model depend on the distribution of conditional decision rules in a population, along with resistance to influence and social networks of interaction.

Although some decisions for some individuals may be unconditional, or nearly so, the aggregate behavior of a group can (and should) be represented by a conditional decision model whenever some portion of individuals in a group make decisions that depend on others' decisions. Conditional decision models are not new to the social sciences; there is a long tradition of research into the formal dynamics of action and opinion when people make decisions that are conditional on those around them.[12] The dynamic properties of conditional decision models are complex, and often highly nonlinear, in the sense that a change in one person's actions can ripple and rebound throughout the system and may push the system into an entirely different equilibrium state (or level of cooperation or collective behavior). In this section, I briefly review the basic dynamics of conditional decision models and highlight the explanatory factors that produce changes in the expected outcome of conditional models.

Conditional decision models are scattered across multiple disciplines and substantive topics, with a resulting proliferation of terms and modeling approaches. Rolfe (2009) reviews a range of literatures and related conditional decision models and identifies the key parameters used in existing conditional decision models. These key parameters are classified systematically into aspects of actions, rules, information, and networks. For example, the action of a model may vary along two dimensions: the type of action or decision to be modeled, and the length of time that an action or decision remains fixed.[13] A complete review of this systematic classification of conditional decision model parameters is not essential to an understanding of either conditional choice or voter turnout, but some further details appear in the discussion of simulation parameters in Appendix A.

Regardless of model parameters, conditional decision models produce a dynamic decision-making process characterized by *initial activity*, a subsequent *trajectory* of changes, and ultimately an *outcome state*. Like game theoretic models, conditional decision models are often characterized by a set of stable outcomes (equilibria or "attractor states"). In addition, conditional decision models produce dynamic trajectory of sequential changes in decision making, or *states of activity* in the group. First, the group of decision makers is in an initial state of activity (i.e., no one is voting, group members hold initial opinions). Next, one or more people

---

[12] There are many well-known examples of research into conditional decision making (French 1956; Harary 1959; Abelson 1964; Schelling 1973; Granovetter 1978). See Rolfe (2009) and Watts and Dodds (2009) for reviews of the literature.

[13] The action modeled may be treated as discrete (binary, categorical, or nominal) or continuous. Previous decisions may be changed almost immediately (i.e., daily decisions about what to eat for lunch) or only after some longer period of time (i.e., car purchases).

change their mind or start doing something different (i.e., unconditional cooperators start voting, or extremists moderate their opinions.) Any small change sets off a chain reaction of interdependent decision making (i.e., the trajectory of the system), with additional people changing their mind until the system stabilizes again at some stable outcome state.

The important insight here is that conditional decision models exhibit behavior characteristic of nonlinear dynamical systems. In other words, when a group of individuals make decisions that are conditional on the decisions of those around them, the social outcome is not a simple linear combination of individual choices. The parable of a butterfly flapping its wings in South America and producing a tornado in Texas captures one noteworthy aspect of nonlinear systems: a very small change in a group of conditional decision makers may produce outcomes that are well out of proportion to the original stimulus event. This insight has two key implications for social scientists who seek to provide explanations of social outcomes in situations where individuals make conditional choices.

The first implication is that when people make decisions that depend on those around them, it is rarely possible to make straightforward directional hypotheses along the lines of "an increase in costs of voting leads to a decrease in participation." The impact of a change in one factor that affects the system is often contingent or conditional on the other factors that affect decision making. For example, Chapter 5 shows that small, dense social networks may assist in the spread of innovations in some situations but slow down diffusion in other situations represented by a different distribution of decision rules. A simple, general claim about how network size affects the likelihood of diffusion is not possible, given the nonlinear dynamics produced by conditional decision making.

Thankfully, this implication is less devastating than it might appear. Whereas the specific outcome and trajectory of most conditional decision models are characterized by nonlinear or complex behavior, general model dynamics are nonetheless affected by only a handful of formal mechanisms. Three of these mechanisms affect the basic dynamic[14] of the decision model: initial activity, distribution of decision rules, and resistance to influence. Three additional mechanisms affect the networks of social interaction between conditional decision makers: the size and

---

[14] The basic dynamic of the model is simply the expected trajectory and outcome of a given distribution of decision rules when actors are members of global (or all-see-all) networks. In some models with fixed actions, including threshold models, the basic dynamic of the model incorporates resistance to influence, although other parameters that introduce resistance to influence may be considered part of the extended model.

structure of social networks, social cleavages, and social location. More details on each of these mechanisms, and links to both evidence and the conditional choice framework, are taken up in the following section.

The second implication is that even scholars working within the traditional rational choice framework cannot entirely ignore the nonlinear dynamics that characterize social systems. Conditional decision making cannot be reduced to simple, linear payoffs for pro-social or cooperative behavior; such a simplification would ignore the inherent interdependence of individual action. Incorporating the conditional aspect of decision making into a standard maximization framework would render the resulting mathematical system essentially equivalent to a conditional decision model (Lopez-Pintado and Watts 2008), although with important potential differences in the nonlinear functional form (Young 2009). This is not to say that costs and benefits have no explanatory power, but that it is equally important to acknowledge the explanatory role of initial activity (or history), social meaning, resistance to influence (often related to power), and social networks in most social situations, regardless of whether or not the researcher is working within the conditional choice tradition.

ENGINEERING A MODEL AND MID-LEVEL THEORY

This book's ultimate goal is to develop a new theoretical model of turnout and provide evidence for that theory by testing a series of empirical hypothesis derived from it. The conditional choice research paradigm cannot proceed deductively from assumptions about the true motives of voters. Rather, conditional choice requires a formal model built painstakingly from empirical evidence about (1) the contemporary social meaning of voting, and (2) the various ways in which people make decisions about whether or not to cooperate, in social situations with structurally similar meanings. This model will then yield predictions that can be tested empirically. The approach requires a considerable investment on the front end in building and justifying the decision-making model, but yields a considerable payoff in empirical explanation.

The previous section introduced the mathematics of conditional choice, highlighting the nonlinear dynamics produced when actors follow conditional decision rules. Existing mathematical results suggest that turnout rate is likely to be affected by variables related to six formal mechanisms (Rolfe 2009): initial activity, distribution of decision rules, resistance to influence, network size and structure, social cleavages, and

TABLE 2.1. *Formal Mechanisms and Empirical Variables*

Formal Mechanism	Empirical Variable	Theoretical Explanation	Evidence of Link
Initial activity	Costs	Affects probability of unconditional cooperation	Chapter 4
Distribution of decision rules	Social meaning	Social dilemma among equals	Chapters 3, 4
Resistance to influence	One-shot "threshold" decision	Probabilistic decision based on prior observations	Assumption (Chapter 2)
Average network size	General friendship networks (12–20 people)	Regular conversation partners	Chapter 5
Initial activity	Electoral institutions Very low salience	Affects probability of unconditional voting	Prior studies, Chapter 6
Average network size	Mobilization, electoral salience, political discussion	Increases use of latent social networks as reference group	Chapters 6–8
Social cleavages	Over-dispersion of college education	Distinct social worlds with different latent network	Chapter 7
Social location of politicians	Personal residence, location of personal social activity and direct mobilization activity	Direct and indirect mobilization increases political discussion	Chapter 8

social location. These six mechanisms are like payoffs, discount rates, and information sets in game theory, and serve as explanations of variation in the expected outcomes or equilibria of social situations. Table 2.1 summarizes how the six mechanisms at work in mathematical models of conditional decision making are applied to the empirical study of voter turnout.

The first three mechanisms work together as parameters of a conditional decision model of voter turnout; a model characterized by a basic dynamic as described earlier. This model is developed, and the basic dynamic analyzed, in the first half of the book, Chapters 3–5. The first stage of the research design uses evidence from a variety of sources to build a mathematical model of conditional decision making in situations similar to voting turnout. The model-building stage follows an empirical and inductive approach similar to the multi-method approach to model validation used by engineers (Law and Kelton 1982).

The stage of the research design develops a more complete social theory of voting turnout, based on the turnout decision model from the first stage but adding features specific to the political context. Multiple testable implications are derived from the social theory and then compared to observable behavior. For example, simulations reveal that whereas changes in initial activity shift the range of observed turnout, changes in network size shift average turnout (but not the range). These predictions are compared to turnout in elections that vary in terms of either costs or mobilization/salience, and confirm the plausibility of link between the relevant empirical variables (e.g., costs or election salience) and formal mechanisms (initial activity and network structure). The research strategy places as much emphasis on measurement as it does on hypothesis testing, as careful and accurate measurement of model parameters and theoretical constructs are integral to both the model-building and theory-testing stages.

Properly developing and testing a social theory of a particular phenomenon within the conditional choice framework thus takes considerable patience to work through a multistage process. Careful attention to each step of the process, however, yields numerous benefits. First, the resulting decision model and social theory are based on empirically sound and verifiable assumptions. Second, the incorporation of a formal decision model into the research process produces surprisingly accurate predictions that can be compared to observed social outcomes. Finally, the theory lends itself to easy extension in multiple directions. This book investigates only a few of the numerous test implications that can be derived from a fully developed social theory of turnout.

3

The Social Meaning of Voting

A woman leaves her home, walks through her neighborhood, and enters a building. Upon entering the building, she briefly exchanges words with an attendant, signs her name to a piece of paper, goes to a nearby work-space, and then deposits a paper into a slotted box.

A social scientist might seek to explain the woman's trip to put a paper into the slotted box, or why this woman made the trip and another one did not. To explain her decision to drop some papers into a slotted box, we need to understand something about the meaning of that trip – both to her and to others around her. It is, of course, not enough to observe the action of dropping paper. As surely as we need additional informa-tion about context and meaning to understand whether an eye closing is a wink or a blink in the anthropologist Clifford Geertz's (1973) famous example, the physical action is not intelligible until we know, for exam-ple, whether the paper is a personal letter to her child who just left for college, a bank deposit slip, or an electoral ballot. Assuming that we iden-tify the paper as an electoral ballot, we still need to understand what others might think if they saw her actions. Do some people believe that women should not vote? Would some claim that electoral participation was a waste of time? Might voting appear to lend implicit support to a corrupt regime?

In other words, all social science starts with an interpretation of social activity and practice. We cannot explain variation in voting turn-out without understanding how dropping a ballot into a ballot box has a fundamentally different social meaning from dropping a letter into a mailbox, and indeed without understanding more about the meaning of the act of voting in its particular social context.

The conditional choice framework incorporates social meaning in the basic decision equation in the form of a situational parameter (*s*). This parameter determines the distribution of decision rules that decision makers will apply to that context; in other words, it is the distribution of decision rules across a population that changes as the situation (*s*) changes. The goal of this chapter, then, is to specify a situational parameter for the situation of voting in contemporary American elections. This entails establishing the social meaning of the act of voting and, further, establishing the extent to which that meaning is shared or disputed among different groups of American citizens.

I focus on three basic elements of social meaning: (1) the people or groups involved, 2) the relationship among them, or the "relational model(s)" applicable to their interaction (Fiske 1992), and (3) the relevance of the action to the relationship. Drawing on a combination of survey data, key American texts, newspaper editorials prior to an election, and secondary information about historical social practices, I find that voting is understood as a fundamental act of the American citizen. According to widely shared understandings, all good Americans by definition should vote in elections. American citizens belong to a loose-knit community of equals, but implicit appeals to vote use language invoking additional normative models of the relationship among American citizens. Because the social meaning of voting is uncontested, a failure to vote may be excusable as an accident, but it cannot be justified without casting doubt on one's good standing as an American citizen. While it may seem to reflect unsurprising common sense, this analysis of voting is crucial for defining the situational parameter in the conditional choice model. Once it is established that voting is an essential act of members of a loose-knit community of (formal) equals, a model of turnout can be developed from observing what happens in situations that are equivalent along these dimensions of social meaning.

SOCIAL MEANING: PEOPLE AND RELATIONSHIPS

For the purposes of this book, I argue that the social meaning of a particular social situation can be reduced to two key elements: who is involved and what relationship exists between them. I also investigate the extent to which there is a shared consensus on the social meaning of the action, or if, alternatively, the meaning of the action varies across social divides. Intuitively, we expect that different conceptions of the people or relationships involved in a given situation would produce very different behaviors. For example, citizens in a democracy might be willing to defer to authorities when attending church or at work, but be unwilling to do so in democratic settings such as at the voting booth or in public meetings.[1] Whereas a formalization of social meaning as "people and relationships" may dramatically oversimplify the notion of social meaning, I argue that it is a reasonable and parsimonious approximation of the typical characteristics of social cognition and social interaction across cultures.

Substantial evidence points to the primacy of other people and groups in social cognition. As plentiful evidence shows, associations linked to the agents of social action – both people and social groups – are central to social cognition (Jones and Davis 1965; Hogg and Abrams 1988; Srull and Wyer 1989; Fiske and Taylor 1991; Frith and Frith 1999; Hong et al. 2003; Tajfel and Turner 2004; Hong et al. 2005). These associative maps link together the sorts of information that the individual, as naive scientist, might use to try to predict what other people will do: traits or stereotypes, likes and dislikes, intentions or motives, past interactions, and affective evaluations. In the absence of specific information about a person, information about the group to which the person is assumed to belong can be used to predict behavior instead (Fiske and Neuberg 1990).[2] The "people" aspect of social meaning is closely related to the analytical construct *identity content* proposed by Abdelal et al. (2006), and may include evidence documenting how central the action is to the social identity of the groups and people involved.

As for relationships, I analyze their social meanings in terms of four basic norms or mathematical relationship: communal, authority, equality, and equity (Fiske 1992). Sociologists have long considered relationships or roles an important aspect in assessing the meaning of social interaction, but these relationships are generally described in relatively concrete terms as social roles (e.g., mother, teacher, leader). However, the social meaning and set of behavioral expectations associated with concrete social roles is culturally specific and often debated even within a given local social context, and would therefore be less suited to use as a formal element of social situations than the comparatively abstract principles. Therefore, I

---

[1] Admittedly, interactions in one setting can and do influence interactions in these other settings (Sanders 1997; Mendelberg and Oleske 2000).

[2] An important social motivation is retaining a positive self-image. Therefore, a special form of person memory, self-representation, plays a special role in social cognition. Self representations are also linked to similar traits, motives, and intentions, as well as intrinsic and extrinsic motivations (Markus and Kitayama 1991; Brewer and Gardner 2004).

rely on a growing body of evidence confirming that relationships between actors can be characterized by one or more of these models, across a wide range of cultures (Fiske 1992). These four basic principles help organize social cognition (Fiske and Fiske 2007), and play a role in most individual judgments regarding justice and injustice in resource allocation (Eckhoff 1974; Deutsch 1975; Cook and Hegtvedt 1983; Cook and Whitmeyer 1992). These relational principles govern both the effort that is put into an activity and the expected rewards from that effort. If decision makers involved in social interaction are thought of as playing a strategic "game" (analogous to a game-theoretic situation), then the four basic relational models might be described as the rules of four different games.

Briefly, the four principles are as follows. *Communal* relationships are characterized by a blurring or elimination of the boundaries between self and other (those in the relationship are not merely equal, they are all the same.) *Authority* relationships are inherently unequal and operate according to a winner-take-all principle. Individuals in an authority relationship are placed in a linear order or dominance hierarchy, without a clear metric by which to assess the absolute position of those involved. Tradition is often used to justify or legitimate inequality within an authority ranking interaction. *Equality*-based interactions are characterized by the equality of those involved and operate on a principle of reciprocal exchange, or tit for tat. Each person is expected to match the contributions of others to the relationships, and the relationship can be terminated if those involved do not believe that their efforts have been reciprocated. *Equity* relationships operate according to norms of market pricing and merit, and people are related to each other in terms of value ratios or proportions. Market pricing principles are often quite controversial when applied to human interaction, however, and might be criticized as "taboo tradeoffs" (Fiske and Tetlock 1997; McGraw and Tetlock 2005), the "commodification of labor," or disregard for intrinsic human value. However, equity principles confer only limited power to the more valuable partner in a relationship and provide a reasonable alternative to authority-based winner-take-all norms when it is necessary to distribute power and status in a group. Rational choice is built from the assumption that all relationships are based on equity, as people are assumed to interact on the basis of a calculation of the ratio of costs and benefits of the interaction.

Whereas these four principles are parsimonious and mathematically elegant, the social meaning of everyday social interaction is often messy, ambiguous, and contested.[3] This ambiguity can be understood in terms of competing expectations of the interaction based on different applications of the four basic relational models. For example, in Bearman's (2005) description of the social world of doormen and tenants in New York City, conflict arises when the low-status doormen act as provisional fathers to their wealthy tenants. Doormen who cannot adjust to the ambiguity of their role find themselves demanding favors from the higher-status tenants while also resenting them and complaining about the tenants' inability to manage even the basic job of changing a light bulb. Ambiguity in political debate can also be characterized in terms of relational justice, as political opponents disagree about which relational model should prevail in a given situation (Fiske and Tetlock 1997). Injustice frames highlight how the democratically equal underdog was harmed through the illegitimate use of authority (Gamson et al. 1992). Similarly, claims about responsibility for prior actions seek to hold parties responsible for their failure to uphold the applicable norms governing the interaction (Iyengar 1991). Ambiguity over relative status in an interaction can even produce violent conflict (Gould 2003) Therefore, I also consider whether there are competing interpretations of the action voiced in general or within specific social identity groups. We would expect greater variability in the distribution of decision rules in situations in which the social meaning of an action is ambiguous, actively contested, or less central to the social identities invoked by the action.

DATA AND METHODS

This chapter uses a combination of textual analysis and survey data to measure the social meaning of voting: the people and relationships involved, and whether by all members of the population share a similar understanding of voting. This choice of methods is in keeping with standard practice, as research into social meaning typically draws on some combination of discourse analysis, survey analysis, and content analysis (Abdelal et al. 2006).[4] For the discourse analysis, I selected texts

---

[3] Not that this is a bad thing, as ambiguity of social meaning is necessary for the smooth functioning of social systems (White 1992).

[4] Although it would have been ideal to bolster the discourse analysis with a quantitative content analysis of the same sources, this would have involved constructing and validating word dictionaries for the "people and relationships" constructs described above, and would have added little to the analysis given the relatively straightforward social meaning of voting and the purely pragmatic intended use of this analysis.

to represent three distinct audiences or narratives: historical American sources (both primary and secondary), the contemporary general public narrative as captured on the editorial pages of four major metropolitan newspapers prior to the 2004 presidential election, and the academic literature on voter turnout. For the historical meaning of American voting, I used two key historical texts of different origins: first, the Declaration of Independence, and second, the Pledge of Allegiance recited daily by schoolchildren. Insights from these texts were supplemented with a close reading of Schudson's (1999) study of the historical and contemporary social practice of voting and political histories of democracy and American citizenship (Smith 1993; King 2000; King and Smith 2005). Histories of voting can be very informative, but alternative or contested meanings of voting might not be captured in this analysis if omitted marginal groups hold alternative views or if new understandings of voting are still emerging and evolving. I address this concern by using contemporary data sources, as described in detail later. To represent the contemporary academic literature on voter turnout, I used texts compiled from the prior literature search used as the basis for the literature review in the opening chapters of this book, with key articles in the literature re-read closely with an eye toward determining the social meaning and relational models involved in voting from the social scientists' perspective.[5]

Four newspapers were used as data sources for the analysis of the contemporary meaning of voting. Papers were chosen to include different regional and political perspectives: the *New York Times, Washington Post, Atlanta Journal-Constitution*, and Chicago *Daily Herald*.[6] The texts analyzed included all official editorials, editorial cartoons, and letters to the editor appearing in several major metropolitan papers the two weeks prior to the presidential election on November 2, 2004. To confirm that selecting only these two weeks did not bias the letters or editorials that appeared, additional days were selected at random from the full month leading up to the election. All text selections that referred to the word vote or voting in the editorial pages (and in some cases the news pages as well) were read to determine whether or not the written text included references to American citizenship, partisan categories, the four relational

---

[5] The inclusion of academic works on voting allows for a specific form of model validation, described as expert or face validity (Law and Kelton 1982).

[6] The *Los Angeles Times* was originally intended to be included as the fourth paper, but it proved difficult to access easily. Review of a few selected days did not reveal any systematic difference in the content of the *LA Times*, and therefore the *Chicago Daily Herald* was retained as a replacement.

models, and reasons or justifications for whether or not to vote in the upcoming election. Selections that addressed voter turnout specifically were read by two coders to determine whether any described the act of voting as something that would be interpreted in a negative light by others. In addition, less systematic searches of the Internet were used to identify marginal groups that might not be represented on the editorial pages of major newspapers.

The survey data in this chapter come from two general population sample surveys: the 1984 General Social Survey (GSS), and select years of the American National Election Study (ANES). GSS respondents were asked whether several actions commonly associated with citizenship (voting, male military service during peace and war, staying fully informed about public affairs, volunteering time in the community, and jury duty) were important obligations that a citizen owes to the country.[7] I use this question to measure the centrality of voting to the identity of an American citizen. ANES respondents were asked whether they agreed with the following statements: (1) my vote doesn't matter,[8] (2) my party doesn't have a chance to win,[9] or (3) local elections aren't important.[10] These questions serve as indicators of the extent of consensus on voting as a central act of citizenship.

VOTING IS THE ACT OF AN AMERICAN CITIZEN

> Despite the pain in my legs from standing in the insanely long line, I have exercised my right to vote. No matter what happens, this is the most important part of our democratic nation, and I am content in knowing this.
>
> – Letter to the editor, *Atlanta Journal
> Constitution,* November 2, 2004.

---

[7] All of these GSS questions include the following introduction: "We all know that American citizens have certain rights. For example, they have the right to free public education and to police protection, the right to attend religious services of their choice, and the right to elect public officials. I'd like to ask now about certain obligations that some people feel American citizens owe their country. I just want your own opinion on these – whether you feel it is a very important obligation, a somewhat important obligation, or not an obligation that a citizen owes to the country. Respondents could choose between: "very important," "somewhat important," "not an obligation."

[8] The exact question is somewhat confusing: "so many other people vote in the elections that it doesn't matter much to me whether I vote or not." The normative response required respondents to follow a double negative construction and disagree with the statement.

[9] "It isn't so important to vote when you know your party doesn't have any chance to win."

[10] "A good many local elections aren't important enough to bother with."

The claim that voting involves American citizens, and that voting is an act fundamental to citizenship implies that there is no other way of thinking about the act of voting: dropping a letter into a box is the private act of an individual (although that act may still be subject to social interpretation and judgment) whereas casting a ballot is the public act of an American citizen. The woman mailing a letter faces a very different decision situation than the woman casting a ballot – even though the physical actions are basically indistinguishable. In this section, historical and contemporary discourses about voting affirm that voting is symbolically linked to American citizenship, and that the boundaries of American citizenship have been historically defined through extension of the franchise.

The physical practice of voting and the attendant ideals of the citizenship have changed dramatically over the history of the American nation. Election day has included semifeudal affairs in which voters were rewarded with a drink after casting their ballot in the eighteenth century, boisterous (and at times violent) public ballots that confirmed community membership in the nineteenth century, and the privatized and rationalized aggregation of private interests of the twentieth century. Throughout this time, however, the physical act of voting in an election has remained the most celebrated and fundamental act of a *Good Citizen* (Schudson 1999).[11]

The symbolic link between voting and citizenship is central to the political and historical narrative of the United States. American schoolchildren are taught that the birth of the American nation was a fight for the right to vote. "No taxation without representation" was a revolutionary rallying cry, while the successful fight for voting rights defined the peak of the American Civil Rights movement and inspired revolutionary rhetoric as well ("the ballot or the bullet"). Periods of social change in American have been marked by changes in the constitution, in which inhabitants of the country (African Americans, women, and finally young adults between the ages of eighteen and twenty-six) made claims to full citizenship affirmed by the constitutionally guaranteed right to vote.

Contemporary discourse continues to link voting to American citizenship. Signs at polling places, get out the vote (GOTV) materials, and the GOTV and "I voted" buttons visually reproduce the symbolic link, often featuring the American flag, Uncle Sam, and a red, white, and blue color scheme. A *Washington Post* editorial from the 2004 election

---

[11] Readers are referred to Schudson for an excellent and accessible treatment of the historical and contemporary link between voting and citizenship.

season drew attention to the disenfranchisement of ex-felons, arguing "the stigma of a conviction lingers forever, undermining a person's
citizenship and pushing him away from the community" ("Voting Rights
for Ex-Felons" 2004). The editors describe voting as the "central event of
democratic life."

The "get out the vote" editorial is a staple of election season. The
editors of the *New York Times* state: "Urging Americans to vote on
Election Day should be a motherhood-and-apple-pie editorial topic"
("Vote No Matter What" 2004). On election day in 2004, all of the sam-
pled newspapers featured an editorial urging readers to get out and vote.
The editors of the *Atlanta Journal-Constitution* urged readers to "Make
Your Voice Heard" (2004) and reminded readers that "To be part of history, be sure to vote." The *Chicago Daily Herald* told readers: "That right
[to vote] is like granite; it has never been eroded" ("Take Advantage of a
Good Day Tuesday" 2004). Also on election day, an astounding eighteen
out of forty-four cartoons in the comic pages (not editorial cartoons) in
the *Washington Post* were explicitly about voting, suggesting the salience
of voting at election time even in nonpolitical media.

The strong symbolic linkage between the act of voting and membership in the national community is evident both in the definition of citizenship as a person with the right to vote and in the public discourse on
voting. To what extent, however, do most Americans accept this symbolic
link? Do most Americans agree that voting is the fundamental act of an
American citizen? Voting is clearly linked to American identity in public rhetoric, but there are other acts symbolically linked to citizenship
and community membership (e.g., paying taxes, serving in the military,
following laws, serving on a jury of peers), and not all of these acts are
necessarily going to be seen as central to a positive American identity by
most Americans.

As shown in Table 3.1, 80% of respondents on the 1984 GSS claimed
voting was a very important civic obligation, and only 4% claimed it was
not an obligation. The only other actions that are equally obligatory in
the eyes of respondents are wartime military service for men and speaking
English. Moreover, the perceived importance of voting does not vary significantly across the boundaries of race, class, or education.[12] The nearly
uniform importance of voting among all Americans stands in contrast to
responses to questions about jury duty and reporting crimes, which vary
considerably across the lines of social stratification.

---

[12] Results available from author on request.

TABLE 3.1. *Importance of Civic Obligations*

Civic Obligation	Very Important	Somewhat Important	Not Obligation	*n*
Speaking English	84%	14%	3%	1446
Wartime Military Service (men)	84%	14%	2%	1440
Voting	80%	16%	4%	1447
Jury Duty	65%	29%	6%	1438
Keeping Informed	56%	28%	6%	1439
Peacetime Military Service (men)	33%	49%	18%	1432
Volunteer	31%	56%	13%	1441

Source: General Social Survey 1984.

VOTERS AS AMERICANS: IS THERE A CONSENSUS?

The GSS survey data from Table 3.1 provides compelling evidence that the symbolic link between American citizenship and voting is widely shared in the general population: 80% of respondents indicate that voting is very important to American citizenship. Academic historians and editorial writers describe voting similarly, as the fundamental act of American citizenship. The social science literature on voting, however, raises questions about how widely this consensual understanding is actually shared in the population. Two groups in particular may not view voting in the same light as the general population: partisans and nonvoters.

Partisanship

> Whether Democrat or Republican, every U.S. citizen has a duty to learn about candidates and vote for the best person to serve our country.
> – Letter to the editor, *Chicago Daily Herald*,
> October 27, 2004[13]

Whereas the social identity of American citizen looms large in both historical and contemporary political discourse about voting turnout, the academic literature presents a somewhat different picture of the turnout decision. In the Downsian turnout model, potential voters are not regarded as members of a single American citizenry, but as individual actors with partisan interests. Partisanship continues to play a large role

[13] Evans 2004.

in most formal analyses of voting (Morton 1991; Bendor, Diermeier, and Ting 2004). Is this academic interest in partisanship entirely misplaced? Is it possible to reconcile a view of voters as partisans with the popular treatment of voters as American citizens, and what (if any) impact might partisan identity have on the decision rules used by potential voters?

As the quote at the beginning of this subsection indicates, the contemporary discourse on turnout goes to some lengths to describe voting as fundamental to American citizenship, and not the act of a Democrat or a Republican. There is a clear division in public discourse between the widely circulated nonpartisan appeals to vote and partisan appeals to vote for a particular candidate. Partisan activists and candidates seek to mobilize their own constituents (an issue discussed at length later in the book), but partisan mobilization attempts are either private (via phone or email) or include explicit nonpartisan appeals to vote embedded within partisan appeals. For example, American candidates making a stump speech often urge voters to vote regardless of what choice they make. Very few of newspaper excerpts included in the sample made a partisan appeal, and those that did also stressed the importance of turnout for Americans regardless of partisan preferences.

Thus, it appears that contributors to popular discourse recognizes the importance of partisan social categories to voter turnout, even while speakers go to great lengths to minimize the relationship between partisan categories and voter turnout. It is relatively easy, however, to reconcile these two distinct understandings of the people involved in the act of voting: an explicit public discourse about American citizens, and a political science discourse about partisan voters that is mirrored by popular acknowledgment that many voters implicitly consider the act of voting to involve members of partisan teams. The important distinction to make is between the widely accepted or normative social meaning of the act of voting as the fundamental act of an American citizen and the subjective interpretation of the act of voting by individual citizens or groups of citizens within particular social contexts. It may be that highly partisan and/ or politically knowledgeable citizens (including, presumably, many political scientists) subjectively experience the decision of whether or not to go vote as more related to their social identity of being a politically involved Democrat or Republican than an American citizen.

Whereas it is plausible to regard voting as involving people drawn from all three of these social categories (Americans, Democrats, and Republicans), the crucial practical question from the conditional choice perspective is whether or not partisan actors have a different relationship with one another, or are likely to apply a different distribution of decision rules. Given that all three categories refer to loose-knit communities of equals (the relationship between community members, discussed later), the basic meaning of the social situation would be the same regardless of whether someone considered voting the act of an American or a partisan. Therefore, there is no *a priori* reason to suspect that the distribution of decision rules would be different in the two situations, as they are similar in most respects.[14] Furthermore, the general public has explicitly rejected statements linking the turnout decision to partisan categories. More than 90% of NES respondents have consistently disagreed with the statement "It isn't so important to vote when you know your party doesn't have any chance to win." (See Table 3.2.)

Nonvoters

The academic literature also distinguishes voters from nonvoters, with nonvoters often drawn largely from particular demographic categories (e.g., minorities, young people, the uneducated, and, in earlier times, women.) Could it be that nonvoters do not accept that voting is the fundamental act of an American citizen, or do they in any way reject the shared social meaning of voting described above? A closer look at the reasons given for nonvoting reveals just the opposite: nonvoters also see voting as the fundamental act of American citizens, and justify nonvoting explicitly in these terms.

Survey data suggests that nonvoters and voters share the same understanding of voting. The overwhelming majority of nonvoters surveyed by the 2000 Census as well as in the past (Merriam and Gosnell 1924) claim that they wanted to vote but were out of town, sick, or in some way unavoidably delayed. Thus, the majority of nonvoters do not disavow

---

[14] This is not to say that observed turnout is expected to be similar among citizens who see voting as partisan and those who view it as a nonpartisan act, as discussed in Chapter 2. There is also one obvious exception to this general claim: Individuals who would follow an implicit communal norm when thinking of voting as a contribution to the united community of American citizens but be unwilling to follow the same norm when voting is seen as a conflictual partisan action. Conflict over mutual values is unthinkable within the communal frame (where everyone is assumed to be the same), and this may lead people who are highly cooperative in consensual settings to refrain from participation in high-information bipartisan social environments or following exposure to negative advertising (Iyengar and Ansolabehere 1995). This noteworthy exception to the overlap in social meaning between contributions to a public good and voting turnout most likely accounts for the unexplained findings of Fowler (2006).

TABLE 3.2. *Respondents Agreeing That Voting Is Not Necessary*

Year	Vote Doesn't Matter	Party Can't Win	Local Elections	n^a
1952	12%	11%	18%	1,757
1956	10%	9%	14%	1,733
1960	8%	8%	12%	1,149
1972	10%	9%	14%	2,674
1976	10%	8%	14%	2,209
1978	13%	9%	13%	2,240
1980	9%	8%	14%	1,562
2000	11%[b]	–	–	1,442
Overall	11%	9%	14%	14,766

[a] Statistics are for three different questions with similar number of responses, *n* for question with most responses provided.

[b] A four-category response option was used in 2000, and responses were collapsed to match earlier years.

Source: American National Election Study 1952–2000.

community membership, nor do they question the meaning of voting. Citizens who claim to be alienated make up around 10% of nonvoters on the 2000 Census, and their self-reported reason for not voting implies that they do not feel themselves to be part of the community that participates in elections.[15] Thus, these respondents acknowledge that a failure to vote marks exclusion from the national community, whether legal or self-imposed. Similarly, approximately 13% of female nonvoters surveyed by Merriam and Gosnell (1924) stated that they did not vote because they did not believe that women should be involved in politics.

The ANES has asked survey respondents, around a third of whom did not vote in the most recent election, whether they accepted three basic justifications for nonvoting. Table 3.2 shows the proportion of respondents who accept the justification (i.e., agree that voting is not necessary) for each year in which the question was administered (see also Knack [1992] for a complete discussion). The proportion of respondents accepting the justifications was so low and varied so little from year to year that the questions were dropped after the 1980 survey, and only one of the

[15] This justification for nonvoting fits quite well with the social theory of voting, however, as these citizens are likely to be poorly integrated into social networks that encourage both voting and a sense of belonging to the community. Citizens who live in communities with poor connections to political actors would also be likely to perceive themselves as disconnected from the political community of citizens.

questions was repeated on the 2000 survey as part of a question wording experiment.[16]

Even when respondents are given the chance to agree with the survey designer that voting is not important, only a very small proportion of respondents are willing to excuse nonvoting, exceeding 10% of the population only when considering voting in local elections. There is no sustained objection to this norm of voting, nor are more than 5–15% of respondents willing to give public legitimacy to any possible justification for not voting. Of course, not all of these survey respondents voted; in fact, not all were even registered voters (Knack 1992)!

Although nonvoters are more likely to endorse the various rationales for nonvoting, this does not indicate that nonvoters actually have a different understanding of voting, only that they do not identify so closely with their community and the community of American voters.[17] Even though the NES does not ask whether nonvoters are alienated from their community, there is indirect evidence that increasing inclusion does affect responses to these questions, namely the significant change over time in the attitudes of African Americans toward voting. In the 1952 survey, only 65% of black Americans agreed that they should vote even if their vote did not matter, but the gap with white respondents narrowed considerably by 1960 and became insignificant in 1972. This change in endorsement of nonvoting occurred during a time when many barriers to full community belonging facing black Americans were removed by the civil rights movement.

I was also unable to locate evidence in contemporary text sources that nonvoters held unique views on voting. However, it may be that newspaper editors purposely excluded any dissenting opinions voiced by

[16] The 2000 version added a middle-response category to try to elicit more variation. Although the question change reduced the portion of the population agreeing with statement, it did not affect the proportion rejecting the idea that the norm of civic duty applied to voting.

[17] Respondent answers to the NES question show more covariation with demographic variables that predict turnout (education, age, and race) than did responses to the GSS question about civic obligation reported earlier. However, this difference may reflect acquiescence to a confusing question rather than a true difference in acceptable justifications between various social groups. The questions are given in the negative form, thus a double negative construction is required to agree that voting is the right thing to do under the circumstances. The difficult wording of the questions may increase the number of respondents who accept the justification through acquiescence bias – a particularly plausible scenario as responses to the NES question are more strongly related to years of education than are responses to the GSS questions reported earlier.

nonvoters from the editorial page. Therefore, I also conducted an extensive online search to look for nonvoters with a different understanding of turnout. I found only one example: a small number of extreme individualists or anarchists who believe that legitimate authority rests with the individual, and therefore argued that people should not vote because it legitimates the state. Ironically, their argument does not contest the meaning of voting, but simply takes an extreme interpretation of the formal relationship between American citizens in order to advocate nonvoting. However, this view is not widely shared among the general public, and the speaker and organizer of a campus talk on the immorality of voting under anarchist principles were publicly attacked for the speaker's views on turnout.[18]

AMERICAN CITIZENS: FORMAL EQUALITY, INFORMAL AMBIGUITY

> One nation, under god, indivisible, with liberty and justice for all.
> – *Pledge of Allegiance*

The social meaning of voting is defined not only by the people (American citizens) involved in the interaction, but also by the relational model that characterizes interaction between them. The act of voting is a clear example of an interaction participated in by people who are formally defined as equals; one person, one vote is a prime example of the norm of equality at work. The formal relationship between American citizens is not the whole story, however, as informal or implicit relationships can still affect interpretations of a social situation and the decision rules that are used. Therefore, I look beyond the formal definition of American citizenship to consider whether or not there are other conceptions of the relationship between American citizens, and if these different conceptions might lead voters to use different decision rules.

Throughout American history and continuing into the present, American voters and citizens have been described as relating to one another through the principles of equality, community, and authority. A prime example of this blending of relationships within the American myth is found in the quote from the American Pledge of Allegiance: One nation (community), under god (authority), indivisible (community), with

---

[18] For more information, see the discussion of Wendy McElroy's talk at the University of Wisconsin online at http://lesterhhunt.blogspot.com/2008/02/dont-vote-event-on-campus.html

liberty and justice (equality) for all. Historical and contemporary discourse on electoral participation treats voting as a normatively desirable act according to each of these three relational models. The contemporary academic literature is once again somewhat at odds with the mainstream view, describing voting in equity or market-based terms. Perhaps as a result of the turnout depressing effects of the exposure to the market-based academic meaning of voting, some popular appeals also invoke market-based concepts when making turnout appeals. Therefore, I conclude that no consistent difference in turnout is likely to be motivated by the different relational models applied to American citizens.

All Americans Are Equal

> We hold these truths to be self-evident, that all men are created equal ...
> – *Declaration of Independence*

The American Declaration of Independence invokes the first of the mythical social relationships that bind all American citizens together: all Americans are equal. As discussed earlier, it is clear even in the phrasing of this famous quote that not all people who lived in America were considered part of this citizenry of equals: men without land, women, and slaves were all excluded from citizenship rights. Nonetheless, the formal relationship between citizens in a democracy is that of equality.

Historically, the rhetoric and formal recognition of individual equality in the act of voting was not necessarily matched by the reality of the social experience of voting (Schudson 1999). Although all citizens did have the opportunity to vote, historical social norms and practices emphasized allegiance to a local leader in the early days of the nation and membership in a local community in the latter half of the nineteenth century. However, the Australian ballot reform made voting a largely anonymous and private affair, and reinforced the social meaning of voting as the act of free and equal citizens. Perhaps ironically, the same reform may have decreased turnout by significantly altering citizen's expectations of whether or not other people would vote in the absence of social monitoring.

Contemporary writers stress equality among citizens in public discourse. The editors at the Chicago *Daily Herald* set up a specific contrast between the authority relationships of the past and the equality of citizenship, reminding readers that: "We threw out the kings a long time ago. We were transformed from serfs into citizens, with the right to do what we will do" ("Take Advantage of a Good Day Tuesday" 2004). The equality frame continues to be used to press for extended rights of citizenship, as can be seen in the discussion of felons and the right to vote earlier in the chapter. The popular reference to the "right to vote" implicitly invokes an interaction among equals, in direct contrast to the "civic duty to vote" phrasing that invokes an interaction based on authority relationships.

The American Community

> Most of all, we're going to vote because this is our country, our election, our national future. It's not possible to make up enough rules or roadblocks to discourage us.
> – *New York Times editorial*, November 2, 2004[19]

Interactions that take place between individuals who comprise a unique and undifferentiated whole (e.g., a country, a people, or we/our) are associated with the communal model of interaction. The communal relationship is also implicitly invoked via appeals to the good of the group and the amazing qualities of group members. There is ample evidence of a communal relationship between American citizens in both the historical and contemporary discourse around voter turnout.

The communal relationship between citizens is deeply embedded in classic texts defining American identity. "We, the people" draws on a communal logic, as does the earlier quote from the Pledge of Allegiance. The many symbolic references to America as an infant or child (the nation is born, the cradle of democracy) also reference the communal nature of the relationship between America's parents (the citizens) who have joined together to provide for the health of this new being, "the American nation."

Communal appeals are also characteristic of well-written and inspirational editorials. The *New York Times* editors conclude their election-day appeal with multiple references to community in the quote provided earlier. Another *New York Times* opinion piece, titled "Faith in America" (Krugman 2004), focused on the inspirational efforts of American citizens to vote. As is commonly found in communal rhetoric, other group members (citizens) are described in glowing and positive terms: "majestic," "refusing to be discouraged," "patiently waiting," "refusing to give in to cynicism and spin," and "believing in American democracy." A communal sharing frame was also found in some letters to the editor, as one writer

[19] "Vote, No Matter What," 2004.

noted: "[R]ecent letters on this page have had this implicit message: 'Get out and vote for the good of your country.'" (Dinan 2004)

Authority in America

> The American people have ... been given an ark, in which to deposit the most sacred thing known to man, namely, the ballots of free man; and we should see to it that only those authorized to do so by law be permitted to approach this ark, and that every person attempting to lay unclean hands upon it be overtaken by the wrath of a free people, which should be as destructive as the lightnings of Jehovah.
>
> – John P. Altgeld, Governor of Illinois (1893–1897),
> quoted in Schudson (1999)

The American nation has been made up of ostensibly democratic (or free and equal) citizens from the beginning; however, authority relationships, in which some Americans were simply better than others, have also played a large role in America's political past, and formal authority relationships have been closely linked to political citizenship and voting from the start. While many of these formal authority ranking relationships no longer play a role in voting, authority-based appeals continue to be found throughout the contemporary discourse on voter turnout. A description of voting as a "duty" or obligation (and the attendant threat of social punishment) invokes authority relationships between citizens. Language suggesting that some citizens are better than others has also long been used to argue that the rights of voting and citizenship should be protected from those unworthy of those rights.

Early rights of citizenship and voting and citizen rights were clearly allocated according to an authority ranking conception of citizenship, in which citizenship was restricted to elites who were deemed better than other American inhabitants. As in classical democracies, in early American times, citizens were drawn from a natural aristocracy of sorts. Elite members of society (white, male landholders) were granted the right to vote, whereas other members of society were not. Even with these restrictions on citizenship, the original constitution did not allow for direct election of the president. The framers of the Constitution worried that mass democracy would produce tyrants (bad authorities) instead of leaders of good character (good authorities). According to Schudson (1999), the popular image of citizenship at the time was of the informed citizen. Both citizens and leaders were expected to do what was best for the community, not merely look out for their own interests, invoking an image of the citizen as the good and kindly father and linking into the communal appeals described earlier.

Authority ranking conceptions of citizenship have long played an important role in public debates about voting and citizenship. The quote provided at the beginning of this subsection is from a period of high immigration at the end of the nineteenth century, when progressive calls for ballot reform were linked with an explicit authority ranking symbolism. Early studies of voter competence were inspired by similar concerns, and often contain explicit references to the problem of political participation by uninformed immigrants. As a result, the academic literature on voter competence retains an elitist sensibility (Lupia 2006).

Although poll taxes, literacy tests, and other such limitations on the right to vote have been constitutionally banned, the belief that citizenship should be limited to competent citizens is still part of the American debate over citizenship and voter turnout. This logic surfaced in the controversy over the contested 2000 Presidential election, as Justices Rehnquist (in his concurring opinion) and O'Connor (during oral argument) suggested that voters whose ballots were not machine-readable (the notorious "hanging chads" and "overvotes" of the Florida recount) had in effect forfeited their voting rights by not casting their ballot correctly (Lynch 2001).

Although American citizenship has gradually been expanded in the direction of the egalitarian norms of democracy, the authority-based norms of the informed, deliberative citizen is still very much alive in contemporary discourse. A quote from a letter to the editor appearing in an earlier subsection links the duty to learn about candidates and vote for the best one – a clear reference to authority norms of duty and a belief that the elite, informed citizen is better than the uninformed one. Numerous references to an authoritarian conception of citizenship are also found in a pre-election 2004 *Atlanta Journal Constitution* opinion piece backing the use of photo identification to reduce voter fraud (Wooten 2004). The author uses implicit racial cues (i.e., the MTV Vote or Die campaign, the term "harvest" to describe Democratic votes)[20] to evoke the authoritarian tradition linked to race in the United States (Stenner 2005). Citizen competence is a recurring theme: the Democratic get-out-the-vote literature is described as "the incoherent babble of a political lunatic"; Democratic opposition to voter identification is a product of the "liberal view that

---

[20] "Harvest" may evoke for many readers the former work of slaves in the American South; and slavery is a classic example of an authoritarian relationship.

individuals should be free to behave as irresponsibly as they choose"; and spoiled ballots are attributed to mistakes made by poor voters.

Authority often comes from the past: Those of lower status (present-day citizens) owe debts and allegiance to those of higher status (previous generations). Thus, one author of a letter to the editor drew on the shared meaning of the American Revolution (and other wars) when he wrote urging others to vote: "[E]xercise that obligation that so many have died to maintain" (Stastny 2004). The historical extension of citizenship is invoked in a similar manner. The official election-day editorial for the November 2004 election in the Chicago *Daily Herald* ("Take Advantage of a Good Day Tuesday") reminded readers that "it took mighty civil rights struggles to ensure that right [to vote] is given to all." References to authority are also found in academic treatments of voting, in the form of explanations of values that might inspire voting: the democratic system itself (Downs 1957), the internal satisfaction from doing one's duty (Riker and Ordeshook 1968), and the social rewards or sanctions associated with voting (Riker and Ordeshook 1968).

Appeals to authority were made more often in letters to the editor than in newspaper editorials. The term "duty," typically "civic duty," appeared in more than half of the general letters to the editor on the topic of voter turnout during the time period considered. Although the letter writers disagreed about the source of legitimate authority (past citizens, current citizens, your future self), all agreed that voters owed certain duties and obligations to the authority in question. Within the logic of the authority relationship, the positive duty or obligation to vote corresponds to the negative possibility of social or internal punishment for a failure to uphold those duties. Thus, one letter writer claimed that citizens who were not registered should be ashamed of themselves (Stastny 2004); another claimed that nonvoters might end up feeling guilty (Dinan 2004).

Market Pricing

I have argued that whereas American voters are in a formal relationship of equality as democratic citizens, other relational models enter into the popular, historical, and academic discourse on voting and citizenship. This blurring of the informal relationship between American citizens is not particularly problematic, however, as appeals to vote appear in terms of each of the relational models. The equity or market relationship represents a significant exception to this trend: Actors in a market interaction are not expected to vote.

The assumption of a market relationship between voters is the basis of the academic literature on rationality and turnout. In *An Economic Theory of Democracy*, Downs (1957) questioned the implicit assumption that decision making was determined by the social and normative meaning of an action. Instead, he argued that citizens were like buyers in a political market, choosing from among candidates according to a rational value ratio calculus ($pB - C$). The problem with the market logic is that the probability of influencing the outcome of any election (p) is so small that "no rational man [sic] would ever vote" (Downs 1957). The Downsian logic is so compelling that college students exposed to it become less likely to vote in subsequent elections (Blais and Young 1999).

Perhaps in response to the academic literature, I found evidence that some turnout appeals were cast in terms of market relationships. One article, under the subheading "Vote Your Way to a Fat Wallet," tackled the market pricing logic of voter turnout directly (Tierney 2004). The article opens with a stark reminder of the economic logic of turnout: "you have a much better chance of being struck by lightning on the way to the polls than of casting the decisive ballot in the presidential election." It goes on to summarize research claiming that enthusiasm for voting is a signal of trustworthiness, and that trustworthy voters are therefore more likely to earn higher incomes and do better in business. The researcher is quoted in the article saying: "none of us would ever want to hire the homo-economicus stereotype that populates most economic models." The *New York Times'* 2004 election day editorial ("Vote, No Matter What") outlined the belief that voting was intrinsic to the success or failure of democracy, arguing that "[b]y coming to the polls, citizens are literally giving a vote of confidence in American democracy" and "the more people vote, the more vital is our democracy." One letter writer cited earlier also made a minimax regret appeal: "Do it for yourself.... If you don't vote, you may end up feeling guilty for the next four years if your guy doesn't win" (Dinan 2004).

CONCLUDING THOUGHTS

This chapter has provided evidence for three distinct claims: (1) it is widely understood that the group of people involved in voting are American citizens; (2) American citizens are explicitly equals with respect to voting, but also linked together through communal bonds and respect for a higher authority; and (3) this understanding of voting and American citizenship is uncontested and stable across time, space, and even social divisions.

In both the past and the present, we can identify numerous disagreements about who should be granted the rights of citizenship and allowed to vote, but these concerns all flow from the same central assumption: that an American citizen is one who is granted (and exercises) the right to vote. Taken together, these claims capture the essential elements of the social meaning of voter turnout: Voting is needed to maintain the egalitarian community of American citizens, and thus voting is always the right thing to do.

Another theme running throughout the chapter is that voting is repeatedly recognized as requiring an effort on the part of ordinary citizens, with no obvious reward in terms of potential impact on the election. Thus, voting is understood by most Americans as a social dilemma among equals, as democratic stability is a public good, although individuals are tempted to free-ride on the activity of others (Hardin 1982; Taylor 1987; Green and Shapiro 1994). This is not to say that the popular imagination is correct in assuming that democracy is a public good that depends vitally on the turnout decisions of citizens. Is democracy threatened in America because presidential nominees are so often determined by the votes of several hundred people in an Iowa gym? The answer is probably no. Within the framework of conditional choice, however, individual behavior is conditional on what individuals *perceive* to be true about reality. If people experience the costs and benefits of voting as similar to those in a social dilemma, then they will decide whether or not to vote in the same way that they make decisions in similar social dilemmas. The decision rules used by prospective voters are not (entirely) unique to voter turnout, but reflect a lifetime of experiences in situations involving friends, acquaintances, and strangers where social norms and the public good are perceived to be in conflict with one's immediate self-interest. Therefore, the next chapter takes up the task of finding evidence of how people behave in similar situations, using data from comparable situations from decision-making experiments to develop a conditional decision model suited to the turnout situation.

4

Conditional Cooperation

Voter turnout is (inter)subjectively understood as a social dilemma, a situation in which individuals who are equal members of a loose-knit community are expected to do their fair share and duty for the good of the community. In this chapter, I complete the argument that citizens deciding whether or not to vote in an election use the same sorts of conditionally cooperative strategies that they use in other social dilemmas. In brief, most people are willing to cooperate as long as those around them are willing to do so as well. Drawing on evidence from multiple sources, this chapter also develops a model of conditional cooperation in social dilemmas similar to voting. The first half of this chapter considers which experimental protocols are most similar to voting turnout, using the same conceptual and measurement framework employed in the previous chapter. The second half estimates the distribution of decision rules in such similar situations.

EXPERIMENTAL DECISION SITUATIONS SIMILAR TO VOTING

The previous chapter demonstrated that voting is understood to be the act of an American citizen. Citizens in a democracy are in a formal relationship of equality, but are also implicitly tied together in a loose-knit community characterized by a mix of communal and authority relationships as well. In this section, I argue that the decision to vote has a similar social meaning as the decision to cooperate with other subjects in two basic experimental protocols: public goods games and bargaining games (ultimatum or dictator). I use a similar approach to assess the social meaning of these experimental protocols; however, there is little

in the way of survey data or other direct evidence available documenting how subjects understand the decisions made in the experiments.
Therefore, I rely primarily on academic discourse, indirect self-reports,
measurement of emotions, and changes in behavior following experimental manipulations that may alter the social meaning of the interaction.
First, however, the two basic protocols are introduced below for readers
who are unfamiliar with the experimental economics literature.

In a standard public goods game (see Ledyard 1995 for a review),
multiple subjects are given a sum of money. For example, a group of four
people might be given $10 each. They are told that they can keep the
money for themselves or contribute it to the group pot. Their contribution will then be doubled and redistributed evenly among all four group
members ($5 for each). If only one person contributes her money, and
everyone else fails to do so, she will leave with $5 and the other group
members will get $15. If all the group members contribute their original
sum of money, everyone in the group will receive $20.

In a standard bargaining game (Roth 1995 for a review), often called
the ultimatum game, subjects are divided into pairs. A sum of money is
allocated to each pair of subjects, and one of the two is given the instruc-
tion to "divide" the money between them. This subject, the Proposer,
proposes a division of the money, and the Responder has the opportunity to accept or reject the proposal. If the proposal is rejected, neither
subject gets any money. In the dictator version of a bargaining game, the
Proposer's suggested division is implemented without any opportunity
for the other subject to respond, thus the subject who divides the money
is called the "dictator" or Allocator (Kahneman, Knetsch, and Thaler
1986; Forsythe et al. 1994).

Citizenship in Social Dilemmas

How do subjects in experimental social dilemmas understand the people
or groups involved? Do the subjects understand themselves to be acting
as pure individuals, as is commonly assumed by economists? Or do they
see the situation as invoking other people, groups, or social identities?
Evidence from the writings of economists and self-reports from subjects
suggest that experimental social dilemmas are seen as a reflection of one's
personal commitment to fairness and willingness to be a good citizen in
a loose-knit community of equals.

Economists rarely ask subjects about their subjective understanding of
experimental protocols, as experimental social dilemmas were originally

designed to test the predictions of rational choice rather than to explore the social psychology of decision making. The little evidence that is available suggests that subjects see the experimental decision as reflecting on their personal commitment to treat other people fairly, analogous to an implicit social identity as a good citizen in a community of equals.

Subjects in public goods experiments overwhelmingly report that fairness was a major concern in making their decision, and that making substantial donations to the public good is the fair or right thing to do. Marwell and Ames (1979, 1981) found that experimental subjects could easily identify the "fair" or usual contribution, much as survey respondents almost unanimously identify turnout as the civic duty of Americans. Between 90% and 100% of subjects reported that a fair contribution to the public good was 50% or more of their personal endowment; around a third of subjects said that a fair share was all of their endowment.[1] Just as nonvoters still professed a belief that voting was integral to American citizenship, 75% of subjects who did not invest anything still reported that it was fair to contribute 50% or more of their personal resources. Subjects also report that taking money from a public good reflects poorly on subject (Henrich et al. 2004).

In a slightly modified version of a social dilemma, Tenbrunsel and Messick (1999) find that subjects distinguish between decisions perceived to reflect one's personal ethics or values (fairness, trustworthiness, good citizenship) and those perceived to reflect one's business acumen. When asked to decide whether or not they would comply with a hypothetical agreement between companies to limit pollution, respondents who describe the decision as an ethical one claim that they will cooperate with the agreement more than 90% of the time, and expect that 62% of others will do the same. Of those who describe the situation as a business decision, the cooperation rate is less than 40%, and only 47% of others are expected to cooperate. A further modification introducing an external monitoring authority had a significant impact on subject perceptions, with far fewer subjects viewing the decision as a personal one related to good citizenship.

Many economists writing about experimental dilemmas agree that public goods, prisoner's dilemmas, trust games, and bargaining games

---

[1] The rate was lower among economists, but this is not entirely surprising given the impact of graduate training (Frank, Gilovich, and Regan 1993, 1996). Lest these findings be taken as encouraging prejudice against economists, it is worth noting that many economists were still willing to cooperate.

are similar not only to each other, but also to other "good citizen" activities outside of the lab, such as charitable donations, voting, and other community-spirited activities (Marwell and Ames 1979; Dawes 1980; Frank, Gilovich, and Regan 1993, 1996). The formal structure and written instructions of public goods experiments often emphasize group membership. For example, a public good is called a "group exchange" (Marwell and Ames 1981). In general, economists do not debate whether subjects understand that experimental social dilemmas are a potential reflection of a subject's personal values, ethics, or morality – only the reasons that subjects do or do not comply with community values (Pillutla and Murnighan 1995).

Subject behavior also provides indirect evidence that subjects see the experimental decision as involving members of a loose-knit community with a shared social identity or common in-group status, not merely anonymous individuals. Not only are subjects willing to cooperate with one another, contrary to expectations, but experimental subjects are also willing to punish unfair behavior at a cost to themselves. Community membership is characterized by a willingness to punish unfair behavior and norm violations to enforce community standards (Kahneman, Knetsch, and Thaler 1986; Fehr and Fischbacher 2004). In contrast, subjects do not punish computers that randomly allocate unfair offers (van 't Wout et al. 2006), nor do they experience strong negative emotional reactions to unfair offers by computers (Sanfey et al. 2003). Group discussions during social dilemmas may contain: raised voices; threats of social, material, and even physical harm; and noncooperators described with a host of hostile terms such as "greedy," "cheat," "screw," "double-cross," "liar," and "immoral" (Bonacich 1972; Bonacich 1976; Dawes, McTavish, and Shaklee 1977). On a positive note, fair offers from other humans and mutual cooperation are associated with increased self-reports of happiness and increased activity in the areas of the brain associated with rewarding social interaction (Walter et al. 2005; Tabibnia and Lieberman 2007).

Equality, Communality, and Authority in Social Dilemmas

American citizens are formally equals with respect to voting; each citizen has a single vote that she or he may cast. Nonetheless, Americans see themselves tied together not just through bonds of equality, but also the bonds of communality and authority. Subjects in basic public goods experiments are also formally equal in terms of resources or endowments (i.e., each is given $10).[2] Similarly, subjects in bargaining games who are randomly assigned to the different roles are essentially equal at the start of the experiment, although they play different (and unequal) roles during the experiment. Drawing once again on subject self-reports, subject behavior, and academic discourse, I argue that subjects in an experimental social dilemma view themselves as tied together through similar bonds of equality, communality, and authority.

Subjects in basic social dilemmas perceive themselves as equals, based on both self-reports and observed behavior. In the preceding discussion, we saw that subject self-reports were strongly tied to the concepts of equality and fairness, similar to the commitments to equality found in discussions of voting turnout. Many subjects in both ultimatum and public goods games make decisions based on an equality heuristic, dividing the money fairly between themselves and the other subject(s). Van Dijk and Wilke (1994) show that an equal division rule (or equality heuristic [Messick 1993]) is even used by subjects facing asymmetric social dilemmas.

Subjects are significantly less likely to cooperate in modified bargaining games that alter the relationship of equality between them, reinforcing the claim that generic social dilemmas are commonly understood as situations involving fairness among equals. Modifications that introduce a business or market pricing frame to the dictator game significantly alter subject behavior (Hoffman et al. 1994; Hoffman et al. 1996). Similar changes are found in dictator and ultimatum behavior when subjects can earn the right to be the seller by winning a general knowledge trivia quiz (Forsythe et al. 1994; Hoffman et al. 1994; Camerer and Thaler 1995). When subjects compete for the right to play Proposer or Responder, thus imposing a pure market relationship among subjects, fairness is no longer a consideration for the vast majority of subjects (Camerer and Thaler 1995), and players in both roles use very different decision rules (Roth et al. 1991; Schotter, Weiss, and Zapater 1996).

---

[2] It is possible to imagine that the $10 might have a higher marginal utility to some subjects. This argument is more common in discussions of voting turnout with respect to the value of time, where someone will invariably point out that some working-class people may forgo wages or even risk losing their job if they take time off to vote, and thus voting would be far more costly for them. On the other hand, very high earners are often extremely busy and think of their time as extremely valuable, and thus might see voting as costly even if it does not involve forgoing wages or risking jobs. There is little systematic evidence on this point.

Themes of equality and fairness are commonly found in the academic literature on social dilemmas. Economists have repeatedly questioned whether subjects are motivated by a true desire to be a fair and trustworthy member of the community under all circumstances, or by a desire to simply appear fair to others (Pillutla and Murnighan 1995). In one of the most frequently cited economics articles on fairness in social dilemmas and other interactions, Rabin (1993) argues for an equality-matching version of fairness. An emerging strand of research on cooperation in social dilemmas has taken up the task of better defining and understanding how fairness and equality work at the individual cognitive and emotional level (Stouten, Cremer and van Dijk 2006; van Winden 2007).

The academic literature also contains numerous references that suggest the relationship between subjects is additionally characterized by aspects of communality (pro-social, altruism, community/group) and authority (punishment/duty, enforcement of community morals.) Thus, just like voting, cooperation in social dilemmas is formally defined as a relationship between equals, but there are signs that subjects also see themselves as governed by the injunctive norms associated with communal and authority relationships. Subject behavior also indicates the multilayered nature of the relationship that is understood to exist between them. As described earlier, punishment of noncooperators is common in social dilemmas, and active punishment is characteristic of authority relationships. Subjects' self-reports indicate that many experience anger and contempt in response to noncooperation (Bosman et al. 2001; Reuben and van Winden 2006); the emotion of contempt is generally a response to violation of authority norms (Rozin et al. 1999). Some subjects make large contributions to other subjects without expecting anything in return – a behavior associated with communal relationships.

In summary, generic social dilemmas are understood as involving equal members of a loose-knit community, with cooperation expected of all good citizens. While subjects are formally in a relationship of equality, they are also tied together through the bonds of communality and authority that are associated with community membership.

DISTRIBUTION OF DECISION RULES

The goal of this chapter is to develop a model of conditional cooperation, based on the distribution of decision rules used by subjects facing experimental situations similar to voting turnout. Thus far in the chapter, I have argued that the experimental situations most similar to voter turnout are bargaining games (ultimatum and dictator) and public goods games with equal endowments. We now consider the conditional decision rules used by subjects in these experimental situations, and use existing evidence to estimate the distribution of those rules in the population. We expect to find that subjects in these situations commonly use three basic decision rules, alone or in combination: an unconditional decision rule, a linear or mean-matching rule, and a nonlinear or median-matching rule.

As expected, the experimental literature reveals considerable individual heterogeneity in the use of decision rules. Some subjects regularly contribute most or all of their personal pot of money to a public good, whereas others contribute little or nothing unless there is the threat of punishment. In bargaining games, some subjects are willing to split the pot of money in half with another subject completely voluntarily (in dictator games), but others offer around 10% to 20% of the money to their partner even when that offer could be rejected as unfair (in ultimatum games). In a very thorough review of public goods experiments, Ledyard (1995) proposes that people can best be understood as "types": 10% of subjects play public goods dilemmas in an irrational (i.e., unconditionally cooperative) manner, 40% are responsive to issues of conditional fairness, and 50% respond like dedicated Nash players to purely rational motives.[3]

Ledyard's estimates are a useful starting point for estimating a distribution of conditional decision rules; however, he does not document the process he used to arrive at these estimates. Additionally, it is not clear how well Ledyard's "types" correspond to the three basic conditional decision rules. In the following section, I take a systematic look at available experimental data to assess the distribution of types (a summary of these results appears in Table 4.1). First, I consider results from a unique study that has explicitly asked subjects to provide conditional decision rules. Additional indirect evidence of the use of conditional rules can be uncovered through documented changes in subject behavior following experimental manipulations that affect their expectations of what other people will do (i.e., descriptive norms.)

[3] In all fairness, Ledyard terms his conjecture "outrageous," but the evidence for differing approaches to public goods and bargaining is quite compelling, even if the notion of types deserves further thought.

TABLE 4.1. *Estimated Use of Basic Decision Rules*

Experimental Condition	Average Gift[a]	% Giving Some[b]	% Giving Substantial[c]	Study
Repeated PG, final round	10–15%	25–47%	10–15%	Fehr and Gächter (2000)
Repeated PG, final round	11–18%	†	†	Croson (1996)
Repeated PG, final round	12–24%	30–60%	†	Andreoni (1988)
Repeated PG, final round, students	27%	55%	†	Andreoni (1995)
PG, self-reported rules	10–13%	12%	2%	Fischbacher, Gachter, and Fehr (2001)
DG, U.S. college students	23%	80%	20%	Forsythe et al. (1994)
DG, U.S. college students	27%	80%	12.5%	Hoffman et al. (1994)
DG double-blind, U.S. college students	13%	35–40%	10%	Hoffman et al. (1994)
DG, Middlebury students	33%	70%	42%	Carpenter, Verhoogen, and Burks (2005)
DG high stakes, Middlebury students	25%	80%	22%	Carpenter, Burks, and Verhoogen (2005)
DG high stakes, community college students	33%	85%	50%	Carpenter, Burks, and Verhoogen (2005)
DG high stakes, workers	45%	97%	70%	Carpenter, Burks, and Verhoogen (2005)
Cooperation, anonymous v. known	n/a	n/a	20%	Engelmann and Fischbacher (2002)
Cooperation with uncooperative subjects	n/a	n/a	10–20%	Engelmann and Fischbacher (2002)
(Mean-matching) PG, self-reported rules	n/a	50–65%	25%	Fischbacher, Gachter, and Fehr (2001)

PG is a public goods game, and DG is a dictator game.

† This information was not provided and could not be estimated based on available information.

[a] Average (mean) donation as percent of initial endowment (public goods games) or allocation to Proposer (dictator and ultimatum games.)

[b] Proportion of subjects giving some amount of money to either the public good or the Responder (dictator and ultimatum games.)

[c] Proportion of subjects giving a substantial amount of money to the public good (50% or more of allocation) or the Responder (an even 50/50 split.)

Self-Reports of Conditional Decision Rules

Fischbacher, Gächter, and Fehr (2001) asked subjects to make a traditional public goods allocation decision and to state how much they would be willing to contribute conditional on the contributions of other subjects.[4] The whole range of the rule was elicited, mapping subject contributions for anywhere between 0 and 100% average contributions made by the other subjects. The resulting estimates of conditional rules are reasonably similar to Ledyard's estimates (10%, 40%, 50%), but the results are not perfect because subjects underestimate their own willingness to contribute to a public good.

Two distinct findings suggest that self-reported conditional contribution tables underestimate how willing the subjects are to contribute to the public good. First, 30% of subjects claim that they will not contribute anything regardless of the behavior of others. This is a much larger proportion than we might expect, as only 13% of subjects chose to free-ride completely in a similar study by Marwell and Ames (1979). More importantly, when asked to make an actual contribution (as opposed to providing a conditional contribution table), the average contribution of these alleged free-riders is 5% of their endowment, with some subjects giving up to half of their endowment. A similar underestimation is found in the remaining subjects as well. The average traditional donation was about one-third of the endowment, although this contribution corresponds to an expected contribution rate of 100% by other group members according to the average of subjects' contribution tables.

With this caveat firmly in mind, the relative use of unconditional cooperation is assessed by looking at the amount subjects report that they would be willing to contribute to the public good knowing that other group members did not contribute ($\Sigma d_j = 0$). In the study, approximately 10% of subjects were willing to make substantial (more than 25% of their endowment) contributions to the public good, and the average contribution at $\Sigma d_j = 0$ was 15%.

Turning now to evidence concerning the linear-matching rule, 65% of subjects report conditional rules close to mean matching when average group donations are less than 50%, and the majority of these continue to match contributions close to perfectly after this point. Almost 25% of

---

[4] Economists are generally wary of using stated intentions instead of actual behavior in an experiment, but each subject had a 1 in 4 chance of having their conditional schedule used in place of the traditional contribution response to determine payoffs.

the subjects turned in contribution schedules that were small variations on the mean-matching function. Fourteen percent of subjects submitted a hump-shaped conditional pattern that might have been a utilitarian rule (Elster 1989), whereas the remainder reported a reduced (but still linear) matching rate. Given the aforementioned issues with the data, it seems reasonable to estimate a population level weight of 40–50% on the linear matching rule, with some people using a pure mean-matching rule and others mixing it with other decision rules.

The evidence to support the use of the median-matching rule is not overwhelming, as only a few subjects gave contributions schedules that resembled median matching. However, it is clear that many subjects underestimate their willingness to contribute, and that in the right situation (e.g., manipulations allowing discussion or punishment), even the alleged free-riders would contribute something to the public good. Therefore, subjects who claim that they will not give anything to the public good, those who use linear rules at a reduced rate, and those who make utilitarian contributions are most likely also placing some weight on a median- or focal-point-matching strategy when making contribution decisions. Based on the relative use of the unconditional and mean-matching rules, the relative use of the median-matching rule is most likely 40–45%, although I would consider the range 40–50% as plausible using Ledyard's relatively generous estimate as the upper limit.

Experimental Manipulations and Conditional Decision Rules

Experimental social dilemmas can take a variety of forms, including public goods games, trust games, and dictator and ultimatum games. Subject behavior in these experiments is often affected by experimental manipulations that do not affect the basic social meaning of the experiment. The manipulations with the greatest impact on subject behavior include changing the relative costs and benefits of cooperating, providing the ability to talk with other subjects, and adding the possibility of punishment (Ledyard 1995).

I argue that most of these manipulations do not change the social meaning (or applicable injunctive social norms) of the decision situation, and therefore do not fundamentally alter the distribution of conditional decision rules used by subjects. (Changing costs can shift the distribution at the margins, as considered in the following section.) The manipulations instead impact observed subject behavior by changing the descriptive norms of the situation, or expectations of what other people in the same situation will do. Thus, even with the same distribution of rules, cooperation will increase as expectations of others' cooperation increase, and decrease as expectations of others' cooperation decreases. Therefore, the impact of manipulations on subject expectations, along with associated change in subject behavior, can provide indirect evidence on the relative use of the three basic rules in experimental social dilemmas.

As previously noted, it is possible to estimate the use of the unconditional cooperation rule by identifying experimental situations where subjects do not expect others to contribute. Two treatments are discussed later in the chapter, where the average expectation of cooperation by other subjects is likely to be quite low: (1) the final round of repeated public goods games and (2) anonymous dictator games. Another study manipulating the anonymity of subject contributions provides similar estimates of unconditional cooperation levels as the two earlier treatments.

Subjects in the final round of repeated public goods games have seen contributions slowly decrease, and are most likely to expect virtually no cooperation from other subjects. Previous research has shown that subjects indeed update their expectations of others on the basis of prior play (Offerman, Sonnemans, and Schram 1996, 2001; Kovarik 2008), although very few studies of repeated games elicit subjects' expectations in the final round. The one study that reported subject expectations in a repeated public goods game found that the average expected contribution was around 20% of the endowment in the final round (Neugebauer 2009). As shown in Table 4.1, average final round contributions of between 10% and 20% of the endowment are regularly observed in repeated dilemmas.

Another experimental treatment that isolates unconditional cooperation is the anonymous dictator game, in which the Responder has no ability to punish the Proposer for unfair allocations and thus, absent unconditional cooperators, expected contributions approach zero. Once again, few studies elicit subject expectations in the dictator game; those that exist estimate expected contributions of around 10–30% (Bicchieri and Xiao 2008; Artinger et al. 2009). Furthermore, as shown in Table 4.1, Proposers in a dictator game allocate an average of 15% to the other party. On average, 30–40% of Proposers give the Responder at least some money, whereas 20% of subjects actually give the second player half of the pot of money. Even when faced with a hypothetical dictator game involving stakes of $100 million, two of the sixty-six subjects professed a willingness to give away half of this money to be fair (Pillutla and Murnighan 1995).

Another approach to isolating unconditional cooperation is to assess the proportion of subjects who contribute the same following a manipulation designed to increase cooperation. Engelmann and Fischbacher (2002) find that 20% of subjects are willing to help as much in a purely anonymous contribution situation as they are in a situation where subjects can build reputations on the basis of common knowledge about contributions.[5] In an embedded manipulation that affected expected contributions of others, the same study found that subjects who developed a reputation for being uncooperative were still helped 10% to 20% of the time. Thus, these two different approaches yield quite similar estimates of unconditional cooperation.

Whereas the majority of experimental participants do not make contributions when they are in a dictator-like role, almost all experimental subjects are willing to cooperate conditionally, given sufficiently high expectations of the cooperation of others. Indeed, experimental treatments allowing communication and/or punishment (Ostrom, Walker, and Gardner 1992; Fehr and Gachter 2000) can push cooperation rates up to 100%, and both of these treatments increase expected cooperation of others (Offerman, Sonnemans, and Schram 1996; Vanberg 2008). The willingness of almost all subjects to cooperate given the right circumstances is not unlike patterns in voting turnout, where only "core" (Campbell et al. 1960) voters consistently turn out in all elections, but almost no registered voters who remain in the community fail to vote in at least one election over a five-year period (Sigelman et al. 1985; Sigelman and Jewell 1986).

Unfortunately, no persuasive indirect methods were identified for assessing the relative use of mean matching and median matching on the basis of subject behavior. Therefore, the most parsimonious assumption is that the remaining 80% to 90% of rule usage is distributed evenly between the mean- and median-matching conditional cooperation rules – in line with the estimates produced using direct evidence on the distribution of conditional decision rules.

Costs and the Distribution of Decision Rules

Although both conditional choice and rational choice assume that costs may affect individual decisions, costs figure in the two frameworks in very different ways. Within rational choice, changing the costs of the

[5] Contributions were higher on average in the reputation-building condition.

action can fundamentally alter the decision that a potential voter is facing. Conditional choice, on the other hand, describes the decision situation in terms of social meaning rather than in terms of costs and benefits.
Increasing individual costs do not fundamentally alter the perception of
the situation of voting as a social dilemma among equals, and thus do
not fundamentally alter the injunctive norms that apply to the situation.
However, costs can work at the margins to change participation by shifting the aggregate distribution of decision rules, particularly the proportion of unconditional cooperators.

Results from laboratory settings fit with this conception of costs.
Experiments on decision making can manipulate costs and benefits of an
action in several ways: raising benefits, lowering costs, or allowing punishment. Raising the marginal payoff for contributions to a group good
may result in a small increase in cooperation (Ledyard 1995); lowering
costs can be even more effective at inducing cooperation. Subjects playing a public goods game where no one involved had the opportunity to
be greedy (all subjects pay if the group contributes enough to provide the
good) contributed between 80% and 95% of the endowment, on average (Dawes and Thaler 1988; Ledyard 1995). Thus, significant changes
in behavior result from removing costs entirely – a manipulation that
is likely to alter the social meaning of the situation, as it is effectively
no longer a social dilemma. Marginal changes in costs produce small
changes in behavior at best.

The use of the unconditional cooperation strategy is likely to be particularly responsive to costs, as suggested by Elster's (1989) analysis of
decision making by everyday Kantians. Carpenter, Verhoogen, and Burks
(2005) found that changing the pot from $10 to $100 had no impact
(or even decreased) the proportion of Proposers offering nothing to
Responders, but that the proportion of those offering 50/50 splits fell
from around 40% to around 20%. They report a similar drop in the
proportion of ultimatum game Proposers offering a 50/50 split in the
high-stakes ($100) condition.

Taken as a whole, these findings suggest that once costs are higher than
a certain low level, changes in costs do not fundamentally change either
individual behavior or the social meaning of situations. To the extent that
small changes in costs do affect behavior, the effects are relatively small
and appear to primarily affect the relative use of the unconditional cooperation rule. Therefore, low- to moderate-cost social dilemmas are likely
to be very good proxies for voter turnout, although changing costs may

slightly reduce the likelihood of unconditional cooperation in a situation without substantially changing the social meaning.

In summary, this chapter has closely examined experimental social dilemmas that are analogous to voting, in that they are governed by the same injunctive norms as voting turnout and involve equal members of a generic, loose-knit community. Manipulations of experimental social dilemmas that affect the expected actions of others allow us to distinguish between unconditional and conditional decision rules, and to a lesser extent between the two forms of conditional cooperation. A combination of direct and indirect evidence suggests that 10–20% of subjects are willing to cooperate regardless of what those around them do, with observed rates of unconditional cooperation in lower-cost dilemmas at the upper end of this distribution. Even though evidence on the relative use of the two conditional cooperation rules is not nearly as persuasive, it is reasonable to assume that equal weight is put on the two conditional rules on average.

5

Conditional Voters

Dynamics and Networks

This chapter is the final one devoted to the first stage of the research design: develop and validate a model of conditional decision making in situations similar to voting turnout. Recall that a conditional decision model posits both that most individuals use decision rules that are conditional on the decisions of other people, and that the distribution of individual decision rules in a situation is conditional on the social meaning of the situation. Therefore, to identify a plausible decision rule distribution, Chapter 3 analyzed the social meaning of voting and Chapter 4 isolated conditionally and unconditionally cooperative behavior in experiments with a similar social meaning. This chapter now takes up the task of building and analyzing a model of conditional cooperation based on the parameters determined in Chapter 4: a model with a distribution of 10–20% unconditional cooperation and an approximately even split in the use of the mean- and median-matching conditional decision rules.

Constructing and analyzing this model requires the introduction of several additional concepts through the course of this chapter, including diffusion of behavior, the tools of social network analysis, and the technique of simulating decision making in a large population through agent-based modeling. In nontechnical terms, this chapter will analyze the way cooperative behavior such as voting turnout spreads through a group of people, assuming that these people's decisions are based on the observed or expected activity of those around them. First, I create numerous simulated populations of individuals who make conditionally and unconditionally cooperative decisions. In later sections, these simulated voters are also embedded in social networks created to mimic properties of real-life friendship networks. These simulated voters then make decisions about whether or not to vote based on the behavior of others that they can observe from their location in the network.

Simulations of the basic conditional cooperation model produce turn-out rates that are reasonable, robust, and sensitive to network size. First, simulated turnout rates are *reasonable*, varying between 10% and 100% of potential voters.[1] The simulated turnout rate is most sensitive to the distribution of unconditional cooperation in the population, and only produces reasonable turnout in the empirically calibrated parameter range of 10–20% unconditional voting. This is a noteworthy result in itself, given the difficulty of generating reasonable rates of turnout in models based on rational choice assumptions about voters. Further, these basic results are also quite *robust* to changes in the relative distribution of mean-matching versus median-matching rules. Finally, incorporating more realistic local social networks between voters reveals that *average network size* also has a significant impact on turnout. Voters who are embedded in larger and less dense network structures vote at higher rates than those embedded in networks that are smaller and more clustered. These results will have important implications for the empirical model of voter turnout tested in later chapters.

CONDITIONAL COOPERATION: THE BASIC DYNAMIC

The conditional cooperation model in this chapter produces what are commonly termed contagion, or threshold, or diffusion dynamics, much like many other processes in which choices are conditional or interde-pendent (Rolfe 2009; see also Dodds and Watts 2004; Watts and Dodds 2009). In a model of conditional turnout decisions, voting is contagious (cf. Nickerson 2008) and can spread to friends and family. Widespread contagion or diffusion occurs when at least one more person is willing to cooperate or vote conditional on others over a sequence of points in time, assuming that the decision to vote is fixed once it is made during this time span. The question is: Which distributions of decision rules are likely to lead to the spread of cooperation or voting turnout? Are there some distributions that always produce 100% turnout, and others in which the turnout decisions of initial voters fail to spread to friends and family?

---

[1] While the asymptotic properties of the model are analytically tractable, agent-based simu-lations are necessary to gain more insight into model dynamics in discrete and finite populations of voters.

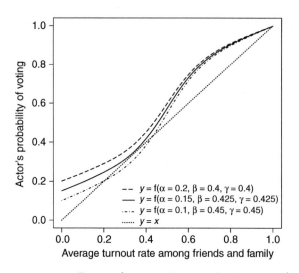

FIGURE 5.1. Expected turnout (cooperation) rate or adoption curve.

Whereas it is possible to characterize the asymptotic properties and general class of conditional decision models (Dodds and Watts 2004), the general properties of threshold-type conditional decision-making models are also easily assessed through the graphical or "cobweb" method. The graphical method consists of first charting the average responsiveness (e.g., the cumulative threshold distribution or influence-response function) of the population and then comparing the resulting function to the 45° line or $y = x$ line. Equilibrium values for the system are found by examining where the function intersects with the 45° line.

Figure 5.1 graphically presents the average conditional responsiveness of a population under three different sets of distributional assumptions, with the $y = x$ line included for comparison. These rules distributions fall at the extremes (10% and 20%) and midpoint (15%) of the empirically observed distribution of unconditional cooperation, with the remainder of the rule usage evenly distributed across mean and median matching. Like most binary conditional decision models, all three models will tend to produce all (100% turnout) or nothing (no turnout) outcomes. Analytically, we would expect both functions with higher numbers of unconditional voters (15% and 20%) to produce universal turnout, whereas the function with fewer first movers (10%) has unstable equilibria where it crosses the 45° line, and therefore will tend toward either no turnout or 100% turnout.

This basic assessment of the conditional choice functions in Figure 5.1 assumes an idealized distribution of population responsiveness. In real life (and in samples drawn from this distribution), actual responsiveness is probabilistic, and therefore expected to be much messier. Additionally, the decision to vote (or not vote) is a one-shot decision made on the basis of multiple prior observations, and is therefore better represented as a threshold type decision as opposed to a changeable, responsive repeated choice (Rolfe 2009). Therefore, a particular sample from each of the distributions will have a tendency to get "stuck" at unstable equilibrium values and other places where the function approaches but does not intersect the 45° line.

Looking back at Figure 5.1, we can therefore form expectations of the patterns likely to be produced by simulated turnout in finite samples using threshold rules. The 10% unconditional rule distribution intersects the 45° line at two places ($x \approx 0.20$ and $x \approx 0.43$), and both of these equilibrium values are unstable. Therefore, we would expect the majority of simulated voting populations to stabilize around 20% turnout, with some populations reaching 30–40%, and only a very few passing the 40% threshold to reach 100% turnout.

The distribution with 15% approaches and almost touches the 45° line at around $x \approx 0.34$, and therefore as many as half of the simulated voting populations may get stuck around 30–40% turnout, with the rest reaching higher levels of near-universal turnout. The distribution with 20% unconditional turnout falls well above the line and is unlikely to dip below it even in a probabilistic sample so long as the simulated population contains at least a few hundred voters. All three distributions also approach the line $y=x$ near the top, and turnout rates may stabilize slightly below 100% as a result (near universal turnout).

Purely on the basis of inspection, we already now know a good deal about the behavior of the conditional turnout system. Turnout rates are expected to be much higher when more people use the unconditional cooperation rule. Turnout at the lower end of the spectrum (10% unconditional) is likely to hover between 10% and 20%. Turnout in the middle of the spectrum (15% unconditional) will be the most variable, but often get stuck around 30% turnout. Turnout rates approaching 100% will be most common at the high end of the range (20% unconditional).

As a confirmation of the results of the visual inspection, I conducted 100 agent-based simulations of "elections" for each of three specified distributions of decision rules among 1,000 "voters." (Simulation procedures are described in Appendix A.) Figure 5.2 reports average turnout rates across one hundred simulations of each of the three specified distributions of decision rules. Simulation results are exactly as expected.

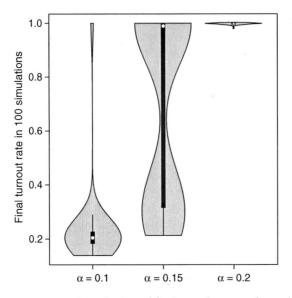

FIGURE 5.2. Distribution of final-round turnout for each parameter combination. Simulated cooperation (turnout) among 1,000 agents in all-see-all (global information) networks. Simulations run in RePast; see Appendix A for more details.

On the basis of simulation results, we can now consider whether the estimated range of unconditional cooperation developed in the previous chapter produces turnout rates that are *reasonable*: Are simulated turnout or cooperation rates similar to those observed in real elections and/ or experimental social dilemmas? Observed turnout in elections can vary between extremely low turnout of 5–10% in local American primaries to almost 100% in countries such as Australia, Italy, and Brazil with mandatory voting. Similarly, contributions in public goods often vary between 10% or so of the total available and almost 100% when discussion and/ or punishment is allowed. This range of 10–100% cooperation and turnout is almost identical to the range of simulated outcomes.

Model Robustness Checks

Next, we consider whether the model and estimated parameter range are *robust*: Does the model produce reasonable cooperation rates throughout its entire parameter range, or do the results break down for certain distributions of decision rules? Two issues are of particular importance. First, is the model robust to changes in the relative distribution of mean- and

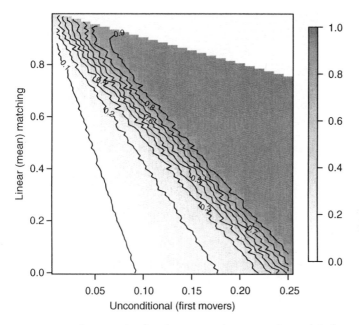

FIGURE 5.3. Average simulated turnout when voters have global networks.

median-matching rules? Recall that it was difficult to estimate this relative proportion from empirical evidence from public goods experiments; it is therefore critical that the model results are robust to changes in the ratio of the two conditional rules. Second, the model should produce reasonable results only within the empirically estimated range for unconditional cooperation, as that would suggest that the estimated model uniquely produces reasonable turnout levels. Therefore, I also conduct a full "parameter sweep," simulating "elections" in communities of 1,000 agents with a complete range of combinations of unconditional and conditional cooperation, to assess whether reasonable cooperation rates are obtained outside of the estimated range of unconditional rule usage (10–20%) or only within this range.

Results from a "parameter sweep" of the model appear in Figure 5.3. In the parameter sweep, the unconditional rule distribution varied between 1% and 25%, and the remainder varied between fully weighting mean matching and fully weighting median matching.[2] In Figure 5.3, the relative

---

[2] To produce Figure 5.3, 100 simulations of 1,000 agents were run using the following parameter ranges, with steps of 0.01 for each parameter: $\alpha \in (0.1-0.25), \beta \in (0.0-(1-\alpha)),$ $\delta \in (0.0-(1-\alpha-\beta))$.

use of the unconditional rule appears on the x-axis, whereas the relative weight put on the mean-matching rule appears on the y-axis. The proportion of median matching does not appear in the figure, but comprises the remainder of the rule distribution (i.e., $1 - unconditional - mean$ $matching$). Turnout rate varies between 10% and 100%, and is indicated by both the graph shading and contour lines at intervals of 0.10.

Figure 5.3 also provides additional insight into the robustness of the model outside of the estimated parameter range. It appeared that the model would fail to produce meaningful turnout below 10% unconditional cooperation and would consistently produce turnout levels approaching 100% participation when the use of unconditional cooperation exceed a rate of 20%. Simulation results confirm these expectations, with participation almost nonexistent below 10% unconditional rule use, and hovering around 100% above the upper end of our estimated range. The sole example of somewhat reasonable results is produced by parameter combinations similar to the uniform distribution threshold model described by Granovetter (1978) but with slightly higher first-mover rates. Although this suggests that a modified Granovetter threshold model may be applicable to some situations, such a model cannot replicate the full range of observed turnout unless we assume significantly higher levels of mean matching (and lower levels of median matching) than is typically observed. Thus, models with fewer than 10% first movers do not provide empirically plausible alternative models of decisions in situations similar to voting turnout.

In summary, the conditional cooperation model both reasonably and robustly reproduces observed patterns of turnout and cooperation in social dilemmas. Furthermore, parameter combinations outside of the estimated range did not produce reasonable cooperation rates: Either all voters would participate or only unconditionally cooperative "first movers" would participate. With this initial check of model plausibility complete, we turn now to consider an extension to the basic conditional cooperation model: the introduction of local social networks in place of global information about other agents.

CONDITIONAL COOPERATION IN LOCAL SOCIAL NETWORKS

Recall that our hypothetical voters are conditional decision makers, such that their probability of voting is a function of the behavior of others. But which others? Simulations in the preceding discussion assumed interaction within a "global" or "all-see-all" network. In other words, potential voters reacted to the average turnout in the entire population, as opposed to the turnout rate only among people that they know. In reality, however, most people's decision making puts more weight on the decisions of friends and family members than on statistics about general rates of activity in the larger population. A voter may care more about his/her friends because he/she has more information about their decisions; because his/her friends are more likely to observe, sanction, and/or reward his/her actions; or because of some other intangible quality of face-to-face contact.[3]

It is quite possible that simulated turnout rates based on global information will be misleading if local social networks serve as the appropriate reference group for conditional decisions about activities such as voting turnout. Therefore, this section looks at the impact of local social networks on simulation results. The model remains reasonable and robust with the inclusion of local network information, although network structure can substantially impact the simulated turnout rate. The size and direction of this impact is contingent and nonlinear, depending both on the level of unconditional cooperation in the simulated population and the average size and density of personal networks of people who are directly and indirectly connected to the decision maker. Smaller local networks do a far better job of fostering compliance with social norms when cooperation is relatively costly, whereas larger networks do a better job of fostering compliance when cooperation is relatively cheap.

Simulating Personal Networks

If voters are to rely on local networks for information, then each simulated voter will need to be given "friends," or a set of other agents on whom the voter bases his/her conditional turnout decision. This, in turn, requires the construction of realistically simulated social networks, because previous research has shown that network composition, as well as the placement of first movers, can have a large impact on the subsequent spread of innovation (Granovetter 1978; Gould 1993; Chwe 1999; Moreira et al. 2004).

---

[3] It is probably important not to discount the potential importance of face-to-face contact, given the effectiveness of face-to-face mobilization efforts in encouraging turnout (Gerber and Green 2000; Green, Gerber, and Nickerson 2003; Niven 2004), or in changing behavior in public goods (Ostrom, Walker, and Gardner 1992). Experimentalists often use computers as intermediaries between partners when conducting experiments, precisely because of the potent influence of face-to-face contact.

First, the networks used in these simulations were created as realistically shaped "random networks." Traditionally, social simulation researchers interested in the impact of local networks have relied on grid-based Moore or Von Neumann local neighborhood – a two-dimensional grid where each agent occupies a square and interacts with the four or eight people closest to them. Grid-based methods may be adequate when modeling the relationships between trees, states, or other geographically contiguous entities, but they are not a good representation of human networks of everyday social interaction, and may produce misleading simulation results (Rolfe 2004). Therefore, the simulations used in the remainder of this book use local networks created following the biased random method introduced by Jin, Girvan, and Newman (2001) to create more realistic personal networks. This method is ideal for this purpose because it allows direct manipulation of personal network degree and clustering in the simulated networks. (More details on the biased random network simulation method appear in Appendix A.)

Second, these random networks were constructed to reflect the structure of real-world social networks. Real-world social networks vary in many ways, with many methods of mathematically describing their important elements (Wasserman and Faust 1994; Bruggeman 2008, for a thorough introduction). Any or all of these characteristics of networks or individual social location might in theory affect the spread of cooperation, but I focus on the impact of two characteristics of local social networks: average personal network size and average personal network density.[4]

The average size or degree of personal networks is a well-known network property, representing simply the average number of friends (or "ties") that each individual possesses. For example, if John has eight friends and Mary has twelve friends, the average network degree in this two-person population is 10 (k_{John} = 8, k_{Mary} = 12). Density is another important property of personal networks, measuring the extent to which a person's friends are friends with one another.[5] If any actor, i, has k_i neighbors, then, at most, $k_i(k_i-1)/2$ ties can exist between these neighbors, assuming symmetric ties. Personal network density, c_i, is equal to

---

[4] This term can be confusing, because personal network density is calculated using an egocentric network. Thus it will not correspond to the sociocentric measure of network density, although whole network density measures do correspond to average personal network degree.)

[5] When describing sociocentric or whole network structure, average personal network density is also sometimes known as the clustering coefficient.

the total number of ties present divided by the maximum number of ties potentially present. For example, if John has four friends who know two of his other friends, and two friends who know one of his other friends, then John's personal network density is 0.36.[6]

Even though it might be ideal to consider more complicated network properties, or even the correlation between network properties and decision rules, there are compelling practical and theoretical reasons to limit the inquiry to network degree and clustering. From a practical perspective, survey data on personal networks is easily available and based on general population samples. To represent interesting sociometric properties such as centrality, cliques, and structural equivalence (Wasserman and Faust 1994), it is necessary to have social tie information from a complete and bounded population. Creative examples of data collected on sociocentric networks include marriage and business relationships between medieval Italian families (Padgett and Ansell 1993), coauthorship or citation networks (Newman 2001), actors in the same movie (Amaral et al. 2000), and cosponsorship of legislation in the U.S. Congress (Skvoretz 2002, citing Burkett 1997). The major drawback to these data sets is that they typically reflect only verifiable and/or very specific interactions within a bounded population, not the structure of more general and intimate interpersonal relationships within a broader population.

Mathematically, a correlation between decision rules and network position/centrality can have a significant impact on the spread of innovations (Gould 1993, Chwe 1999). However, these models assume pure "types" whereas the conditional cooperation model assumes greater levels of individual heterogeneity in the use of the three basic rules. Given that around 50% or more of subjects in experimental social dilemmas were willing to make unconditional contributions at least some of the time, it is impossible for that many probabilistic first movers to occupy central positions in the network. Furthermore, the only available evidence suggests that there is no significant correlation between network centrality or position and the use of conditional decision rules (Goeree et al. 2008; Brañas-Garza et al. 2010). Therefore, simulations that randomly assign relative rule use across a network are probably good proxies for the relative rule distribution in real-world political discussion networks as well.

In summary, simulations of turnout in local networks will only investigate the impact of variation in average personal network size and density.

---

[6] $(4 \times 2) + (2 \times 1) = 10$ ties present out of $8 \times (8 - 1)/2 = 28$ possible, for a density of $10/28 \approx 0.36$.

The next step is to consider which networks to simulate, and to generate empirically grounded estimates of crucial network properties on which to base the creation of networks for the simulated voter populations.

Empirical Estimates of Personal Network Degree and Density

Although discussions of network properties can become quite technical, considering network degree reflects an important substantive question about who is likely to influence a prospective voter's decision. After all, we might consider several different types of friendship ties: networks of close friends, general friends, or mere acquaintances. But which network is likely to diffuse cooperative behavior such as voting? I will argue for modeling the spread turnout through general friendship ties, but to do so requires a brief introduction to personal network data and its collection, at each level of friendship.

Collecting information about ego-centered networks is similar to collecting information about other individual attributes. A set of individuals is surveyed and asked about personal relationships, and their responses can be used to estimate the shape and composition of personal networks in some larger group. A handful of methods are commonly used. Frequently, surveys employ name generators: "with whom do you discuss important matters?"; "to whom do you turn for help?"; "with whom do you socialize?"; "with whom do you discuss politics?" (Fischer 1982; Burt 1984; Huckfeldt 2000). Other methods include small-world and reverse-small-world experiments used to elicit the composition of larger functional personal networks, as well as phone book and first-name list methods used to generate weak-tie or acquaintance networks (Milgram 1967; Travers and Milgram 1969; de Sola Pool and Kochen 1978; Killworth and Bernard 1978; Bernard, Johnsen, Killworth, McCarty, Shelley, and Robinson 1990; Killworth et al. 1990; McCarty et al. 1997). Studies of personal network size and density are summarized in Table 5.1 and discussed in greater detail later in the chapter.

This literature produces rough but remarkably consistent estimates of the average degree and density in three distinct types of personal networks (Dunbar 1992, 1993, 1998; McCarty et al. 1997). The three types of networks can roughly be described as: *acquaintance* networks (past and current), *general friendship* or regular contact networks (past and current), and *core* personal networks. These three types of networks are characterized by differences in average degree and density, and information on the networks is often collected using different methods, as indicated in Table 5.1.

TABLE 5.1. *Estimates of Personal Network Size and Density*

Study	Method	Degree (s.d.)	Density
Gurevich (1961)	contact log	500–2,000	–
de Sola Pool and Kochen (1978)	phone book	3,000–4,000	–
Killworth and Bernard (1978)	Reverse Small World	35–210	–
Hammer (1980)	observation	39	–
Wellman (1979)	"feel closest"	4.7	0.33
Fischer (1982)	11 support items	18.5	0.44
Killworth et al. 1984	Reverse Small World	134 (65)	
Marsden (1987)	GSS important matters	3.0	0.40
Willmott and Young (1967)	non-kin support	12	0.34
Campbell and Lee (1991)	neighbors	14.7	0.52
McCarty et al. (2002)	free list	60	0.27
McCarty et al. (1997)	first names	432[a]	0.36
Freeman and Thompson (1989)	phone book	3,000–5,000	–
Killworth et al. (1990)	"How many X do you know ..."	5,000	
Bernard et al. (1990)	GSS important matters	6.88 (4.89)	
–	Fischer 11 items	21.8 (16.7)	
–	Reverse Small World	128.6 (67.6)	
–	phone book		

Adapted from Campbell and Lee (1991) and McCarty et al. (1997).

[a] Subjects named, on average, 14 alters based on the 50-name list they were shown, and this result was scaled up to provide an estimated network size of 432.

Acquaintance networks are very large, ranging from 500 into the thousands, and include people who the respondent would recognize and call by first name. Typical methods of eliciting acquaintance networks include phone book methods (de Sola Pool and Kochen 1978; Freeman and Thompson 1989; Bernard et al. 1990) and subpopulation estimates (Killworth, Bernard, and McCarty 1984). Past acquaintance networks (i.e., "Name people you have ever known") are much larger than current acquaintance or "weak tie" networks (Granovetter 1973), which can be collected through use of a contact diary (de Sola Pool and Kochen 1978, reporting findings by Gurevich 1961). Acquaintance networks are very similar to scale-free networks (Newman 2001) in that the distribution of degree is very skewed to the right-hand side (a few people have very many contacts) and are probably well represented by the small-world network topology (de Sola Pool and Kochen 1978; Freeman and Thompson 1989).

There are no good estimates of the density of acquaintance networks, although it is likely to be low.[7]

Regular contact or *general friendship* networks are much smaller, ranging from ten to sixty people, and include neighbors, coworkers, and family members with whom the respondent has regular social contact and from whom the respondent receives help and support. Examples of name generators used to elicit regular contact networks include the following: neighbors to whom you speak regularly; friends with whom would you spend Saturday night; friends from whom would you borrow a cup of sugar; friends who would watch your house while you were away; and longer (unlimited) friendship or discussion network lists (Fischer 1982; McCarty et al. 1997; McCarty 2002). A larger network of up to 300 current and past friendships is often elicited by use of the small-world and reverse-small-world methods (Killworth and Bernard 1978; Bernard, Shelley, and Killworth 1987; Bernard et al. 1990). The distribution of degree in regular-contact networks is still somewhat skewed, but much less so than in acquaintance networks.

Core personal networks are very small, egocentric networks, ranging from zero to ten people, and include people with whom the respondent discusses "important matters" (Wellman 1979; Fischer 1982; Marsden 1987). The variation in average degree in these networks is quite small, and clustering varies with size of the network and respondent attributes. In general, if the costs associated with maintaining ties are low, then degree distributions are often exponential; otherwise, they tend to return to slightly right-skewed but otherwise relatively normal distributions (Newman 2001).

In some cases, a respondent is asked if his/her friends know one another, producing an estimate of the density of his/her personal networks. These estimates typically range from about 0.25 to 0.45 in both core and regular contact networks. However, attempts to validate the existence of close ties between the friends of a respondent through use of a snowball sample[8] have found that respondents may overestimate the existence

---

[7] Imagine an individual with acquaintances in many spheres: high school friends, parent's friends, family members from two to four extended families, coworkers, perhaps coworkers from a previous job, friends from church or another organization, etc. Although density within the spheres will be high, there will be few ties across the spheres, resulting in a low percentage of possible ties being present. Thus the network will not be very dense. See McCarty (2002) for more.

[8] A snowball sample is one in which one or more people named by the original respondents are then added to the sample as respondents themselves. In surveys, snowballs are often limited to only one or two additional steps.

of ties among friends (Fischer and Shavit 1995). Also, use of different questions to measure tie existence between alters (i.e., do j and k "know each other" or "know each other well") complicates comparisons across studies. Including household members in density estimates also greatly changes them: Campbell and Lee (1991) find that an average personal network density of more than 50% drops to about 33% after household members excluded. A variety of considerations suggest that median (not mean) density in personal networks may be approximately 15% to 35%.

In summary, three basic categories of friendship can be identified and elicited using personal network data collection techniques. Close friends are those with whom you are willing to discuss almost anything; people rarely have more than a handful of these friendships, usually between three and five, with a minority of respondents reporting six or more. A person has regular contact with general friends, and will often discuss a wide range of issues with them. Depending on the definition used to measure general friendships, most respondents report having an average of ten to twenty general friends at a given point in time, with some reporting up to sixty. Meanwhile, a person knows acquaintances on a first-name basis but has less regular contact with them, and conversations are less likely to be serious. Studies estimate the typical number of acquaintances at a given point in time to be approximately 500 to 2,000, although again the distribution has a long tail. A clustering coefficient of anywhere between 10% and 50% is reasonable, depending on the closeness of the friendship networks under consideration.

Which friendship networks are most likely to influence the likelihood that a person will vote in an upcoming election? A few close friends? A few dozen general friends? Or hundreds or even thousands of acquaintances? Acquaintances are probably least likely to influence a turnout decision, as individuals are likely to discuss politics or attitudes toward voting only sporadically with someone that they do not know very well or converse with at least somewhat regularly. Distinguishing the impact of close friends and general friends is more difficult. The vast majority of Americans discuss upcoming presidential elections with their closest friends (Klofstad, McClurg, and Rolfe 2009), but many also discuss politics with a wider range of general friends as well (Walsh 2004). Males in particular report a wider range of friends included among political discussants. Measurement criteria provide limited additional insight: One prompt for general friendships includes political discussion as a criterion (Fischer 1982), whereas many people consider politics to be an important matter to discuss with close friends (Bearman and Parigi 2004). Therefore, it seems reasonable to expect that whereas close friends are likely to influence turnout decisions in most elections, many decision makers might look beyond their immediate circle of friends for cues about turnout behavior when candidates and activists invest substantial resources into the campaign process to raise the salience and discussion of an upcoming election.

Simulating Turnout on Local Social Networks

The first part of this chapter introduced and analyzed a basic model of conditional, with parameter estimates based on observed behavior in experimental social dilemmas. Simulations of the model with 10% to 20% unconditional, and a relatively equal split between mean- and median-matching conditional cooperation, proved both reasonable and robust. These simulations, however, made the unrealistic assumption of "all-see-all" global networks. Here, we incorporate more realistic assumptions about actual social networks into similar simulations. Because network size has a significant impact on cooperation rates, the prior section was devoted to making empirical estimates of the size and density of personal social networks. I estimate that turnout decisions are most likely influenced by close and general friends, yielding estimated personal social networks with between three and twenty people, with clustering ranging from 0.15 to 0.5. Are realistic turnout levels generated by conditional voters who interact with between three and twenty other citizens who may (or may not) know each other as well? Once again, the answer is a resounding yes. Simulated turnout levels vary within the ranges observed in actual elections, whereas other combinations of decision rules and network properties typically produce turnout that is either too high or too low.

Figure 5.4 summarizes results produced when 100 simulations are run for each of the three prototypical decision models (10%, 15%, and 20% unconditional cooperation), and voters interact on local networks covering a wide range of network parameters.[9] To systematically investigate

[9] To produce Figure 5.4, simulations of 1,000 agents were run using the three prototypical decision rules distributions: 1) $\alpha=0.10, \beta=0.45, \delta=0.45$; 2) $\alpha=0.15, \beta=0.425, \delta=0.425$; and 3) $\alpha=0.20, \beta=0.40, \delta=0.40$. The goal was to run 100 simulations of each decision rule distribution at each unique combination of average network degree ($\bar{k}\in(3, 4, 8, 12, 16, 20)$) and clustering ($c\in(0.2, 0.3, 0.4, 0.5)$), with the exception of the combination of high clustering (0.5) and low degree (3). The simulated networks did not fall exactly into the desired categories (i.e., some had smaller, larger, or more clustered personal networks, on average), and therefore simulations were run for each basic model on 2,300 unique networks that approximated the desired range. The simulation sequence was repeated for the moderate and easy distributions ($\alpha=0.15$ and $\alpha=0.20$), with different start points, and thus Figure 5.4 gives results from 4,600 simulations in total for these distributions.

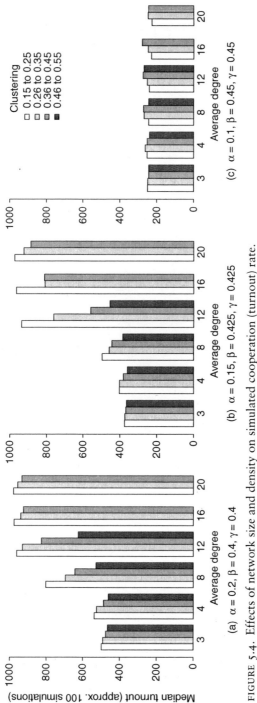
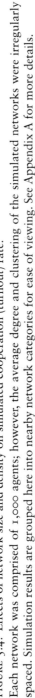

FIGURE 5.4. Effects of network size and density on simulated cooperation (turnout) rate. Each network was comprised of 1,000 agents; however, the average degree and clustering of the simulated networks were irregularly spaced. Simulation results are grouped here into nearby network categories for ease of viewing. See Appendix A for more details.

the impact of personal network properties (network degree and cluster-ing), it is necessary to hold the distribution of decision rules constant (or vice versa). Therefore, I will look at the impact of relative changes in network properties and decision rule distributions in turn.

Looking at Figure 5.4, the clear and substantial effects of network size are obvious when turnout is expected to spread very easily (20% uncon-ditional cooperation) or exhibit significant variability (15% uncondi-tional cooperation.) Median turnout in simulations where voters put a 20% weight on the unconditional rule, pictured in Figure 5.4(a), goes from around 50% in three-person groups to nearly 100% on average in twenty-person groups, with average density of under 0.45. Results from the 15% unconditional rule model – Figure 5.4(b) – look very much like those in the 20% model. Turnout rates start lower, under 40% in three-person networks, but increase sharply to almost 100% in twenty-person networks. The smaller friendship networks cut the expected turnout in half, whereas turnout rates when voters have around twenty friends who are not particularly likely to know one another look very much like turn-out rates in the case of global information.

Even large personal networks, however, were not enough to overcome the contagion-suppressing effects of having very dense and tight-knit personal networks. When personal networks are very dense, isolated communities often form and the impact of first movers cannot spread across the social cleavages dividing the various tightly knit communities from one another. In both the 15% and 20% unconditional coopera-tion models, network density has a suppressing effect on turnout. For extremely dense personal networks ($c > 0.45$), the suppressing impact of clustering increases as average personal network size increases. When moderate density levels ($c \in (0.25, 0.45)$) characterize personal networks, the suppressing impact of clustering is highest at the intermediate net-work sizes.

As expected, the effects of network and density are considerably less pronounced in simulations with very low levels of unconditional cooper-ation, pictured in Figure 5.4(c). When turnout is not expected to spread easily in a population, smaller and denser networks can actually work to increase expected turnout rates. The impact of network characteristics, however, is quite small compared to those seen in the 15% and 20% models.

Why do smaller networks impede the spread of cooperation in some situations (i.e., distributions of decision rules), but encourage nascent cooperation in others? The answer lies in the effect of network size on the probability of being located near both unconditional cooperators and the early movers inspired by them. Assuming that unconditional cooperators are randomly distributed throughout the population, small friendship networks make it less likely that each group of friends will have at least one first mover. Therefore, first movers will affect fewer people initially, and the initial influence of first movers will not spread easily. Especially when networks are dense, innovative behavior can get stuck in a small section of the group and never spread to other areas – a result also reported by Macy (1991).

On the other hand, in situations where cooperation is more difficult (as in the case where there are only 10% first movers, or a much lower relative use of the mean-matching versus median-matching rule), any initial first movers are unlikely to be followed by early movers, and thus set off a cascade of behavioral change when personal networks are large. In situations where cooperation is difficult, the influence of unconditional cooperators is essentially diluted by large groups, but has a better chance of catching on (and making it past the "tipping point") when first and early movers are concentrated within small, dense networks.

Therefore, small groups – especially those kept effectively smaller by having more inward-turning ties – can incubate hard-to-sustain new ideas or actions better than large groups can. These extremely costly forms of activity may still fail to generate widespread social action, but there is a better chance that a small group may get "lucky" if it is comprised of a larger-than-usual clump of either first movers or early adopters who then reinforce each other's cooperative tendencies. Alternatively, careful selection and social isolation of people who are willing to unconditionally contribute can form the basis for either an army committed to social stability or a terrorist cell committed to revolutionary change.

Still looking at the same simulation results, I will now consider the impact of changes in unconditional rule usage in networks of similar size and density. Simulated turnout when voters have only four friends on average varies between slightly more than 20% and slightly less than 50%, with higher turnout in the simulations occurring when there is greater use of the unconditional turnout rule. These estimates are clearly lower than turnout in most national elections, both in the United States and elsewhere. However, this choice of network size is toward the lower end of the empirically estimated range. Substantively, a four-person network implies that people only discuss an upcoming election with their spouse, parents, and perhaps one or two close friends – an unlikely state of affairs for major elections. When voters discuss the election with a larger set of friends, the overall turnout rate is higher, as shown in the following simulations using estimates of both twelve and twenty friends.

Turnout is substantially higher when voters based their decision on the actions of a more general set of friends, most likely including a few coworkers and neighbors. Once again, turnout increases as a function of the percentage of first movers in the population. With larger personal networks, however, the increase is much sharper than it was with only four friends. When voters have, on average, twelve friends, turnout varies from less than 20% of the population when first movers make up 10% of the population to almost 80% of the population when first movers make up 20% of the population – a large range of possible outcomes. The same basic pattern is observed when voters have twenty friends on average, although the impact of an increase in initial activity or unconditional cooperation is even more pronounced. This is expected, as the larger, twenty-person networks do not present significant barriers to the spread of innovations in models where widespread contagion is expected.

Are these findings on the impact of group size reasonable, based on what we know about cooperation rates in social dilemmas? Olson (1965) predicted that large groups would have a harder time providing collective goods than small groups, although he made important algebraic mistakes, which Oliver (1980) later clarified. Oliver and Marwell (1988) claim that larger groups should be more able to provide goods, as long as the cost of the good is held constant. Experimental evidence upholds the claims of both Oliver and Marwell (1988) and the conditional cooperation model: Larger groups provide goods more often and average contributions often increase in larger groups (Isaac, Walker, and Williams 1994). However, when the marginal value of a contribution decreases as the size of the group increases, contributions do decrease (Ledyard 1995; Falkinger et al. 2000). Once again, then, the conditional cooperation model is in line with available evidence.

CONCLUSION

To recap, I have suggested that voters make decisions regarding turnout in the same way that they make decisions in social dilemmas – a claim that underlies the transformation of the conditional decision-making model into a social theory of voter turnout. Earlier chapters provided support for the claim that voting is a social dilemma and that relevant participants are Americans – members of a relatively loose-knit imagined community. Voting is widely seen as a positively valued action regardless of which injunctive norms are invoked, and shares this characteristic with several experimental social dilemmas. Therefore, experimental social dilemmas were used to place bounds on the likely distribution of decision rules. This chapter went a step further and also used empirical data to place bounds on the network properties of everyday social and political discussion networks. Simulations of voter turnout within these bounds, and only within these bounds, produce reasonable and robust variation in rates of voter turnout.

Looking across simulations with the three paradigmatic local social networks, we can see that most of the action in turnout takes place within the broad range of first-mover percentages established using experimental data. When unconditional cooperation dips as low as 10% or less, we see very little cooperation regardless of the remaining distribution of the population between mean and median matching or the size and shape of personal networks. Once the population contains at least 20% first movers, uniformly high voter turnout (approaching 100%) is virtually assured, largely irrespective of how the other parameters are set. Thus, the only real variation in turnout levels occurs within the range of 10% to 20% unconditional voters, particularly when the relevant social networks affecting turnout include more than the closest friendships.

It is very striking that the vast majority of variation in turnout rates lies only within the expected range, especially considering that the data used to establish the likely parameter ranges were taken from an entirely different context and then incorporated into a formal model based on a combination of theoretical insight and mathematical simplicity. (If, for example, the likely range of first movers had been established to lie between 15% and 25%, the results would suggest that these estimates are simply too high: There is still plenty of variation in simulation results outside of this range.) Therefore, the overall success of the model appears to be quite high.

6

The Social Theory of Turnout

This chapter fully details the theoretical logic and empirical implications of conditional choice as a new way of understanding voter turnout. Here, I develop the social theory of voter turnout more completely, for the first time placing conditional decision-making voters in the context of a political election rather than simply a generic social dilemma. This political context features candidates and other political actors who work strategically to mobilize potential voters during the election cycle. This new theoretical synthesis provides a full account of all the empirical turnout patterns currently thought to support a resource-based view of turnout, as well as new predictions to be tested against the resource-based view in Chapters 7 and 8.

In the social theory of voter turnout, conditional decision makers vote because campaigns mobilize them, either directly or by creating discussion that works through networks to spur conditional decision makers to act. In brief, I suggest that strategic politicians work to generate political discussion and other behaviors that make the election more visible and more salient among potential voters; next, added political discussion and other signals increase the size of relevant social network reference group for potential voters; finally, larger effective social networks then increase voter turnout through the working of conditional decision making.

This view contrasts with the prevailing view of political participation, developed most thoroughly by Verba, Schlozman, and Brady's (1995) resource-based theory of voter turnout, in which individuals choose to vote because they can, they like to, and they are asked. In this view, variation in turnout rates is basically a function of individual utilities, or costs and benefits. Voters are different from nonvoters because their resources, interests, and contacts either reduce the costs of voting (making it easier to figure out how to register, for example, or get to the polls) or raise the benefits (because voting is more meaningful to those interested in politics). There are numerous critiques of the utility- or rationality-based understanding of voter turnout (Green and Shapiro 1994, for a prominent example) and empirical anomalies that undercut our current understanding of the true meaning of individual variables such as education (Brody 1978; Miller 1992). As yet, however, there has been no coherent alternative that can both account for the same range of empirical patterns and provide more convincing explanations for consistent individual correlates of voter turnout, particularly education. The social theory of turnout aims to provide such an alternative account.

The argument takes several steps. First, I provide a more complete exposition of my claim that all turnout is mobilized. I then demonstrate that the social theory of turnout can account for a wide variety of previously documented empirical observations about turnout. These prior observations include aggregate patterns such as cross-national variation and cross-election variation, and individual-level correlations with political interest, civic resources, and requests to participate. Finally, the conclusion of this chapter lays out ground where the social theory and resource-based view diverge, setting the stage for empirically testing the theories against one another in the chapters to follow.

STRATEGIC POLITICIANS AND CONDITIONAL DECISION MAKERS: A THEORETICAL SYNTHESIS

The social theory of voter turnout is essentially a synthesis of the conditional model of individual decision making developed in earlier chapters with the strategic mobilization perspective on turnout and campaigns. In the strategic mobilization view, turnout levels are affected by politicians and other political actors with an interest in mobilizing people to vote (for their side, of course). Empirically, Rosenstone and Hansen (1993) provide support for this view, showing convincingly that aggregate turnout levels vary in response to varying mobilization efforts by candidates and officeholders. Cox and colleagues (Cox and Munger 1989; Cox, Rosenbluth, and Thies 1998; Cox 1999, 2005) have extended the strategic mobilization approach into a sophisticated formal view of campaign activity, demonstrating that campaign activity is likely to reflect the race in question as well as national considerations of portfolio formation. So, in higher-stakes races, candidates and other actors will have more resources to spend on mobilizing the electorate, leading to higher rates of voter turnout.

Although the strategic mobilization account of aggregate turnout variation is empirically and theoretically satisfying, it is incomplete as an explanation of turnout variation at the individual level. Why are individuals who are mobilized, directly or indirectly, more likely to vote? Why do individuals respond to campaigns? How do campaigns affect individual decision making? To solve the macro-micro problem (Coleman 1990) in this case, moving from aggregate explanation to the individual level, we need a model of individual turnout that includes a mechanism to translate candidate efforts into changes in individuals' propensities to turn out.

The conditional decision-making model provides such a mechanism: changes in effective size of social networks. Higher-intensity campaigns make politics and the upcoming election more salient, not only in increased political discussion among friends, but also in other prominent cues that may indicate to citizens that their friends, neighbors, and coworkers care about the election. Increases in media coverage, campaign signs, mail and phone contact from candidates, and the like – all of these signals increase the size of the effective reference group for any potential voter when making the turnout decision. As political discussion and awareness increases, more of one's social network becomes relevant for the turnout decision. Thus, in effect, the social networks relevant to the turnout decision become larger as mobilization increases the salience of the election. As seen in the previous chapter, larger social networks increase the likelihood that low-cost cooperative behaviors such as turnout will snowball, and thus ultimately increase aggregate turnout rates.

One convenient aspect of this representation is that individuals are not required to know anything about the candidate or political process to make a turnout decision (although in practice, discussion is likely to increase political knowledge). Voters can simply respond to cues in their environment about the importance or closeness of an election when deciding whether or not to vote, rather than trying to use their own political knowledge to make such estimates (Rosenstone and Hansen 1993).

Of course, potential voters might not ask their friends directly whether or not they plan to vote, nor are they necessarily likely to be asked about their own voting intentions. Political discussion is likely to be casual or incidental; a mention of a candidate or an issue might serve as an indicator of interest or involvement. So might the proliferation of yard signs in a neighborhood, which is itself likely to be another contagious activity

(Chwe 2004). The turnout decision, like many other decisions, is made under uncertainty and without the ability to directly observe the decisions of others. This does not preclude conditional decision making. Even if individual voters do not know who among their friends voted, they are likely to be much better at estimating the proportion of their friends that voted. That does not mean that individual voters will be aware of consciously calculating this probability; they would be more likely to refer to social pressure, or a social expectation, if they were aware at all of the impact of others on their decision to vote. Perhaps even more important, as shown in Cialdini's street musician study described in Chapter 2, conditional decision making can occur even without conscious awareness of others' actions.

Strategic politicians can affect turnout patterns not just through their choices about how much energy to devote to the campaign process, but also through their choices about whom they try to mobilize. For example, seeking to maximize the impact of their campaign, politicians will try to speak to people in large groups. This might involve large rallies of unconnected individuals gathering for extremely high-profile candidates, but in most campaigns this will involve focusing appearances on organized groups, thus increasing the probability that voters who belong to social, civic, or religious organizations will be directly or indirectly mobilized by campaign activity. Politicians are also likely to reach out to another group with a low effort-to-reward ratio: their own friends and acquaintances (Rosenstone and Hansen 1993). These observations, although not unique to the social theory, provide the basis for the social theory's new interpretation of crucial correlates of turnout, such as education, church attendance, and organizational membership, as indicators of social location rather than individual characteristics.

CROSS-NATIONAL VARIATION: FIRST MOVERS AND COSTS

Cross-national variation in aggregate turnout is often used as the primary evidence that voters weigh costs and benefits when making a turnout decision (Green and Shapiro 1994). Voter turnout is considered a relatively low-cost affair by many (Aldrich 1993), but it is clear that even relatively minimal institutionally imposed costs vary across different contexts and affect turnout behavior (Kim, Petrocik, and Enokson 1975; Wolfinger and Rosenstone 1980; Powell and Whitten 1993; Rosenstone and Hansen 1993; Highton 1997). In the social theory of turnout, costs do play an important role in explaining cross-national variation in turnout.

Costs are incorporated into the theory as a small shift in the percentage of the population using the strategy of unconditional cooperation. Thus, the social theory of turnout includes an alternative account for a finding widely thought to constitute one of the strongest arguments in favor of utility-maximizing voters. Indeed, as shown later in the chapter, point predictions from simulations of this shift in first movers replicates closely the difference in turnout ranges between the United States and the lower-cost European democracies.

I argue that costly barriers are best represented as variations in the distribution of unconditional cooperation. In decision-making studies, costs do have a small impact on the willingness of first movers to cooperate unconditionally. The conceptualization of registration requirements as an additional cost to the potential voter is common in the literature as well (Kim, Petrocik, and Enokson 1975; Rosenstone and Hansen 1993; Highton 1997). Neglecting to make election day a public holiday may also increase the cost of voting, although this might affect decision making through a social logic as well: A holiday might make the event more public, and thus increase the opportunity for effective social sanctions that raise rates of unconditional cooperation.

Therefore, in simulating elections, I represent changes in registration barriers across institutional settings as a change in the situation faced by voters in the aggregate. Increases in costs are associated with a decrease in the use of the strategy of unconditional cooperation in the population (closer to the lower bound of 10% to 13%) and a subsequent increase in the use of conditional cooperation. Conversely, the elimination of these barriers and increase in social observability is modeled as an increase in the use of unconditional cooperation, up to 15% to 20% of the population, on average.

I begin by simulating an approximation of U.S. presidential elections, characterized by relatively high institutional costs of turnout (as well as very high salience). The intense media coverage of the event implies that there are likely to be high levels of political discussion. Depending on a number of factors (e.g., age, education, urban or rural residence, etc.), larger personal networks range from ten to twenty people, on average. These are the networks elicited by asking respondents about their casual friendships with fairly regular contact: people with whom they work, from whom they borrow things, or with whom they socialize.

Having established further bounds on the simulation parameters, a series of simulations was run within these bounds. I ran 100 simulations at each of the various combinations of network parameters used as the basis for Figure 6.1. The graph shows how turnout (averaged across all

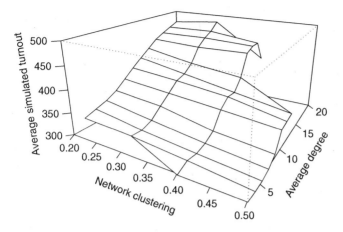

FIGURE 6.1. Average turnout when first movers are 12.5% of the population.

100 simulations) varies with respect to first-mover percentage and network size. This is a smaller subset of results from the general results in the previous chapters, and the tables are read as described in the previous chapter. As can be seen in these graphs, turnout ranges from about 40% to 65% in the agent populations with larger personal networks (average degree greater than 10).

Now we can compare these results to simulations from lower-cost elections, as approximated with simulations with networks of the same size and with 15% of the population as first movers. Results from these simulations appear in Figure 6.2. (The graph is read in much the same way as Figure 6.1.) Comparing average turnout in this graph to turnout in Figure 6.1, it is easy to see that turnout is much higher when there are more first movers in the population. Turnout ranges from 60% to 90% in the simulations, in networks of the right size. Thus, a 5% difference in the number of first movers is translated into a turnout gap of a substantial and highly realistic size.

For the purposes of comparison, a distribution of voter turnout in both U.S. and European national elections appears in Figure 6.3. Figure 6.3(a) is a histogram of state-level voter turnout figures in U.S. presidential elections between 1980 and 2000 (McDonald 2002). Figure 6.3(b) is a histogram of nationwide turnout in parliamentary elections in select Western European national elections between 1974 and 1997 (International IDEA 2005).[1]

---

[1] The countries included are those generally cited as having institutions that encourage voting (compulsory voting, weekend voting, universal registration), excluding Switzerland

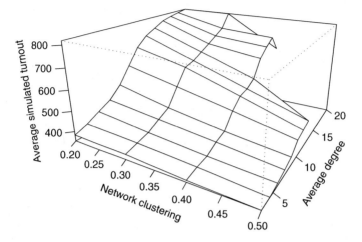

FIGURE 6.2. Average turnout when first movers are 15% of the population.

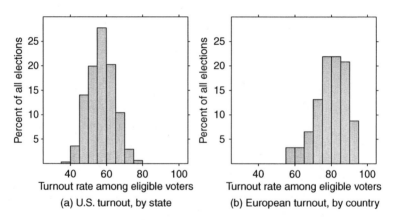

FIGURE 6.3. Histogram of voter turnout rates (national elections, 1980–2000).

As comparison of the two histograms reveals, there are significant turnout differences associated with costs, as expected. U.S Presidential turnout at the state level ranges between 40% and 73% of the population, with the vast majority of the states registering turnout rates between 50% and 65%. European national election turnout ranges between 60% and 95% of the voting-age population, with the vast majority of the

(Powell 1986). Figures for the United States are based on percentage of the voting-eligible population (VEP) voting in each of the fifty states in each election; European figures are based on percentage of voting-age population (VAP) in each country in each election.

countries boasting turnout rates of greater than 70%. The difference in turnout between the two institutional settings is substantial, averaging about 20 percentage points or more between the two institutional settings, with almost no overlap between the two turnout ranges.

These data match up remarkably well with the simulation results described in detail earlier. Obviously, the parameters used in these simulations were approximations, and better estimates would need to account for the remaining variation in institutional barriers among U.S. states (Wolfinger and Rosenstone 1980) or European countries (Powell 1986). However, the ranges produced by the simulations are very similar to the ranges observed in the real data. Looking back to simulations with 12.5% first movers, we see that the turnout range is about 40% to 65% of the population, whereas the simulations with 15% first movers produce turnout in the range of 60% to 90% of the simulated population.

One common criticism of agent-based modeling is that the researchers can easily create the results they want by picking the parameter combinations that produce those results. With such uncanny similarity between previously reported simulation results and real-world turnout data, it is reasonable to wonder whether that criticism applies to these results as well. Much of the work in the previous chapters was aimed precisely at preventing this objection: All of the parameters used in the simulations have been established using empirical data from studies of decision making in other contexts. I argued that these contexts were structurally similar to voting, making it appropriate to use them to simulate elections, but at the same time different enough to ensure the integrity of the simulation exercise. The first-mover percentages used earlier – 12.5% and 15% – were not only those most often encountered in the experimental results (rounded to make the numbers easy to work with), but are centrally located within the identified range of possibilities instead of at an extreme point.[2]

Thus, a social theory of turnout can account for aggregate shifts in voter turnout associated with institutionally imposed costs of turnout, one of the pillars of many arguments for utility maximizing voters. A formal model of decision making, then, can incorporate costs without modeling decision makers as utility maximizers. In conditional decision-making models, costs shift the use of unconditional cooperation instead.

---

[2] The fact that rounded numbers produced these simulation results further suggests that I did not attempt to manipulate the simulation to produce the results.

Specifically, in the social theory of turnout, I assume that voters are more likely to cooperate unconditionally in lower-cost elections – an assumption supported by subject behavior in experiments. Thus, the social theory of turnout provides a sound theoretical account of the effects of costs on turnout, and has the advantage of producing empirically veri-fiable estimates of how costs affect decision making. Furthermore, the point estimates of how costs affect turnout in a cross-national setting obtained from simulations are eerily accurate, providing further support for the ability of the social theory of turnout to explain empirical turnout patterns.

VARIATIONS ACROSS ELECTIONS: CAMPAIGN ACTIVITY AND POLITICAL DISCUSSION

In addition to aggregate variation cross-nationally, turnout also varies across elections within a geographic unit. Some of that variation is straightforwardly related to the scope and importance of the office at stake in the election. National elections for the U.S. president or U.S. senators typically attract more voters, even as a percentage of the eligi-ble electorate, than races for the office of mayor or school board mem-ber. Another portion of that variation is more shifting, seemingly related to the closeness of the race in question and the excitement surround-ing a particular election. In this section, I show that variation from each of these sources can be explained as the result of mobilization-induced changes in political discussion and other visible signals of political aware-ness or interest. Thus, I can again provide an account for aggregate shifts in turnout that is at least as compelling as a utility-based account of how strategic politicians affect individual voters.

Local elections and primaries typically attract far fewer voters than large national elections, especially in the United States. From the point of view of a strategic candidate or political party, this variation in turnout rate makes perfect sense. When there is less at stake, candidates, donors, and political activists are not as willing to invest the capital (financial or human) into winning an election. Thus, positions with a relatively low payoff in terms of political power (or the ability to redistribute resources) are unlikely to attract much investment from candidates and their sup-porters, and are likely to have low turnout (Cox 1999, 2005). Similarly, very close elections, in which investors have a real chance to affect the election outcome, will also increase mobilization activity (Key 1949; Cox and Munger 1989).

As I argue earlier in the book, strategic politicians are at the root of almost all voter participation. Without any mobilization activity by politicians, few, if any, voters would show up – even many of the citizens willing to cooperate unconditionally would be unlikely to know of the upcoming election. As candidates put increasing effort into mobilizing the electorate, their efforts affect voters both directly and indirectly. Indirect mobilization generally works through an increase in salience of the upcoming election. Candidates who are particularly good at reaching the media or who have particularly noteworthy ideas or campaigns, or just lots of money, can create a "buzz," or popular excitement, surrounding an upcoming election. Their efforts are translated into political discussion: As citizens increasingly know about the election, it is an easy and relevant topic of conversation with friends, family, and coworkers. Potential voters in a race with a very low level of buzz may only discuss the upcoming election with one or two of their friends, whereas voters in a very-high-salience race are likely to discuss the election with or observe the political involvement of most or all of their more general discussion network of everyday friendships, up to twenty or thirty people.

This approach makes sense of at least two major logical shortcomings of the explanation of aggregate turnout shifts in a utility-based model of individual turnout decisions. First, a utility-based model claims that voters vote more often in close elections because their probability of casting the decisive vote in the election is greater. But if any voters hold out hopes of casting the decisive vote in an election, the chances of this highly unlikely event are vastly greater in smaller local elections than in the national elections that draw the most voters. Presumably, a utility-maximizing voter would be, if anything, more likely to vote in a local election than in a national election. Similarly, an economic calculus predicts that individuals are more likely to vote when the outcome of the election affects them more. But most individuals have a much greater opportunity to interact with (and be personally affected by) local instead of national officials. Many voters do not even pay federal income taxes, but they do pay state taxes.[3] Thus, it is at best questionable whether an economic logic would suggest higher rates of voting in national elections or local elections.

There has been a real attempt to adapt the underlying economic view of turnout into an individual-level theory compatible with strategic

---

[3] To further this analogy, one candidate reported that he had more daily contact and requests for assistance from constituents as a district representative on the city council than as an at-large member. Even at this very local level, then, lower-profile candidates have more opportunities to affect individual citizens than higher-profile candidates.

mobilization attempts (Verba, Schlozman, and Brady 1995). This attempt, however, has its own logical shortcoming: Why are utility-maximizing decision makers more likely to vote simply because they are asked? It is not clear how a campaign postcard or a visit from a door-to-door canvassing campaign (Gerber and Green 2000) makes voting more beneficial or less costly. Thus, the effects of mobilization are not easily incorporated into a view of individual decision making that assumes that people's decisions are based on costs and benefits of their actions.

A social theory of voter turnout provides a greater degree of logical consistency, as well as accurate point estimates for the effects of changes in mobilization activity on turnout patterns. The basic logic of why turnout varies in close races is provided by strategic mobilization, with additional mobilization efforts translating into increased political discussion at the level of the individual voter. Thus, the individual-level mechanism through which mobilization exerts influence on turnout is an increase in the size of the relevant reference group for the voting decision.

In the previous chapter, a wide range of possible discussion partners was established. We might imagine that potential voters look to only their closest friends (two-to-six people) as a reference group for their decision. Or, perhaps they might look to their general friends (fifteen-to-thirty people), or their casual acquaintances (in the hundreds), or, alternatively, some might not look to anyone else as their reference group. Which network, then, to incorporate into our model of the turnout decision? The network of casual relationships seems an unlikely candidate, because it is unlikely that most people would even have much of an opportunity to discuss the election or their voting intention with their acquaintances. However, the remaining possible range of friendships is still quite large, anywhere between zero and twenty or so people. Thankfully, the estimates can be further revised on the basis of expectations of the effects of campaign activity and election salience on political discussion.

Recall that campaign salience does not increase turnout because citizens exchange promises to vote or threaten to sanction nonvoters. Instead, the spread of turnout is more akin to a fad or popular taste; simple discussion of the event increases the salience of the choices made by other people for an individual's decision making. There is undoubtedly at least some indirect information gathering about the turnout intentions of one's friends in the process of political discussion. A friend who has spent time learning enough about politics to intelligently discuss an upcoming election (or even identify the potential candidates) is signaling a willingness to go to the polls (a much smaller investment in terms of time). For the most part, however, campaign activity results in common knowledge of an upcoming event (Chwe 1999, 2001), which increases the portion of a citizen's social network relevant to the turnout decision.

Salience Equals Network Size

For predicting turnout in the social theory, then, average network size is used as a proxy for differences between elections that reflect differences in campaign activity. Very-high-salience elections, such as a presidential election in the United States, involve extensive free and paid media coverage of the event, a near-universal knowledge of the impending election, and an increase in the level of casual conversation devoted to the upcoming event (Huckfeldt, Johnson, and Sprague 2004, Klofstad, McClurg, and Rolfe 2009). Whereas the average network size activated by very-high-salience activities will depend in part on various demographic characteristics such as age and education, the range of likely choices lies between twelve and twenty people, with a relatively low level of overlap or clustering.

Very-low-salience elections, conversely, will be represented by no discussion of an upcoming election at all, or an effective network size of 0. In the United States, there are often municipal primaries or runoffs with turnout levels of less than 5% of the eligible registered population. Often in these cases, there are no televisions advertisements, newspaper editorials, or any of the other mass media tools used to reach a broad audience in use – even when the elections are contested, which is not always the case. In fact, often only a very small portion of the eligible voters are directly informed of the upcoming election by the candidates or parties. Runoff candidates with limited funds may choose to send out postcards only to registered voters who have made it to at least eight of the last ten elections,[4] effectively limiting both knowledge and discussion among many voters. As campaign activity increases and as the amount of mass media time, paid or unpaid, devoted to the election increases, we are likely to see an increase in discussion of the election and its general visibility to potential voters. Thus, for many elections – off-year Congressional elections, or hard-fought municipal elections – some but not all of the general friendship network might become the relevant network reference group.

---

[4] This exact criterion was mentioned to me by several candidates in the course of interviews (discussed in detail in Chapter 8), and by political candidates in Chicago during casual conversations as well. Huckfeldt (1979) also finds that candidates use similar criteria.

There is no clear mechanism for converting hours of media coverage into discussion frequency and then into network size, but the range is likely to shift in response to these factors.

As shown earlier (see Figure 5.4), small changes in the average degree of voter social networks relate to substantial changes in simulated turnout. Voters who rely on fewer friends when making their decision are significantly less likely to vote than those who discuss the upcoming election with a greater portion of their social network.

Not all citizens, however, face the same campaign environment during a given election – some are exposed to intense mobilization whereas others are barely made aware that an election is forthcoming. Some of this may be due to targeted mobilization, but much of the variation may reflect exposure to different local campaigns. Residents in some local, state, and county districts will be exposed to tight election races with substantial spending, whereas others will live in areas with an unopposed candidate who does not bother with more than a few obligatory yard signs and fliers. Therefore, we would expect to observe that even in a single election, turnout rates at smaller geographic levels of aggregation to vary across the same range that changes in average network size produced in simulated turnout (see Figure 5.4). This range of possible turnout, from around 10% to 60% of the eligible population, is predicted to be observable across all classes of elections outside of presidential elections, although elections of extremely low salience, such as runoffs or unscheduled special elections, may dip even lower.

In Figure 6.4, average turnout rates in three different types of elections are shown. In Figure 6.4(a), statewide turnout rates are given for U.S. congressional midterm or off-year elections between 1982 and 1998. As a point of comparison, Figure 6.4(b) shows precinct-level turnout rates for the 1999, 2001, and 2003 municipal elections in Charlotte, North Carolina, a large southern U.S. city discussed in more detail in Chapter 8. Finally, in Figure 6.4(c), precinct-level turnout during the 1998–2004 federal primaries is given for the same city. As the reader can see, the range of turnout rates is quite similar in the three elections: turnout ranges from around 10% at the lowest end to slightly more than 60% at the highest end – very much in line with the range produced by the simulations in Figure 6.2. Not surprisingly, turnout in the federal primaries has a slightly smaller range than either city or federal general elections. The average turnout levels are quite different across the three types of elections, however, exactly as would be expected, given that the average salience of the elections is presumed to be different. Average turnout is around 50% in

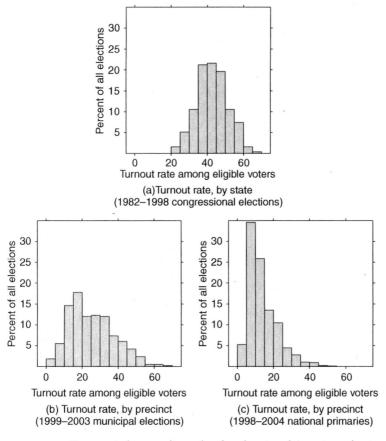

FIGURE 6.4. Turnout in lower-salience local and national American elections.

the federal general elections, 20% in the municipal general elections, and slightly higher than 10% in the federal primary elections.

Low Salience Does Not Equal High Costs

Changes in the costs of turnout are an alternative mechanism that might be used to explain how strategic mobilization efforts translate into individual behavior. Although I have argued that costs vary with institutional barriers but not with mobilization, others have suggested that mobilization activities subsidize the costs of participation for potential voters (Aldrich 1993; Rosenstone and Hansen 1993). Although it may be true in part that lower-salience elections are also more costly to the voter, the

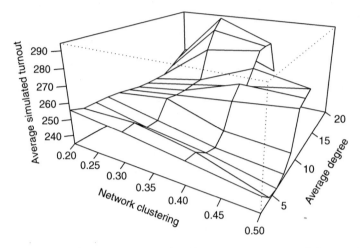

FIGURE 6.5. Average turnout when first movers are 10% of the population.
*Dotted line indicates percent of all respondents giving the indicated response.
Source: 1985 General Social Survey (*n* = 1370).

question is whether this claim provides the bulk of the explanation for
the decline in turnout in low-salience elections. Therefore, let us look
briefly at simulation results if we increase costs even a small amount
more, with a change in costs captured by adjusting the parameters down
to 10% unconditional cooperation. Does this produce plausible results
for a low-salience election?

Clearly, modeling a decrease in election salience as an increase in costs
backfires, as shown in Figure 6.5. The range of average turnout in simulations where first movers comprise only 10% of the population fails to
capture cross-election variability in a realistic way. Simulated turnout here
is uniformly static at around 25–30% of the electorate, which is too high
for low-salience runoffs or municipal primaries, but too low for many
congressional races. Obviously, very small, ad hoc changes in costs might
allow a researcher to fine-tune the model to produce the right results:
say, setting costs such that first movers were 11.5% of the population in
congressional elections and 8% of the population in municipal elections.
Even with this fine-tuning, however, it will be very difficult to reproduce
a significant range of turnout without allowing that mobilization can
change relevant network size and associated political discussion.

Ultimately, modeling changes in mobilization and election salience
as changes in network size seems preferable to a modeling approach
involving costs (and changes in first movers) on the grounds of both

parsimony and greater empirical validity. A network-based approach to mobilization involves the change of only one parameter (network size), while the claim that mobilization affects costs requires the change of two parameters (both network size and costs/unconditional cooperation rate). Furthermore, turnout variation produced by changes in network size at the empirically based estimate of first mover probability, 12.5% (see Figure 6.2), produces a more realistic range of variation in observed voter turnout, as demonstrated in the previous comparison of simulation results with Figure 6.4.

INDIVIDUAL VARIATION IN TURNOUT

Thus, the social theory of turnout provides a clear account of aggregate variations in turnout resulting both from institutionally imposed costs and candidate mobilization, including accurate point predictions of turnout in varying conditions. Now I consider how the social theory of turnout might account for variation in turnout propensity at the individual level.

I argue that individual turnout differences can be traced to three distinct factors: (1) individual tendencies to use different decision rules, (2) structural differences in proximity to and responsiveness to direct mobilization, and (3) structural differences in proximity to and responsiveness to indirect mobilization. This account stands in contrast to the civic voluntarism model of voter turnout (Verba, Schlozman, and Brady 1995), which emphasizes taste (or political interest), resources (or ability to bear the costs of voting), and direct mobilization, and incorporates all of the long-standing empirical correlates of voter turnout, particularly socioeconomic status, political interest, and church and associational membership. In the subsections that follow, I argue that each of these empirical correlates can be understood in the terms of the social theory of turnout, as indicators either of individual heterogeneity in decision-making strategies or of location in social networks.

Individual Tendencies to Use Decision Rules

As I asserted in the development of the conditional decision-making model, individuals are heterogeneous when it comes to making decisions: They make decisions in the different ways, for the different reasons, and, crucially, using different weighted decision rules. Some people place more weight on the unconditional cooperation rule when making a decision about whether or not to turn out; others rely more on mean- or median-matching strategies. These differences should lead to different probabilities of turning out to vote among real individuals, much as they do in the simulations presented in Chapter 5.

But are these differing propensities responsible for the variation we observe in turnout rates across different social groups and classes? I argue that various decision rules are distributed randomly throughout the population; the decision rules used in deciding whether or not to vote are not associated with variation in a taste for politics or civic skills, as Verba and colleagues would have it; nor are decision rules linked to any prominent demographic characteristics. Rather, in the social theory, demographic categories are indicators of variation in social location. It is these changes in social location, rather than demographic categories or any individual-level characteristics associated with demographic variation, that actually cause the observed, varying patterns in turnout rates. Notably, the social theory presumes that the "taste for politics" (or, equivalently in this context, a taste for unconditional cooperation) is distributed randomly throughout the population rather than increasing with education or with membership in other socioeconomically advantaged groups. Thus, the social theory of turnout developed here explains the demographic correlates of turnout without supposing that membership in some groups makes individuals more prone to voting, whether through raising benefits (i.e., political interest) or lowering costs (i.e., civic resources).

As the claim about political interest starkly contrasts with conventional understandings, it is worth an extended, tangential discussion. It turns out that evidence from both experimental social dilemmas and from my own close analysis of survey data on self-reported political interest supports the social theory's assumption that unconditional decision rules are randomly distributed across demographic groups. In experimental settings, unconditional cooperation in social dilemmas is distributed randomly with respect to most (and perhaps all) demographic categories.[5] Those researchers that have collected and reported demographic information find no effect of income, education, and other indicators of social status on cooperation in social dilemmas (Harbaugh and Krause 2000;

---

[5] Unfortunately, the vast majority of experimental studies published to date use as subjects first-year students in college or graduate school, and this nonrepresentative sample makes it difficult to determine whether education does select for (or train for) cooperativeness and civic duty. However, the increasing use of nonstudent samples will ultimately increase our confidence in claims about the relationship between decision rules used in social dilemmas and demographics.

Solnick 2001; Bohnet and Baytelman 2007; Chuah, Hoffmann, Jones, and Williams 2007). Subject pools drawn from the general population are more generous than pools of university students (Carpenter, Connolly, and Myers 2008), as are pools of sixth- and ninth-grade children (Murnighan and Saxon 1998). In a unique and rigorous test, poor children eligible for a private school voucher program participated in dictator games, following a natural experiment in which some of the children were selected by lottery to receive vouchers. The treatment (attendance at a private, college preparatory school) did not affect dictator game allocations to peers, although it did slightly increase contributions to the Red Cross among older children (Bettinger and Slonim 2006). These findings strongly support the claim that education does not impact the likelihood that a subject would cooperate unconditionally in a social dilemma. If anything, the results pointed in the other direction: College students were less cooperative than subject pools from local communities.

However, the ultimate question is not about donations in social dilemmas, but about the randomness of the distribution of the unconditional voting with respect to education. If people use the same rule in similar situations, there is every reason to expect that unconditional voting rules would also be randomly distributed. Preliminary evidence suggests that there is a high – although not perfect – correlation between cooperation in experimental social dilemmas and turnout in elections (Fowler 2006). Additional support for the claim of random distribution of unconditional voting is found in survey self-reports of frequency of political discussion.

Assuming that unconditional voting is distinct from unconditional cooperation in social dilemmas, it seems reasonable that unconditional voting would be strongly correlated with a taste for politics, and in particular repeated, high levels of involvement in political discussion and activity even outside the campaign season. A basic correlational analysis suggests that political interest, or the taste for politics, is not distributed randomly in the population, but instead is strongly linked to demographic characteristics such as education, income, race, and gender. If unconditional cooperation is motivated by a taste for politics (thus making it rational to vote for citizens with this taste), and some demographic subgroups (the college-educated, for example) contain more people with this taste, then it is very hard to sustain the argument that unconditional voting is distributed randomly in the population.

I argue that much of the conventional wisdom on the relationship between education and political interest is misleading on this point.

Previous analysis of empirical associations between demographic variables and political interest have conflated the exogenous and endogenous components of a taste for political activity – as the social theory would predict that only a conditional, not unconditional, taste for politics would be correlated with education and other demographic characteristics linked to social network size and structural position. A closer look at the data provides initial support for my conjecture. Evidence presented later in the chapter (as well as even more striking evidence about unconditional voting in very-low-salience elections in Chapter 8) indicates that a very strong (or unconditional) taste for politics is distributed randomly in the population. It is only at the lower levels of interest, in particular the category of no interest, that large differences related to demographics are found.

Respondents to the 1985 General Social Survey (GSS) were asked how often they discuss politics (*Political Discussion*). They were allowed to choose from four categories, including "almost always" at the top of the scale or "almost never" at the bottom. Respondents who say "almost always" could reasonably be considered to have a true taste for politics. Looking at the distribution of responses to the question by education level of the respondent in Figure 6.6, we see that the proportion of potential unconditional voters with a true taste for politics – those who report discussing politics "almost always" – is similar across educational backgrounds and does not increase systematically with education.[6] The only systematic variation in political interest on the basis of education occurs among more casual political discussants; these would figure into the social theory of turnout as conditional discussants who would be drawn into conversations by those around them.

Even though previous studies have found that the mean levels of political interest and discussion vary with educational attainment, this does not mean that respondents with more education are more likely to have a truly unconditional (or endogenous) taste for politics. College-educated people are slightly more likely to say they are somewhat interested in politics and less likely to admit being not that interested. I claim that this variation is entirely endogenous to social context and is linked to the same mobilization and diffusion process that drives education-related voting turnout. The proportion of citizens with a true taste for politics

---

[6] Even though respondents holding advanced degrees are more likely to report discussing politics "almost always," the difference is not significant given the small number of respondents in this educational category.

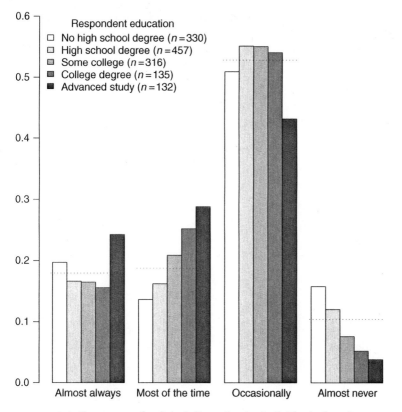

FIGURE 6.6. Frequency of political discussion by individual education.

is quite similar across the two populations – whether defined by individual educational attainment or educationally related social context. Thus, empirical tests of the social theory of turnout assume that unconditional voting is distributed randomly throughout the population turnout.

Even if unconditional voters are distributed randomly throughout the population, as I have argued, there is still a question about the distribution of decision rules among the remainder of decision makers. Could it be that education and other demographic variables are instead related to the use of mean matching versus median matching? Or could education actually be a resource used to reduce the costs of voting, as is commonly argued (Sanders 1980; Schram and van Winden 1991; Verba, Schlozman and Brady 1995, for examples)? Changes in the distribution of conditional decision rules seem to be unlikely suspects, given that the relative distribution of the rules has little impact on simulated turnout within a moderately large range. If education did subsidize individual costs, this would be reflected in a conditional decision model as an increasing the number of first movers among the educated – a possibility that has been ruled out in the earlier discussion.

In summary, I claim that individuals in groups who are more likely to vote – older voters, or those with a college degree, for example – are not more likely to cooperate unconditionally than younger or less educated citizens. Although individual turnout probability is correlated with these demographic variables, this relationship does not come from variation in use of decision rules (or, more loosely, to "personalities"). Rather, as I show, this stems from social structural variables discussed later. Meanwhile, even if the "political junkies" that act as first movers for political participation are distinct from unconditional cooperators in social dilemmas in general, my argument for random distribution of decision rules still stands. High levels of political interest and discussion are not strongly associated with education. Average political interest may still be higher among some portions of the population, but I argue that this is a result of the same political processes and social structures that, in the social theory, produce higher turnout rates in these groups at the same time. A more casual political interest is endogenous to the processes that generate turnout, while a true taste for politics seems randomly distributed in the population.

I will now turn to the remainder of my argument how direct and indirect mobilization drives turnout variation associated with demographic variables. I save these arguments for last not because they are the least important; indeed, they are critically important as they produce the crucial tests that allow us to differentiate between the social theory and the civic resources theory. However, the link between mobilization, demographics, and social networks is also perhaps the least intuitive conceptual link in the theory, and requires the preceding steps in the argument to make sense. The remainder of this chapter is devoted to spelling out more carefully how direct and indirect mobilization by strategic politicians produces variation in turnout linked to demographics and individual social location.

Direct Mobilization

Voters can vary in terms of personal tastes and choice of decision strategies, but they can also vary in terms of social location, which might have a strong influence on turnout if candidates choose to focus campaign resources on specific subgroups of citizens. In this section, I argue that direct mobilization can affect individual turnout in several ways: candidates can boost the turnout of first movers in very-low-salience races where knowledge of the upcoming election is very limited; candidates can mobilize some segments of the population during high-salience elections through canvassing and personal appearances[7]; and candidates can reach out to friends, acquaintances, and organized groups to whom they have social connections during low- to moderate-salience elections.

In low-salience elections, how will strategic candidates organize their mobilization efforts? Strategic candidates will tend to focus resources on areas that yield the greatest returns (Cox 1999). In low-salience elections, they will focus limited resources on persuading regular voters to support them or on reaching out to voters who are relatively easy to mobilize. For example, many candidates send out mailings to regular voters and strong partisans (Huckfeldt and Sprague 1992) in low-salience races, seeking to influence their vote under the assumption that they will turn out regardless of the contact (an assumption that may be somewhat flawed, of course). If only a few voters get these mailings, and if regular voters are distributed essentially randomly with respect to social networks, then direct mail is unlikely to increase general visibility of the election (see Chwe 2001 on common knowledge). Instead, contact with regular voters is likely to be useful simply for informing unconditional cooperators about the occurrence of the upcoming election. I expect that this sort of campaign activity will have the biggest effect in very-low-salience elections, say state or municipal runoffs of which relatively few citizens will even be aware. Contact with high-interest (unconditional) voters is unlikely to increase political discussion more generally, and therefore mobilization efforts directed only at extremely regular voters is unlikely to boost turnout higher than 10% to 12% of the electorate (i.e., the proportion of voting first movers) in very-low-salience elections.

Candidates are also likely to try to mobilize people who are already tied to strong social networks, whether through informal or through formal

---

[7] In this discussion, mobilization is treated as if it worked to increase turnout solely through the individual-level mechanism of encouraging discussion (perhaps by priming the salience of politics), even among those canvassed door to door (Gerber and Green 2000). Canvassing might also increase turnout more immediately, by either: (1) altering individual weights on decision rules (perhaps by priming the salience of social identities or impression management goals), or (2) increasing expected turnout among reference group members (perhaps by priming significant alters). More focused experimental research is needed to identify the actual mechanism(s) involved in face-to-face canvassing, although it is likely that all three are involved to some extent.

organizations. Rosenstone and Hansen (1993) argue that candidates will contact and mobilize people to whom they are tied either directly or indirectly in their own personal social networks. Cox, Rosenbluth, and Thies (1998) find evidence that candidates in Japan reach out to groups with higher levels of social capital, or preexisting network resources for network-based indirect mobilization. The social decision-making model predicts that campaign activities that create common knowledge of the election in a localized population will increase turnout, perhaps dramatically, in that small group. This is even more likely within the candidate's own weak-tie networks, where common knowledge of the candidate at a personal level creates an additional point of discussion.

The social decision-making view predicts that localized mobilization efforts will increase discussion of an election among those reached by a candidate, and thus indirectly increase the number of conditional voters. The candidate who speaks to a neighborhood association may be reaching many unconditional voters, with their greater propensity for contributing to group goods such as voluntary associations. They may also, however, be generating discussion among conditional voters who join the organization for other reasons. Even door-to-door campaigning may generate very localized "buzz." As one candidate explained about door-to-door campaigning,[8] "people will hear that you were there, even if you don't talk to everyone." Thus, we expect to see higher turnout as a product of localized interest in and discussion of a campaign in places where candidates make face-to-face appearances, even if the election is not talked about widely in the population at large.

Politicians also work to directly mobilize voters during high-salience elections, although their efforts may be harder to detect given the overall increase in the turnout level in national elections. However, survey data (Rosenstone and Hansen 1993; Verba, Schlozman and Brady 1995) and field experiments (Gerber and Green 2000; Green, Gerber and Nickerson 2003) confirm that direct mobilization can have an impact on individual propensity to turn out. In looking at national election turnout form the 1984 election in Chapter 8, we will explore the possibility that direct mobilization of certain groups who were the subject of particularly vigorous mobilization efforts during that race (e.g., African-American churchgoers in the South) did increase turnout in the mobilized groups.

---

[8] This quote comes from one of a series of interviews I conducted with political candidates, detailed in Chapter 8.

The civic voluntarism model also includes direct mobilization as a predictor of individual activity. Mobilization is tacked on to the civic voluntarism model despite not fitting well with its logic. On the other hand, it fits neatly into the social theory of turnout. Nonetheless, these two theories do not make very different predictions about direct mobilization: Both claim that people who are asked to participate are more likely to do so. The differences between the two theories are more apparent when examining indirect mobilization, as shown in the subsection that follows.

Indirect Mobilization

Although direct mobilization clearly cannot be left out of an explanation of turnout, it is equally clear that direct mobilization alone cannot account for all voting. Campaigns and activist groups simply do not have a chance to personally speak to all potential voters. The social theory and the civic voluntarism theory make similar predictions for direct mobilization, but the theories differ dramatically on the possibility of indirect mobilization. I argue that all turnout is, in a sense, mobilized, with much of the mobilization occurring indirectly through increases in political discussion and general visibility of the upcoming election among potential voters. In this section, I introduce the final factor that accounts for individual turnout variation – latent differences in the potential of individuals to be mobilized indirectly – and argue that these latent differences are rooted in the differences in social structure that, in fact, cause much of the variation in individual turnout probabilities.

Because politicians are strategic, and campaign in areas where they think they can get votes, I expect to see that many demographic characteristics may serve as indicators of mobilization activity: High-income households, racial minorities, and members of churches and associations are all likely to be approached by a candidate or an activist in the course of an election. Moreover, according to the social theory of voter turnout, people in these social categories, even if not approached directly, are still more likely to turn out because of the carryover effects of indirect mobilization (Leighley 1990; Kenny 1992; Huckfeldt, Beck, Dalton, and Levine 1995; Gerber and Green 2000; Green, Gerber, and Nickerson 2003; McClurg 2004), paired with the assumption of homophily in friendship choices (McPherson, Smith-Lovin, and Cook 2001). In this sense, essentially all turnout is mobilized, and much individual variation can be explained by the direct and indirect effects of mobilization. Survey questions that query only whether an individual was directly approached by a party or a candidate are likely to vastly underestimate the overall effects of mobilization (see, e.g., Nickerson 2008 on spouse influence).

How does indirect mobilization work? Although I cannot pin down this process as precisely as might be ideal, we can speculate that citizens communicate to each other their own level of involvement in the political system through a variety of means, and that this communication increases the effective size of the social network relevant to the turnout decision. Even citizens who do not directly meet with a candidate, or see a candidate's ad on television, or watch the presidential candidates' debate on TV still have an opportunity to discuss an upcoming election with their friends. Much of this discussion is likely to be casual, perhaps dwelling on personal characteristics of the candidates rather than their issue positions or more substantive political content, of course. Regardless of the conversational content, however, exposure to higher levels of political discussion, I suggest, increases the likelihood of voting. In terms of the model of social decision making, additional discussion increases the size of the reference group used by a citizen when deciding whether or not to vote, thus in effect increasing the size of one's social network.

As we saw in Chapter 5, average network size is one of the most important determinants of aggregate voter turnout in a population. Simulated populations in which agents systematically make decisions on the basis of larger social networks turn out at higher rates, on average, than populations where social networks are smaller. Thus, one implication of the social theory of voter turnout is that citizens who are in larger social network contexts are advantaged in terms of voter turnout: Potential voters who have many friends, and whose friends have many friends, are more likely to vote than people who have fewer friends, regardless of any other characteristic of the voters or their friends.

Why "social network context" rather than simply social networks? Crucially, it is not just the number of friends an individual has that determines her likelihood of voting, but rather the size and density of the network structure in which she is embedded. To clarify the difference between personal social networks and social network context, I present the visual illustration of Figure 6.7. Here, we see two people, *Gray* (on the right) and *Black* (on the left), each of whom have two friends. Based on looking only at the personal friendships of *Black* and *Gray*, we would have no expectations that one would be more likely to vote than the other; both have two, and only two, friends. However, our expectations

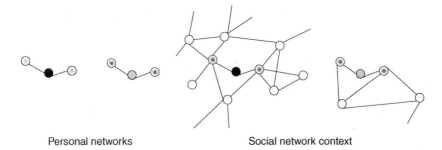

Personal networks   Social network context

FIGURE 6.7. Personal network size and social network context.
Source: 1985 General Social Survey (*n* = 1395).

change dramatically if we look at the larger social network context of these two individuals.

In Figure 6.7(b), we see the friendship networks of the friends of *Black* and *Gray*. We see that all of *Gray*'s friends have only a few friends themselves. However, *Black* is in a much larger social network context, as each of her friends has five or six friends apiece. *Black*'s network context has a greater latent ability to spread mobilization efforts indirectly to *Black*. The larger network has greater latent potential to spread voting in several ways. First, there is a greater probability of indirect exposure to first movers, and second, there is a greater likelihood that the network context will contain low-threshold conditional cooperators who can amplify first movers' actions and eventually induce higher rates of turnout throughout the network. In other words, the friends of *Black*'s friends are more likely to contain first movers, and also the mobilizing impact of any first movers is more likely to spread through the network to reach *Black* and increase her likelihood of voting.

This point only strengthens in importance when thinking about a whole social world rather than limiting our gaze to friends one step away from the person in question. Full social networks comprise a social world, including friends of friends of friends of friends and so on, with systematic differences in the sizes of personal social networks within those worlds. When we find such differences – across social groups, for example – then the social theory would predict differences in voting turnout to appear as well. As it turns out, formal education, long known to be a strong correlate of voter turnout, is also a useful indicator of larger network context. Early studies of personal social networks found that respondents with college educations reported more close personal friendships and

acquaintances than less educated respondents. This finding has been rep-
licated using multiple methods, and appears consistently across different
settings and different levels of friendship (de Sola Pool and Kochen 1978;
Killworth and Bernard 1978; Marsden 1987; Freeman and Thompson
1989; Bernard et al. 1990; Cochran 1990; Huang and Tausig 1990;
Killworth et al. 1990; Campbell and Lee 1991; Straits 1996).

Individual education, however, is not a perfect indicator of the larger
structure of social relationships in the United States. In Chapter 7, I use
survey data on personal networks and voter turnout to develop a more
refined measure of social network context within the U.S. population. I
use a simple binary indicator of social "worlds" derived from the overdispersion of college-educated friends (Zheng, Salganik, and Gelman 2006).
Networks in these social worlds vary in network size and structure, and
thus vary in ability to spread mobilization efforts indirectly. This indicator of social network context represents a view of education that is clearly
distinct from the resource-based view in the civic voluntarism tradition.
Strikingly, it turns out to be a better predictor of turnout probability than
individual educational attainment, as shown later.

In Chapter 8, I look at another implication of this understanding of
social networks and latent ability to convert direct mobilization into
indirect mobilization. While the logic is laid out in greater detail in that
chapter, the goal is to demonstrate that when systematic differences in
social network size are rendered insignificant (as is the case in very-low-
salience elections where there is little or no political discussion among
friend about the upcoming election), education is no longer a good predictor of individual voter turnout; exposure to direct mobilization and
personal links to candidates are the only factors that affect individual
turnout decisions.

In summary, the social theory of turnout stands in more direct contrast to the resource-based theory of turnout when explanations of individual turnout variation are considered. Whereas the civic voluntarism
model focuses on (1) the desire to vote, (2) the ability to vote, and (3)
being asked to vote, the social theory of turnout accounts for the same
correlates of turnout rate in terms of individual decision rules and social
context, and makes further predictions on this basis as well.

7

Education and High-Salience Elections

We have now seen that changes in social structure can plausibly produce changes in turnout, as predicted by the social theory of turnout. In simulated elections, people embedded in larger social network contexts were more likely to turn out than those in smaller network contexts.[1] In this chapter, I test this implication of the social theory empirically, using survey data on individual turnout in high-salience elections. In the end, I provide evidence showing that education and turnout are associated only because education is a strong proxy for social network context. Although the literature has yet to agree on the right mechanism (Sondheimer and Green 2010), there is a long-standing consensus that formal education actually has a causal impact, increasing the probability that a given individual will turn out to vote. Thus, this chapter directly challenges a key element in prevailing empirical understandings of political participation.

Years of formal education is one of the "usual suspects" in empirical survey research, and is of particular interest given the influence this variable appears to exert over a range of political behaviors. Education is associated with not only political participation and political engagement, but also attitudes such as political tolerance (Stouffer 1955; Bobo and Licari 1989; Nie, Junn, and Stehlik-Barry 1996), support of racial equality (Schuman et al. 1997), and support of gender equality (Bennett and Bennett 1992), among others. Education has been theorized to instill a sense of civic duty among students (Wolfinger and Rosenstone 1980),[2]

---

[1] The impact of social networks depends on the distribution of decision rules, and larger social networks increase turnout only when turnout is relatively low cost (as it always is in the United States).

[2] At least among those not exposed to Downs's turnout paradox (Blais and Young 1999)!

teach the civic skills necessary to register and vote (Rosenstone and Hansen 1993; Verba, Schlozman, and Brady 1995), or increase political interest (Verba, Schlozman, and Brady 1995).

In other words, education is presumed to transform individuals because of the prevailing emphasis on how education influences the individual costs (available resources) and benefits (political engagement) of turnout.[3] Based on the simulations in the previous chapter, I argue that social structure – or the average size and density of personal networks in a population – is highly correlated with education but has an independent influence on cooperation levels.

Moreover, this chapter further validates the conditional choice framework as an alternative view of decision making. Current empirical theories implicitly assume that the voting decision is driven by costs and benefits, and that the empirical correlates of voting must therefore represent variation in either a taste for politics (benefits) or civic skills (costs). If this underlying decision-making model is wrong, however, and potential voters do not make forward-looking decisions to maximize their utility, then there is a good chance that empirical measures presumed to capture differences in the costs and benefits of turnout are being misinterpreted.

In the analysis that follows, I use the conditional choice framework to choose alternative indicators of social networks and social structure, and use survey data to compare the implications of the social theory to those associated with civic voluntarism (Verba, Schlozman, and Brady 1995).

SOCIAL THEORY: IMPLICATIONS OF THE MODEL

Although the social theory of turnout is similar in spirit to theories of social influence embodied in sociological models of vote choice, from the early Columbia School studies to more recent work by Robert Huckfeldt and colleagues, it carries more radically structuralist implications. Social-influence models typically look at the ways in which alters (or friends) influence the person whose ego-centered network is under consideration. The attitudes and behavior of ego are altered either through the logic of balance theory and cohesion (Heider 1944; Coleman, Katz, and Menzel 1966) or through the power of structural equivalence (Burt 1980). Like the conditional cooperation model, such theories would expect that person i is more likely to vote than person j if i has more friends who vote than j.

---

[3] Notwithstanding notable exceptions (Huckfeldt 1979; Huckfeldt and Sprague 1992; Knack 1992; Rosenstone and Hansen 1993, on social networks).

In this chapter, however, I analyze a further question: How does *i*'s network come to have more voting friends than *j*'s? Are *i*'s friends better citizens – blessed with more civic duty, or better equipped to navigate the electoral system? Although this might correspond with typical empirical conceptions of voter turnout, I suggest that the differences may lie not in the individual characteristics of the people in *i*'s network, but rather in the structure of interpersonal interactions in which citizen *i* and his/her friends are all embedded. The size and shape of a social network can determine the extent to which a behavior spreads through a society, independent of any variation in the characteristics of the individuals composing the network (Granovetter 1985; Macy 1991; Gould 1993).[4]

As an illustration of network size and clustering and its possible roots in educational attainment, imagine two men, James and Wade.[5] Wade is a college graduate working in his adoptive hometown of Miami; James is a high school graduate in his original hometown of Cleveland. Network studies suggest that the networks of these two men will vary with respect to size (number of friends) and density (number of friends who know each other) (Killworth and Bernard 1978; Bernard et al. 1990; Cochran 1990; Straits 1996). James's closest contacts are very likely to have close ties among themselves – they may consist largely of family members, or neighbors, most of whom know one another, as well as knowing James. Wade, on the other hand, may be close with his immediate family but also stays in close contact with a former college roommate now living in Milwaukee and a business associate living in Boston. Unlike James's family and neighbors, who are likely to know each other very well, Wade's ex-roommate does not know his business associates, and his coworkers do not know his extended family. Wade's network is less dense, or less tightly clustered, than James's, in this case due to Wade's experiences in higher education and resulting employment.

---

[4] Roger Gould's paper in particular speaks strongly to this point, and this work owes him a major intellectual debt.

[5] Resemblance to NBA basketball players is not meant to be taken too literally, as some of these details no longer or never did apply to LeBron James and Dwyane Wade. Most notably, once reaching similar positions as NBA superstars, the two men's networks likely became more similar in structure as well as overlapping considerably – although many attributed LeBron James' move to Miami rather than New York or Chicago to his social networks, whether his reliance on a small circle of friends from his high school days who became his business advisors, or his desire to recreate the feeling of a small, dense network of friends by choosing to play on the same team with two of his closest friends in the NBA.

TABLE 7.1. *Average Turnout Rate in Simulations, by Network Size*

First Movers	Small Core Network		Moderate Core Network		Extended Core Network	
	$\bar{k} \approx 3$	$\bar{k} \approx 4$	$\bar{k} \approx 8$	$\bar{k} \approx 12$	$\bar{k} \approx 16$	$\bar{k} \approx 20$
Low (α = 0.10)	35%	37%	39%	41%	40%	41%
Medium (α = 0.125)	47%	50%	55%	74%	76%	89%
High (α = 0.15)	60%	67%	78%	94%	95%	97%

Source: Results generated using *Repast* simulation package.

What are the implications of this systematic difference in social network properties? I claim that different voter turnout rates may be a result of variation in social structure, instead of a function of variation in the characteristics of the individuals who make up these social networks. As a brief reminder of earlier results, Table 7.1 contains the numeric estimates of average turnout in simulations depending on the size of networks in question.[6]

Two results stand out. First, in all combinations of first-mover percentage and network type (core, moderate, or extended), the simulated world with larger social networks of a given type (numbers that appear in the right-hand column) produces higher rates of turnout, with the difference ranging from 3 to 19 percentage points. Intuitively, this finding represents the fact that individuals in larger networks have indirect access through these networks to more information about other people. Thus, if a small group just happens by chance to include several first movers, cooperation will rapidly build in that area of the social space and then will spread easily to others who are indirectly linked to the initial cooperators. Cooperation in very small groups tends to get "stuck" in those groups, whereas in extremely large groups, the initial contributions of first movers may be diluted by the mass of noncooperators.

The model, therefore, provides an alternative explanation of why some people vote more often than others. If more of person i's friends cooperate then person j's, it may be because of differences in the latent structural potential of the networks themselves rather than differences in the characteristics of the individuals composing the networks. Of course,

[6] The reader is invited to refer back to the discussion of Figure 6.1 and Figure 6.2 from the previous chapter, as well as earlier discussions in Chapter 5, for more details on the process used to obtain these estimates and the combinations of network size and network clustering used to produce them.

from the perspective of the individual voter, the only relevant information is the turnout rate of her friends. From the perspective of the researcher, however, this distinction is both tractable and consequential.

Why is this difference meaningful? As mentioned earlier, the properties of personal networks vary systematically with respect to some demographic variables, particularly education. To the extent that these demographic variables also mark the existence of relatively segregated subgroups of individuals who relate almost exclusively to people similar to them (Blau 1977), variables presumed to capture important individual characteristics may actually capture meaningful differences in the structure of social interactions. For example, a highly educated prospective voter may be more likely to vote, not because either he/she or his/her friends have a stronger personal propensity to vote or an easier time figuring out how to register, but because the patterns of relationships among highly educated individuals are more conducive to social cooperation than are the patterns of interaction among less educated citizens. The remainder of this chapter is devoted to demonstrating that the social theory of turnout offers a coherent framework for interpreting the effects of education on individual turnout that outperforms a resource and interest based view in empirical tests.

A NEW LOOK AT EDUCATION

The social theory of turnout (and associated conditional decision-making model) points to an important theoretical mechanism to be examined in this chapter: People in larger social networks with fewer overlapping ties cooperate more often than those in smaller and denser social networks, at least in social dilemmas with properties similar to the situation posed by voting. The claim that social network properties are more important than individual costs and benefits of turnout is a clear departure from two important tenets of the civic voluntarism model: People are more likely to participate if they have more civic resources (lower costs) or political interest (greater benefits) (Verba, Schlozman, and Brady 1995). In considering the relative merits of these two views of turnout, I proceed as follows. First, I describe and validate an important link between education and social network structure. Second, I compare the social theory to the civic resources theory on three counts: (1) the relationship between education and political interest, (2) the relationship between education and turnout, and (3) a multivariate comparison of the two theories.

I rely here on the 1985 General Social Survey (GSS). Of appropriate
and available data sets, at present only the 1985 GSS contains direct
measures of personal social network size, density, and personal characteristics of friends.[7] I also note other variables available for a multivariate comparison of the social theory and civic voluntarism in the GSS,
with the caveat that such variables could and should be subjected to the
same treatment as education in the future before simply being included
as "controls" (Achen 1992).

Social Network Size

The 1985 GSS contained a network battery, in which respondents were
asked to generate a list of up to six people with whom they "discussed
important matters," and then provide additional information about each
of the first five people named, including characteristics such as gender,
education, race, the nature of the relationship (kin, coworker, neighbor),
and the respondent's estimate of the strength of each possible dyadic tie
among the five alters. In all, almost 1,400 out of possible 1,530 respondents provided the name of at least one friend, and only about 60 of these
failed to provide educational information on every one of the friends they
named. These data provide a measure of ego-centered or *Core Network
Size* (Wasserman and Faust 1994), a count from 0 to 6 of the number of
responses to a name generator about core social networks (Fischer 1982;
Burt 1984; Marsden and Campbell 1984; Huckfeldt 2000).[8]

The dynamics of conditional decision making in situations like voting,
however, suggest not just that individuals with more social ties are more

---

[7] Other surveys have included social network name generators, such as the 1992 American
component of the CNES and the 1984 South Bend study. Unfortunately, there is significant bias in both the survey sample and in nonresponse to name generators. For example,
respondents in the 1992 CNES did not provide educational background for more than
half of all friends named. Those respondents willing to respond were much more likely to
have college-educated friends – regardless of the respondents education, further confirming the general cooperativeness of individuals who are part of a social world with a social
structure conducive to the spread of generalized cooperation. The 2004 GSS included
a replication of the 1985 GSS "important matters" module that produced significantly
lower estimates of social network size (McPherson, Smith-Lovin, and Brashears 2006),
sparking a fierce debate over whether the 2004 estimates are reliable (Fischer 2009).

[8] Other name generators are possible (Milgram 1967; Travers and Milgram 1969; de Sola
Pool and Kochen 1978; Killworth and Bernard 1978; Bernard et al. 1990; Killworth
et al. 1990; McCarty et al. 1997). There is a strong correlation among responses to core
network generators and other generators, so there is good reason to think that individuals are ranked appropriately even if the absolute size of the networks may be measured
inaccurately.

likely to vote, but that individuals who are part of a community characterized by large networks are more likely to vote, regardless of the size of their own personal network. Therefore, a measure of personal network size does not capture the key insight needed to develop a social theory. The necessary measure would instead tap into the average personal network size of the friends of friends of the respondent. Furthermore, given the dynamics of conditional decision making, an appropriate measure would also take into account the average size of all of the personal networks of friends of friends, gradually moving out through paths of network ties until reaching the boundaries of the larger social community. Thus, the ultimate goal is to identify a relevant social cleavage that defines larger but distinct social communities, and then estimate the average size of personal networks within these densely connected social communities.

There is no easy method of measuring the personal network size of the friends of respondents directly. Various solutions such as snowball samples or multiple samples from the same neighborhood are perhaps the best approaches. However, there is a rich literature on how network size varies systematically in relation to demographic variables (see de Sola Pool and Kochen 1978 and McCarty et al. 1997 for examples). Therefore, I approach the problem using a two-step process. First, I look for evidence of a social cleavage, using a method similar to that used to identify the over-dispersion of friends with particular social characteristics (Zheng, Salganik, and Gelman 2006). Second, I look for systematic differences in the average personal network size and degree between the identified subgroups. The key is that to serve as a relevant marker of structural network differences, there must be a relatively distinct line between those who belong to the subgroup and those outside of it. In what follows, I examine the extent to which traditional demographic variables define groups that are stratified or segregated into recognizable communities with pertinent differences in network structure. I also consider whether recognizable subgroups in the population may vary on the basis of their exposure to political mobilization during the 1984 presidential campaign.

Education

Education is typically thought of as an individual-level variable, influencing the extent to which an individual acquires skills or interests pertinent to politics, such as political interest and information, cognitive skills, or a large vocabulary (Verba, Schlozman, and Brady 1995). In contrast, I argue that the apparent influence of individual education on

TABLE 7.2. *Ties to a College-Educated Alter, by Individual Education*

Respondent's Education Level	College-educated Discussants as Percentage of Total[a]	n
No High School Degree	11%	345
High School Degree	13%	463
Some College	27%	318
College Degree	54%	137
Advanced Study	62%	132
All Respondents	24%	1,395

[a] Discussants with missing information about education are coded as having no college degree.

Source: General Social Survey 1985.

turnout arises because individual educational attainment is an indicator – albeit an imperfect one – of membership in one of two distinct subgroups in American social life. These two subgroups are distinct in both their patterns of ingroup and outgroup relationships and the average size and density of personal networks within the subgroups, and thus would be likely to influence turnout accordingly.

In thinking about social segregation along educational lines, it is useful to think first about the degree of educational homophily, or the tendency for individuals to choose others similar to themselves as friends, in the United States. In order to measure this tendency, I looked at how likely respondents were to name friends with similar educations using the 1985 General Social Survey (GSS).

As Table 7.2 shows, higher education is a significant social dividing point in U.S. society. Each of the table's cells represents ties to a college graduate, as a percentage of all social ties listed by all respondents with the indicated educational background. Thus, on average, only 13% of the ties of high school graduates were to individuals with a college degree, whereas, on average, more than half of the alters named by college-educated had a college degree.[9] Overall, 84% of the ties named by respondents with less than a college degree were to someone who also did not have a college education.[10] On the other side, about 58% of the

[9] We would not expect the distribution of educational attainment of friends to mirror the distribution of educational attainment in the population. College-educated respondents have larger self-reported network, and thus we expect that those with university degrees will be overrepresented in social networks relative to their population distribution

[10] This is the average if respondents from all three categories with less than a college degree are combined.

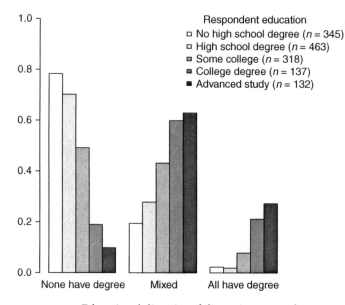

FIGURE 7.1. Educational diversity of discussion networks.
Source: 1985 General Social Survey (*n* = 1534).

ties of respondents with a college education were with someone who also had at least a college degree.

However, the numbers in Table 7.2 are simply aggregated on the basis of education, and as such may be misleading if people with larger networks make different choices than those with smaller networks. A clearer picture of educational segregation emerges from examining the percentage of people in each world who exist in completely segregated networks – that is to say, those individuals who name only alters either with or without a college degree. Evidence on this point is presented in Figure 7.1. As an example, 78% of those without a high school degree named no college-educated friends, whereas 3% of those without a high school degree named only college-educated friends, leaving 19% of respondents who named both high- and low-education friends.

High school dropouts are not alone in not naming degree holders as friends, as 70% of GSS respondents who completed high school do not name a college-educated person as a member of their core network. Even more startling, half of respondents with only some education beyond high school do the same. That is to say, half of the respondents who attended college but did not graduate maintained no close ties with anyone who went on to obtain a college degree. Two-thirds of those Americans who do not have a college degree have minimal contact with anyone with a college education (Bailey and Marsden 1999), although not at the closer levels of contact recorded by the GSS. This educational cleavage in friendship persists despite the fact that most university graduates have educationally diverse networks: Less than a quarter of college degree holders have social networks composed exclusively of those with similar educations.

These data suggest that education of one's friends, not one's own education, serves as a clear dividing line in the American electorate. There appear to be two distinct subgroups in the American population: low-education respondents whose close friends are drawn exclusively from a community of low-education members, and respondents of diverse educational backgrounds whose personal networks include one or more individuals with a college education. Having identified a convenient social cleavage, I examine the extent to which this clear division is related to average network size and density within the groups. Estimated network size appears in Figure 7.2, with confidence intervals marked for network size at each level of education.

These descriptive statistics confirm the existence of two distinct subgroups in American life, the low-education world and the multieducation world. Furthermore, they blunt the possible objection that highly educated people are more comfortable or more thorough as survey respondents, and thus provide more names than less educated people. Individuals with low educational attainment who are members of the multieducation world generate, on average, about the same number of ties as those who themselves possess a college degree (and in fact more than the individuals who bridge the two worlds – those who have college degrees but claim to have no college-educated friends). Thus, education of one's friends serves as an indicator in membership of one of two social world; worlds that are distinct both in terms of membership and patterns of interactions (as indicated by personal network size and density) that take place between group members.

Therefore, I use educational social worlds to proxy for the average social network size and density of the extended social context of respondent. Respondents with no college-educated friends are given an indicator for *Low-Education World*. In multivariate analysis, individual education should no longer pick up the influence of this previously omitted variable, but capture only the individual effects of education on individual costs and benefits.

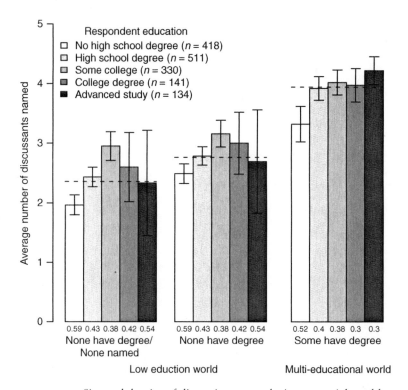

FIGURE 7.2. Size and density of discussion networks in two social worlds. *Source*: 1985 General Social Survey (*n* = 1486).

Looking closer at Figure 7.2, one group of respondents does stand out as markedly different: those without a high school degree. These respondents clearly have much smaller social networks than others in their social world, and therefore it may be inappropriate to include them in the same community context as high school graduates. This is true even of the respondents who name one or more close discussion partners with a college degree but do not themselves have a high school diploma. There are a few indicators that these respondents are, at best, marginally incorporated into either of the core social worlds.

First, failure to complete high school is relatively uncommon among most of the cohorts represented in the 1985 study. Whereas less than 50% of 1985 GSS respondents born prior to 1920 had a degree (respondents age sixty-five and older in 1985), less than 25% of those born after 1935 failed to do so. Among the postwar cohorts, lack of an education was likely to greatly reduce an individual's ability to find a job, a home, or become a member of a stable community. Therefore, we would expect to find that among respondents over age fifty-five, the social-world variable might be less indicative of their social incorporation. Respondents older than fifty-five who have any education beyond high school (and in some cases merely a high school degree) were part of the social elite in their birth cohort.[11] Conversely, respondents under age fifty-five without a high school degree are more likely to be less-than-fully integrated – both economically and socially – into mainstream society.

Given that there are clear signs that most respondents without a high school education are not fully integrated into their respective social worlds, I use a dummy variable for *Social Isolation* for respondents without a high-school degree. Although this decision may to some extent confound the impact of education and social world, it is equally difficult to simply include these respondents as if they were part of the same social context inhabited by respondents with a high school degree. To check for robustness, therefore, I remove this variable and replace it with better specified and more nuanced indicators that take into account differences in cohort. The results are generally robust to these changes, although removal of the indicator does increase the estimated effect of education on turnout to the point of significance if no replacement indicators of cohort and social isolation are included. At no point, however, do changes to the indicator of social isolation result in a decrease in the estimated impact of the variable that is our primary interest: membership in one of the two social worlds.

Mobilization

Also critical to the model are variables that might proxy for likelihood of political mobilization in the absence of a measure of direct recruitment. These include: (1) an indicator for *Work for the Government* (Rosenstone and Hansen 1993); (2) an indicator of *Religious Liberalism* to account for the strong countermobilization against Reagan in 1984 (a reverse coding from the three category GSS variable of denominational fundamentalism); (3) a more careful specification of race to account for the mobilization efforts during the 1984 election, which reached African

---

[11] Therefore, knowing someone with a high school degree might be a better indicator of social worlds in this cohort (Nie et al. 2006). Additional analyses were conducted with this specification, and the adjusted social world indicator did better distinguish among members of this cohort. However, the results did not change dramatically, as only thirty to forty subjects over age fifty-five moved into the higher-education social world with the replacement indicator.

Americans in the South, particularly female churchgoers (Tate 1991; Calhoun-Brown 1996), including *Black Female* and *Black Southerner*; and (4) *City Size* (Oliver 2000; Kelleher and Lowery 2004) from the six-category ordinal SRC belt variable. It is also possible that the indicators of network social structure will pick up on preexisting stocks of social capital – a key factor predicting the probability of elite mobilization according to Cox, Rosenbluth, and Thies (1998).

Other Measures

Beyond the mobilization variables, there is a substantial difficulty in coming up with measures to allow direct comparison between the civic resources model and the social theory of turnout. The 1989–1990 Civic Voluntarism study included direct measures of political engagement, vocabulary, high school activity, and recruitment – all of which had a significant impact on turnout probability. The 1985 GSS, upon which I rely to create the needed indicator for membership in social worlds, has a direct measure only of political engagement, lacking measures of the other three Civic Voluntarism variables.

I can nonetheless approximate the civic voluntarism model using indirect indicators of recruitment and other exogenous factors.[12] Verba, Schlozman, and Brady (1995) often must rely on structural 2SLS estimates to disentangle the various causal pathways through which individuals acquire civic skills, resources, and political interest and information. The exogenous variables they use to capture the structural components of civic resources include: citizenship, education, vocabulary, English spoken at home, family income, working, retired, job level, organizational affiliation, religious attendance, Catholic, number of children under eighteen, preschool children at home, sex, spouse working full or part time, black, Latino, parental education, age, and indicators of political interest, information, and partisan strength measured in a screener survey six months before the main survey. Most of these variables are present in the 1985 GSS, and are therefore used in the following analysis.[13] Gender (*Female*),

---

[12] The inclusion of direct measures of both vocabulary and high school activity are already questionable on theoretical grounds. Vocabulary is likely to represent a spurious correlation, and thus it is actually preferable to omit this variable. To see why this is the case, imagine what might happen to voter turnout if motivated activists gave everyone vocabulary lessons!

[13] The structural predictors of high school involvement and recruitment are included in the analysis, and there is good reason to suspect that the remaining variation in high school

race (*Black*), occupational prestige (up to one hundred) (*Occupational Prestige*), age (*Electoral Experience*), *Religious Attendance* (eight-point ordinal scale), categorical *Household Income*, a cumulative measure of *Parental Education* and marital status (*Married*) are used both directly and as indirect instruments by Verba, Schlozman, and Brady (1995), and merit further discussion.

Gender was historically an excellent predictor of turnout probability (Merriam and Gosnell 1924) and is still used as an instrument for resources in contemporary empirical models. The social theory of turnout would predict gender-based differences in turnout if some women still professed a belief that women should not vote, as was common in the early twentieth century. If this were the case, there would be a conflicting social meaning of voting (and resulting social norm governing turnout), and simulation results based on normative consensus would no longer apply. But as this competing norm has been abandoned or disappeared through generational replacement, there is no longer an expectation that women should differ systematically from men in turnout rates.[14]

Religious attendance is one of the best predictors of political activity. The skills learned in the process of religious involvement, as well as the additional bump in general activity associated with organization involvement, are presumed to be the mechanisms for this effect (Verba, Schlozman, and Brady 1995). But even after controlling for these pathways through which it might exert influence, religious attendance retains an independent association with higher rates of turnout. Based on candidate interviews, I expect religious attendance to play an important role in turnout as well, but my expectation is based on two different factors: first, the probability of being mobilized, and second, the nature of casual conversation in such an organizational setting.[15]

---

activity represents individual differences in activity that should be orthogonal to the other variables in the analysis. Thus, omission of these three direct measures should not bias the estimates.

[14] Note that the same expectation may not necessarily hold for the relative likelihood of donating time or money to political activity, because normative expectations are mixed. Anecdotally, I have found that many female students in class discussions have expressed a strong conviction that it was more appropriate to donate time than money to a cause – a behavioral pattern among women that frustrated female organizers trying to raise money in the past.

[15] It also may be that churches simply contain more first movers – an entirely reasonable expectation given the manner in which unconditional cooperation has been defined relative to willingness to contribute to a public good.

First, religious communities provide a setting where many citizens are likely to be linked through weak ties to candidates and other political activists. I found that both white and black candidates in the county I examined mentioned church repeatedly as a source of their weak-tie contacts that played a role in their campaigns. Even though some of this is undoubtedly an artifact of conducting interviews in a very religious community in the Southeastern United States, it is nonetheless clear that religious institutions provide the sort of social structure and support that bind a community together and which political candidates are likely to draw on. Regular religious attendees are more likely to be exposed to candidates and political activists in both formal and informal settings. Given that much of the exposure is likely informal, it may be often overlooked rather than reported as direct mobilization in response to a survey question. Second, religious institutions (as well as other formal associations and organizations) provide a forum that encourages casual discussion among members, and is an ideal setting for the discussion of civic concerns.[16]

The impact of income, much like that of occupational prestige, can be interpreted in different ways. Based again on my interviews with candidates, I expect income to have an independent effect on political activity, even turnout, because politicians spend so much time and energy trying to reach potential donors. People with very high incomes would clearly be very likely to be contacted directly by a politician relative to the rest of the population. In previous work, however, income – usually thought of as a resource for overcoming the costs of participation – has been found to be highly correlated with turnout only in bivariate analysis, before controlling for educational attainment.[17]

Age is often included as a control variable, although the theoretical basis for its inclusion is not necessarily agreed on. The social theory of turnout both provides a clear theoretical prediction that older citizens will vote more often and suggests an alternative specification. Simulation

---

[16] Particularly in Protestant churches, which are less likely to contain neighbors who know each other in contexts outside of church, local issues may be one of the few reliably acceptable common topics for small talk, as long as major partisan disputes are avoided. The difference between the types of social networks typically encouraged by Protestant and Catholic churches provides one possible alternative explanation for the advantage found to accrue to Protestant churchgoers by Verba, Schlozman, and Brady (1995). Protestant churches may also be advantaged by the greater number of Protestant candidates, as well as other forms of mobilization activity.

[17] Not surprisingly, income retains a strong link to political contributions (Verba, Schlozman, and Brady 1995).

results predict a logarithmic increase in turnout as a function of electoral experience, as opposed to the more commonly used exponential speci-fication of age.[18] Age, in the social theory of turnout, is an indicator of increased electoral experience,[19] and therefore of an increased probability of having observed multiple friends turning out to vote in prior elections. In the civic voluntarism model, age is used as an instrument for several key concepts, but is expected to make no independent contribution to increasing turnout rates.

Race is used in the civic voluntarism model as an indicator of system-atic variation in both resources and political interest. The social theory of voter turnout does not expect racial group membership to have any impact on voter turnout through these pathways, because the variation attributed to resources and interest should be picked up by the overall smaller size, on average, of African Americans' social networks. However, I do expect that race will play an important role in turnout decisions when it is an explicit mobilization criterion for Democratic candidates looking to increase their vote share (Tate 1991; Rosenstone and Hansen 1993; Calhoun-Brown 1996; personal interviews). Therefore, as previ-ously explained, race is included in a modified form into the model as an indicator of mobilization, but there is not an expectation that race will influence turnout directly.

Two direct indicators of political interest are available: *Political Dis-cussion* frequency (four-point ordinal scale) and *Partisan Strength* (four-point ordinal scale built from folded partisan identification). Additionally, marital status and parental education are used as instruments for political interest and resources in the Civic Voluntarism model (Verba, Schlozman, and Brady 1995). However, I do not expect either of these variables to have any independent impact on turnout. Marital status may be associ-ated with increased pressure to vote from one's spouse (Nickerson 2008), but this effect is likely to be picked up in the increase in personal network size, unless spouses are presumed to have a unique ability to influence the turnout decision, more than a best friend or unmarried partner. Parents' education may be an indicator of social structure during the formative years of early vote eligibility, but such an interpretation would stretch the data more than reasonable.

---

[18] Logarithmic transformations of age can be found in other studies of voter turnout (e.g., Cassel 2004), but with no justification beyond the well-known nonlinear relationship between age and turnout.

[19] This is similar to the explanation of age provided by Rosenstone and Hansen (1993).

COMPARING SOCIAL COOPERATION AND CIVIC VOLUNTARISM

In this section, I provide a comparison of social cooperation and civic voluntarism on three counts. First, I look briefly again at the two theories' conceptions of the relationship between education and political interest. Second, I conduct a direct test of the two interpretations of education: social world versus individual costs and benefits. Finally, I extend this test to a comparison of the two theories in multivariate statistical analysis. The social theory proves a better explanation of turnout on all three counts.

Education and Political Interest

In the previous chapter, I argued that a true, exogenous taste for politics is distributed randomly with respect to educational attainment, and that any correlation between political interest and education is endogenous to the process that produces voter turnout. Here I return briefly to that discussion to see if our improved measure of social network context alters or supports these earlier conclusions. Are high levels of political interest distributed randomly with respect to both individual education and social location?

A closer look at the data further supports the social theory in its conception of political interest. A true taste for politics is distributed uniformly throughout the population, without regard for education or social location. Table 7.3 gives the percentage of people who report engaging in both the maximum and minimum level of political discussion.[20] The percentage of potential first movers with a true taste for politics is almost identical across education levels, as noted earlier in Chapter 6 (see Figure 6.6). I also examine discussion with respect to social worlds, finding perhaps a slight difference in the percentage of people who claim to talk very often about politics (19% in the multieducational world and 16% in the low-education world), but this difference is not distinguishable from chance, even using generous standards of statistical significance (one-tailed t-test, $p = 0.13$).

Education and Turnout

A more critical difference between the civic voluntarism model and the social theory of turnout is in the treatment of the relationship between

---

[20] Political discussion is taken from the GSS and is measured in four categories. I look only at those who claim to talk about politics "almost always" or "almost never."

TABLE 7.3. *Political Discussion, by Individual Education and Social World*

	All Respondents		Multieducational		Low Education	
	Always	Never	Always	Never	Always	Never
No High School Degree	20%	16%	26%	11%	17%	17%
High School Degree	17%	12%	17%	9%	17%	13%
Some College	16%	8%	18%	6%	14%	10%
College Degree	16%	5%	16%	5%	15%	8%
Advanced Study	24%	4%	24%	3%	23%	8%

Source: General Social Survey 1985.

education and turnout itself. Civic voluntarism, like most empirical models of political participation, predicts that individual education increases individual probabilities of voting. The social theory, on the other hand, predicts that individual education will have no impact on turnout rates once education-segregated social worlds are taken into account. The social theory predicts that within social worlds, turnout rates will not vary much with individual educational attainment, but that turnout rates will be much higher in the multieducational social context, where networks are larger and more conducive to the spread of cooperative behavior.[21] The simple graph in Figure 7.3 offers a preliminary but telling test of the two theories' predictions.

Figure 7.3 summarizes reported turnout rate in the 1984 presidential rate by individual education and social world.[22] Complete integration into the multieducational world makes a substantial difference in aggregate turnout rates. On average, about 80% of respondents in the multieducational world claim to have voted, as compared to only 61% of those in the low-education world. This difference in turnout rates, a staggering 19%, is both substantively and statistically meaningful ($p < 0.001$, two-tailed t-test). Moreover, even given the small number of college degree holders without similarly educated friends ($n = 39$), it is likely that the drop in turnout rate of 10 points that we observe between these individuals and high school graduates with college-educated friends is not the product of random sample variation ($p = 0.07$, one-tailed t-test). Finally, and perhaps most impressively, the scale of differences in turnout

---

[21] One exception may be among those with very little education who appear to be socially isolated individuals.

[22] See Appendix B for a discussion of vote misreport and other sources of bias in these estimates.

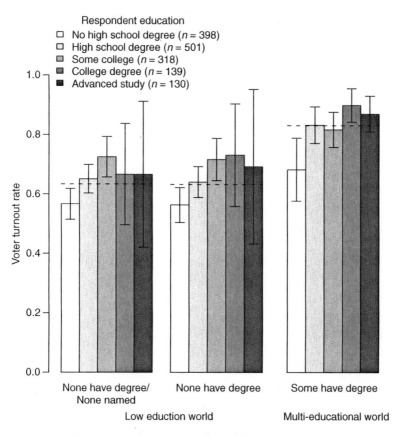

FIGURE 7.3. Voter turnout in two social worlds.

(10–20 percentage points) between the social worlds is very much in line with the scale of differences in simulated turnout reported earlier in the chapter in Table 7.1.

There is a possibility that individual education retains some positive effect on turnout, but the evidence for this is much weaker than one would expect, given prior research and theorizing on voter turnout. In the multieducation world, those without even a high school degree voted less often. Just as expected, however, most of this variation was the result of younger respondents without a high school degree. Approximately 80% of older respondents from the multieducational world without a high school degree reported voting in the prior election.[23]

---

[23] This turnout rate was still lower than that reported for older respondents with at least some college education, but this is not surprising either. The older citizens with a degree

In the low-education world, turnout gradually increases as we move from respondents with no high school degree to those with at least some college. However, the difference in turnout between college degree holders and high school graduates may well be the product of chance ($p = 0.18$, one-tailed t-test). The remaining difference in turnout may also stem from the use of a very crude measure of social world, particularly in light of earlier suggestions that those without a high school degree were singularly socially isolated, and that college-educated citizens cannot truly belong to a low-education world, but only to a border of it.[24] There is no easy way to sort out which explanation of the remaining difference is more appropriate.[25]

Multivariate Estimates

The simple test in Figure 7.3 is impressive, but the results clearly fly in the face of the accepted wisdom in American politics. Education has long been assumed to affect turnout at the individual level by increasing political interest, civic skills, or civic duty, and has proven a stubbornly strong predictor of turnout in previous analyses. The simple cross-tab used in the previous section is a perfect test of the two theories and is unlikely to be overturned by the inclusion of any other variables, but bivariate analysis is unlikely to prove convincing to most readers. Therefore, in this section I test the theories against each other using a variety of additional statistical controls. In Table 7.4, I present estimated models that include indicators of the social theory either alone or in conjunction with additional indicators for the civic voluntarism model. The analysis is

---

were clearly among social elite, and were most likely closely connected to political elites in their community throughout most of their lives.

[24] I also considered other indicators of social cleavages (e.g., religion and race of friends), and some of these sorted some of the college-educated members of the low-education world with higher (not lower) social status.

[25] Huckfeldt (1979) finds that participation among low- and high-socioeconomic-status (SES) individuals is suppressed by living in a neighborhood social environment unlike their own SES and educational status. Here, I replicate the finding that participation among high-education individuals is suppressed (relative to their peers) by ties to the low-education world, but find that participation among low-education individuals is much higher if they do indeed claim ties to a high-education setting. This apparent contradiction is mitigated by the difference in how social environment is measured. GSS respondents define their own social environment, as opposed to having it effectively chosen for them in the form of residential neighborhood demographics. Taken in concert, these two sets of findings suggest that participation rates are increased by integration into a world of high education, but perhaps not by mere residential proximity to it.

TABLE 7.4. *Estimated Effects of Education and Social Network Context on Voter Turnout*

	Civic Only	Social Only	Social and Civic	Social, Civic, and Political
Social Networks				
Low-education world	–	–0.34*** (0.09)	–0.26** (0.10)	–0.23* (0.10)
Personal network size	–	0.31* (0.15)	0.27 (0.15)	0.26 (0.16)
Social Networks or Resources				
Casual discussions (Occupation)	0.59* (0.28)	0.64* (0.26)	0.44 (0.29)	0.41 (0.29)
Social Isolation (No HS degree)	–	–0.39*** (0.10)	–0.18 (0.13)	–0.23 (0.13)
Mobilization Potential				
Black Female	0.42 (0.25)	0.40 (0.21)	0.53* (0.26)	0.64* (0.26)
Southern and Black	0.47 (0.27)	0.11 (0.18)	0.48 (0.27)	0.52 (0.27)
Religious Liberalism	0.37*** (0.11)	0.42*** (0.11)	0.37*** (0.11)	0.42*** (0.11)
City Size	0.11 (0.14)	0.20 (0.13)	0.16 (0.14)	0.20 (0.14)
Government Job	0.17 (0.11)	0.14 (0.11)	0.17 (0.11)	0.16 (0.11)
Mobilization or Resources				
Household Income	0.52*** (0.18)	0.59*** (0.15)	0.48** (0.18)	0.45* (0.18)
Church Attendance	0.98*** (0.12)	0.95*** (0.12)	0.92*** (0.12)	0.90*** (0.12)
Electoral experience				
Log of Age	1.66*** (0.23)	1.38*** (0.17)	1.72*** (0.23)	1.67*** (0.24)
Resources and interest				
Education	1.41** (0.36)	–	0.78 (0.44)	0.70 (0.45)
Father's Education	–0.39 (0.26)	–	–0.47 (0.27)	–0.50 (0.27)
Mother's Education	1.37*** (0.31)	–	1.32** (0.32)	1.45*** (0.33)
Female	0.18* (0.09)	–	0.15 (0.08)	0.10 (0.08)
Married	0.24* (0.11)	–	0.23* (0.11)	0.21 (0.12)
Black	–0.35 (0.28)	–	–0.39 (0.28)	–0.54 (0.29)
Political Engagement				
Political Discussion	–	–	–	0.26* (0.13)
Partisan Strength	–	–	–	0.99*** (0.13)

Missing data imputed using Amelia, and probit model estimated using Zelig in R.
Additional controls for working status, spouse's working status, presence of preschool or other children, and Catholic are included in all models.
Significance levels are indicated as: *** $p < 0.001$, ** $p < 0.01$, * $p < 0.05$.
Source: General Social Survey 1985 (n=1486).

also reproduced including a measure of political interest, although I have serious concerns about whether interest should rightfully be considered exogenous to the political discussion process that produces the individual turnout decision.

Again, the question is whether or not education has an independent influence on voter turnout, above and beyond its indirect influence as a point of access to a larger, more diverse social world – both in terms of close friendships and acquaintances. The answer, once again, is that individual education appears to have little, if any, independent influence on an individual's turnout probability. This is a significant accomplishment. There have been few instances in which individual education is insignificant in a model of turnout despite numerous attempts to do so by uncovering and controlling for the mechanism through which education works. Rare exceptions typically involve using education as an indirect predictor of either registration (Timpone 1998) or political engagement and civic skills (Verba, Schlozman, and Brady 1995). Perhaps the most striking prior instance in which individual education is largely insignificant is reported by Huckfeldt (1979), who finds neighborhood education level to be a better predictor of turnout – a finding in line with the argument presented here.

The effects of social context are clear and compelling. In the *Social Context Only* model in Table 7.4, all of the measures of social network structure (*Small Network Context, Social Isolation, Personal Network Size,* and *Occupational Prestige*) have a substantive and statistically significant effect on turnout probability. Even after controlling for both individual and *Parental Education,* all of the measures remain significant. The effects of *Low Education World* are particularly compelling. Members of the low-education world consistently have a significantly lower probability of voting, for a substantive change of about 10% in the predicted probability of voting holding other variables at their medians.

The poor showing of individual education is not attributable to any idiosyncratic properties of the GSS 1985 sample. In Table 7.4, an estimate of the civic resources model alone is also given. In this model, individual education has a clear substantively and statistically significant effect on turnout probability. I include here the variables that I use to proxy for mobilization potential, given that no direct measure is available. However, removing these proxies from the equation does not have a noticeable effect on the magnitude of the education variable. Moreover, although not shown in this table, the further inclusion of the social isolation dummy variable for individuals without a high school degree has only a small and insignificant effect on the magnitude of the individual education variable in this specification. The estimated impact of the education variable is reduced only by the inclusion of the social network variables, chief among these the (binary) indicator of membership in one of two social worlds, with members of the low-education world having systematically smaller social networks than those in the multieducational world.

The magnitude of the impact of social structure is more evident when considering the contributions of both personal network size and social network context. Holding other variables at their medians, the turnout probability of an isolated person who has no high school degree and with only one close friend without a college education (*Personal Network Size*=1 and *Low Education World* = 1) is more than 30 percentage points lower than a similarly educated citizen with five close friends who is part of a broad, multieducational world (*Personal Network Size*=5 and *Low Education World* = 0). As expected, both social world and personal social network properties contribute independently to turnout probability. And once again, the scale of the change in turnout probability associated with social network context are very much in line with the scale of differences in simulated turnout associated with moderate (twelve-person) and larger (twenty-person) network degree social worlds, as reported earlier in the chapter.

One variable worthy of note is *Occupational Prestige*, considered to be an indicator of civic skills by Verba, Schlozman, and Brady (1995). However, there is long-standing evidence that occupational status is associated with greater acquaintance network size and density, as well as higher levels of casual social interaction of the sort that encourages exchange of political information (Milgram 1967; de Sola Pool and Kochen 1978; Campbell, Marsden, and Hurlbert 1986; Feld and Grofman 1989; Watts 2003). Thus, the significant impact of occupational status on turnout probability is just as easily interpreted as an indicator of an additional dimension of network structure as it is of civic skills. Further study will be necessary to distinguish between the two interpretations.

Parental Education, however, retains a distinct and significant effect on voter turnout.[26] Parental education adds little to the explanatory power

---

[26] Interestingly, it turns out that this effect is almost entirely attributable to differences in the education of the respondent's mother and not of his or her father. Given that childhood development of language and social skills is more closely linked to maternal than to paternal involvement (particularly among the cohorts in the 1985 GSS), this may not be so surprising.

of the model, but instead seems to borrow influence from the indicators of social context, suggesting that parental education may be a very powerful determinant of the social context of their adult children. Also, the initially borderline positive effect of student status is decreased by parental education, suggesting that students may be more likely to participate because of their social background, and not because of the unique political or individual experience of going to college.

I reestimated the model on respondents over the age of twenty-five,[27] to assess whether parental education continued to be such a powerful determinant of social class as individuals age and create their own social niche. I found that whereas the estimated impact of individual measures of social context (except personal network size and no high school degree) and income were less attenuated by the inclusion of parental education in the model for respondents over age twenty-five, parental education continued to exert a positive influence on voter turnout even well after the age when individuals are likely to establish their own social world. Moreover, parental education remains significant, whereas the influence of the respondent's own educational experience remained nonexistent. This is clearly a finding worthy of future consideration, as it suggests that the social world one inhabits as a child may influence an adult's behavior long after the childhood social world has been left behind.

As with any survey analysis, there are additional issues with the estimates provided here. I address several of these – survey nonresponse, item nonresponse, and turnout misreport – in Appendix B. Although a worthwhile goal, purging estimates of these various sources of error and bias would not be likely to change the substantive conclusions of this work: Individual education does not affect turnout through changes in pertinent resources or through civic duty, but rather is a proxy for social context, and a poor one at that. As predicted by the social theory of turnout, citizens who are surrounded by larger number of close friends and acquaintances are more likely to vote than those with more narrow social worlds, as are those citizens who are likely to be politically mobilized either because of their group membership or personal wealth.

DISCUSSION

The social theory of turnout is a theory of how social context influences individual behavior; however, it goes beyond typical social context

[27] Results not presented, but available from the author upon request.

models in claiming that social structure has an independent effect on individual behavior. Demographic variables capture important variations in social context introduced by differences in the volume and diversity of personal contacts. Within this framework, social context does not merely amplify initial individual differences, but actually creates different outcomes among otherwise similar individuals.

The social theory of turnout offers a radical view of the importance of social structure, a view complemented by a focus on political context and the interaction of political and social contexts.[28] In addition to being supported by the evidence I have presented, this perspective offers a much-needed corrective to the tendency among social scientists to ballyhoo the benefits of education. It is quite understandable that scholars and researchers, for whom university education has been a crucial formative influence in their lives and careers, would be inclined to believe in the importance of a college education for citizenship, particularly given the strong and consistent statistical associations between education and many seemingly desirable political behaviors and attitudes. For many others, however, college might mean an opportunity for technical vocational training, or a source of useful business connections, or even a four-year way station of partying en route to adult life, but not anything that transforms them into more aware, more dutiful citizens, nor a necessity for fulfilling everyday chores such as the filling out of registration forms. Rather, college may simply open the doors to higher-paying jobs, more sought-after housing, and social and geographic spaces rich in broad-ranging and politically relevant social ties. The greater likelihood of voting among the educated, then, is not a testament to the power of civic education but rather to the power of social structure, and to college education as a substantial, if permeable, border between different social worlds.

The claim that education does not create regular voters by transforming individuals into more skilled or civic-minded citizens is likely to be somewhat unsettling, given the presumed association between voter turnout and good democratic citizenship. It is important, therefore, to bear in mind that democratic citizenship requires more than a trip to the polls, and that both public and private political discussion may do much to increase the quality of democratic political life in America without

---

[28] One point of interest is that political mobilization only makes sense for parties when there are clear overlaps between social and political cleavages. Thus, even the possibility of political mobilization is contingent on social context.

serving to increase the quantity of relatively low impact involvement. The individual educational experience may also influence other, more meaningful forms of political involvement – despite the fact that education apparently influences turnout merely by serving as a partial sorting mechanism for social class in contemporary America.

8

Mobilization in Low-Salience Elections

In this chapter, I show that the social theory of voter turnout offers a better explanation of patterns of turnout in low-salience primary elections than does the more traditional economic or resource-based model. Prior research has shown that citizens with higher incomes and more formal education are more likely than others to vote in these elections, and, further, has attributed these associations to these citizens' possession of superior civic resources. Scholars have conceived of income and education as providing resources that make it easier to overcome the costs of voting, particularly crucial in low-profile elections that require more effort and information seeking from voters. Alternatively, they have argued that such civic resources make voting more beneficial, and thus rational, for voters high in socioeconomic status and the sense of civic duty that seems associated with such status. In this chapter, I argue instead that it is citizens whose social networks are geographically or socially more proximate to political candidates or other sources of political mobilization who are actually more likely to vote in low-salience elections. The relationship with income and education does not indicate any causal impact of these individual characteristics; rather, the resource-rich are usually more likely to be mobilized, directly or indirectly, by campaign activity. Using data from local elections in a large metropolitan county, I show that high rates of turnout are more closely associated with areas rich in social ties and high in proximity to candidates and campaign activity than with high levels of education and income.

TURNOUT PATTERNS IN LOW-SALIENCE ELECTIONS

Low-salience elections provide a useful arena in which to test the two models of individual turnout decisions – civic resources and social decision making – with the strategic mobilization view of aggregate patterns in turnout as a backdrop. As strategic environments, races for low-profile offices with little power, or primary elections with little difference between the candidates, are likely to be low-intensity campaigns that reach few voters. Candidates, donors, and political parties are strategic investors in the political process, and therefore invest fewer resources in offices that provide fewer opportunities for power and decision making. Both the civic resources and the social decision-making perspective predict that low voter turnout will result from low levels of investment in the campaign activity. However, the two models offer different rationales for this prediction, leading them to make different predictions about who is likely to turn out in low-salience races (summarized in Table 8.1).

The civic-resources perspective predicts low turnout in low-salience races because voting is more costly in such elections. This is in part due to the relative scarcity of information; with minimal media coverage in low-profile races, it is more difficult for citizens to gather information about the candidates, making voting more costly (Aldrich 1993; Rosenstone and Hansen 1993; Nicholson and Miller 1997). Moreover, candidates have fewer resources to use for mobilization efforts that subsidize the costs of turnout. The buses to the polling stations, absentee-ballot efforts, and other turnout-encouraging activities present in a high-profile general race may not be affordable for campaigns in low-profile races. As a result, the civic-resources model predicts that only those most able to bear the costs of turnout in low-profile races are likely to vote. In other words, if low-salience elections are low-turnout affairs because they impose additional costs on the potential voter, individuals with the civic resources obtained via a college education or involvement with church or another organization would be the most likely to vote according to the civic-resources model.

The social theory also predicts low turnout in low-salience races, but the differing logic behind the prediction leads to two sets of divergent testable implications. Low-salience races do not generate much of the high-profile media coverage that would result in increased casual discussion of the upcoming election. This lack of discussion limits turnout, because it is this sort of discussion that encourages voting among conditional cooperators. In terms of the conditional cooperation decision

TABLE 8.1. *Predictions of the Social and Resource Theories of Voter Turnout in Low-Salience Elections*

Candidate Mobilizes...	Network Size	Social Theory Turnout Rate	Social Theory Who Votes?	Resources Theory Who Votes?
No one	0	< 10%	Random	High SES
Regular voters	0	10–12%	Random	High SES
Organized groups	Small	15–30%	Some High SES	Med-High SES
Personal friends	Med/Large	15–50%	Some High SES	Med-High SES

model, the effective reference group for decision makers should be set at zero when citizens do not discuss the campaign. In such circumstances, only unconditional cooperators would vote.

First, unlike the resources theory, the social theory makes an approximate point prediction in very-low-salience races: No more than 10% to 12% turnout (i.e., the proportion of unconditional cooperators), probably less in most cases because many citizens, even those who would be likely to vote unconditionally, may not know about the upcoming election. Turnout should increase up to the 10% to 12% barrier if there is enough activity such that regular voters are aware of the election (often through heavy use of direct mail) (Huckfeldt and Sprague 1992), but not enough activity to generate widespread visibility and common knowledge (Chwe 2001) of the election.[1]

Second, the theories make divergent predictions about which potential voters are more likely to turn out in low-salience elections. The civic-resources model predicts that people with more resources, such as the college educated, can better bear the increased costs of turnout. The social decision-making model, on the other hand, predicts that first movers will be more likely to vote than conditional voters, who are normally stimulated to vote by discussion about the campaign in higher-stakes races. How does this bear on correlations with education, income, or other civic resources? Earlier in the book, I argued that individual propensities for unconditional cooperation – for example, personal tastes or a strong sense of civic duty – are distributed randomly throughout the population,

---

[1] Actually, even under these circumstances, turnout may be low in some precincts if candidates, like researchers, make mistakes and conflate the demographic predictors of regular voting in national elections with being a likely unconditional cooperator. Some first movers, particularly those low in socioeconomic status, may be willing to vote but never find out through direct contact or otherwise that an election is coming up.

without any relationship to education or income. Therefore, the social theory predicts that when turnout in low-salience elections is made up exclusively of unconditional voters, turnout in these races should be unrelated to these indicators of civic resources. Note that this is a radical departure from the established consensus in the literature, which holds that education in some way causes higher turnout rates, and should be particularly likely to do so in low-salience elections.

This story holds in full only when candidates have virtually no resources with which to mobilize citizens. In slightly higher-profile races, in which candidates have some ability to mobilize, the story changes somewhat. The two theories' divergent expectations for the impact of mobilization in low-salience races are also summarized in Table 8.1. In brief, the social theory of turnout predicts that mobilization will strengthen the correlations between turnout and its typical demographic correlates, whereas the resources model should predict that these relationships are strongest in the lowest-salience races, those lacking any mobilization efforts. Why? In the resource-based view, mobilization subsidizes the costs of turnout, thus bringing in voters with fewer resources for whom voting would otherwise be too costly. The lowest-salience races should see voting among only the most resource-rich, with mobilizing activity gradually broadening the electorate to include those with fewer resources – less income, less educational attainment, and so on.

In contrast, for the social theory of voter turnout, mobilization stimulates discussion and increases public visibility of a campaign, directly for those personally contacted or present at campaign activities and indirectly for others in these people's social networks. Thus, assuming social decision-making voters, we expect to see higher turnout as a product of localized signals of interest in a campaign among certain social groups or within certain social networks, even in a low-salience race that is not talked about widely in the population at large. To figure out who these voters will be, we need to know something about candidates' mobilization strategies in specific low-resource campaigns, as well as something about the social networks that are more likely to help spread cooperation.

Why does mobilization strengthen the association with income and education? This occurs simply because those with higher socioeconomic status are usually more likely to be mobilized, or to be friends with those who are mobilized. As argued in Chapter 6, candidates with limited resources are likely to reach out to three types of citizens during an election: regular voters, personal social contacts, and organized groups and associations (Rosenstone and Hansen 1993). Whereas contact with regular voters is likely to be a largely private activity, the public nature of appearances and requests to personal friends and other groups and organizations is more likely to inspire additional indirect mobilization through increased political awareness and discussion within a particular social network. Moreover, candidates' social contacts and organized group members are likely to be disproportionately high in education and income. Even though this is not always true – and indeed it is cases that defy these easy expectations that allow me to test the social theory of turnout against the civic voluntarism model – it may well occur often enough to account for the observed association between socioeconomic status and voting in local elections in which campaigns make some attempts to mobilize voters.

If indirect mobilization is effective, and candidates reach out to their own friends as part of the campaign process (Rosenstone and Hansen 1993), a relationship between individual resources and turnout may be misleading. If candidates are generally wealthier than many citizens, then candidates may more easily mobilize their friends and acquaintances, who are also of a high socioeconomic status. This would create an association between socioeconomic status and turnout, but one that would potentially disappear in an analysis that controlled for candidates' social location. The civic-resources model predicts that all citizens with substantial resources would be likely to turn out, whereas the social-decision model predicts that only those educated citizens with social ties to a candidate are likely to turn out.

From this more fully specified version of the model, we can refer back to simulation results from earlier chapters to make point predictions for levels of turnout in different sorts of elections (seen in the third column of Table 8.1). As detailed earlier, in a very-low-resource campaign, candidates may well lack sufficient resources to let even the majority of regular voters know that they are running for office. No simulation is needed to predict turnout in these cases, as only first movers will vote. Thus, less than 10% to 12% of citizens will participate in such elections. Without any discussion or even common knowledge of the campaign, there is no opportunity for voting to spread to conditional decision makers, thus we do not need to simulate this process to make our point predictions. If candidates reach out to friends and other organized social groups, however, localized discussion of the election and subsequent indirect mobilization is possible even in a race that lacks the interest and media attention to generate discussion more widely throughout the electorate. The point predictions for candidate mobilization of these two groups reflect the likely size of the reference group activated by candidate activity. Personal friends of the candidates are more likely to mention the race in casual discussion, so they may discuss the election with the majority of their general friendships – about sixteen to twenty friends, on average. Thus, the higher range of this estimate (50%) represents the simulation results (from Figure 6.1) when networks are large. Less discussion is likely to take place among organized groups less directly connected to the candidate, so the expected range is smaller to reflect the smaller estimate of network size.

The predictions examined here refer to relatively low-salience elections, and also require a fair amount of data about the particulars of a given election campaign and the community in which it is conducted. Thus, I chose to focus my investigation on a geographically bounded sample of elections. The details of how I gathered the data and how I measured each of the important theoretical concepts are presented in more detail in the next section.

DATA

Now that the predictions of turnout patterns in low-salience elections have been derived from the two theories, it is necessary to find a way to measure the important concepts and test the two theories. Measures of socioeconomic status (SES), mobilization activity, voter turnout, and personal relationships to candidates are all needed. I used a combination of voter roll data, census data, and candidate interviews to look at turnout in a series of elections between 1998 and 2004 in Mecklenburg County in North Carolina – a large, metropolitan county in the southern United States that includes the city of Charlotte.

An important element of the testing of these two theories is identification of voters who share social network contacts with candidates for political office. Unfortunately, because this is not a question commonly asked of survey respondents, nor was conducting an individual survey feasible in this case, individual-level data are not available. Therefore, I put together a data set and included a proxy for social relationships with a candidate based on residential location and candidate self-reports, which necessitated that the other data for the project be gathered at the aggregate level.[2]

---

[2] Ecological inference might seem to be a problem here, but the nature of the social theory of turnout focuses on distinct populations of friendships, not just individual characteristics. Thus, looking at aggregate variation is, in a sense, perfectly suited to test the social theory.

Socioeconomic Status

First, a measure of socioeconomic status was available at the census block group level from the 2000 U.S. Census. The Census provides numerous SES measures; I include two in this chapter: percentage of population older than twenty-five with a college degree (*Education*) and percentage of households with an annual income exceeding $100,000 (*Income*). Census block groups largely overlap voting precincts, although not completely. Therefore, I will focus not on statistical analysis of turnout that incorporates the measure of education (although this is presented at the conclusion of the chapter), but rather on a graphical presentation of the data, which serves to make the point without introducing the difficulties of matching census block group information to voting precinct information.

Turnout Rate

I used voter roll data to develop a measure of voter turnout rates at the precinct level. The first task was to generate estimates of total number of voters who had voted in the previous elections at the precinct level. Current voter rolls, available from the local board of elections, provide information about the voter: name, gender, ethnicity, party affiliation, age, date of registration, and whether or not the citizen voted in the twenty most recent elections. Each voter record is matched to voting precinct, census block group, and GIS geocode of spatial location (latitude and longitude). The county provided accurate street information that allowed full identification of all voters on the list, as well as aggregate data on total turnout for each race by precinct. Luckily, precinct boundaries were frozen by the state legislature in 2000 during redistricting of state offices, and thus precincts stayed the same between the 1999 and 2000 elections, with one or two easily identifiable exceptions. Changes to precinct boundaries prior to 1998 were identifiable by the researcher but could not be verified with the county board of elections.[3]

[3] Unfortunately, there appears to be no official record of the old boundaries. However, a county employee told me that the policy was to split precincts in half when the population got too large. However, boundaries of the precincts were defined by major landmarks (streets, rivers, etc.), and thus remained stable. Analysis of the boundaries of the precincts that changed suggested that this information was accurate, and thus it was possible to determine what the former precinct number of current precincts had been. To complicate matters further, however, some political office boundaries contain split precincts. In the analysis that follows, I try to avoid this issue.

To estimate turnout percentages requires an estimate of the voting-eligible population (VEP) in each precinct; here I used standard practices based on McDonald and Popkin (2001). The census provided the state with 2000 voting-age population (VAP) estimates at the block-group level, excluding noncitizens, according to Public Law 94–171. I adjusted these estimates to reflect the percentage of the population ineligible to vote because of their prior criminal record (only those currently on probation or imprisoned are disenfranchised by state law) and to reflect growth in the area on an annual basis.[4] I estimated ineligible populations from the demographic makeup of the area, using gender and race to reflect the percentage of the population currently on probation according to data from the state prison system. These are far from ideal proxies for probation status, but no better instruments were available for this study.[5]

Based on these adjustments, turnout as a percentage of VEP in the county was calculated at the precinct level by summing the number of voters recorded on the voter rolls and dividing by VEP. Note that these numbers may be slight underestimates if voters in previous elections were purged or removed themselves from the voter rolls. On the other hand, it may be more likely that these figures are overestimates if the voter rolls

---

[4] Two options were used for predicting growth. The first was to take projected rates of growth between 2000 and 2003, which were available at the zip-code level from the Chamber of Commerce in the county. Yearly estimates were arrived at using linear extrapolation. Precincts that contained multiple zip codes were adjusted appropriately. To estimate growth in precincts that included multiple zip codes, the sum was taken of the percentage of the VEP in a precinct living in a zip code multiplied by the growth rate of that zip code. However, these estimates seemed abnormally low, probably owing to the low registration rates among fast-growing zip codes. Therefore, I also used linear extrapolation forward (and backward) based on block-level changes in the population between the 1990 and 2000 Census. These estimates, while very accurate prior to 2001, were unfortunately far too high given the extremely high rate of growth in the county in the previous decade. Ultimately, I took an average of the two estimates, which yielded estimates of the population that were both reasonable based on the latest Census estimates of population in the county, and which seemed to accord with the timing of special exception precinct splits over the past four years, once a precinct hit about 8,000–10,000 people.

[5] Ineligible populations (noncitizens and felons) would have nonlinear impacts on turnout in higher-salience elections, but would not have this effect in a low-salience election unless their presence changed strategic candidate mobilization. It is worth noting that in the 2004 election, the national get out the vote (GOTV) groups were working consciously to re-enfranchise previous felons who were no longer on parole. The ex-felons would depress turnout among their social groups if they incorrectly perceived themselves as ineligible in a high-salience election. Whereas this is not likely to have been an issue in 2004, this misunderstanding of voting status may have depressed turnout in some populations in earlier elections.

include significant numbers of people who no longer live in the given precinct, and thus should have been purged from the rolls. In any case, this appears to be a minor issue with the voter roll data, based on a comparison of official vote totals for previous elections with the totals obtained from voter roll data. In a very few cases, only one of the two parties had a primary in a given precinct, therefore not all voters in the precinct should be counted in the VEP, because voters must be either a registered member of the party or unaffiliated to vote in the primary election of that party. VEP was adjusted in these cases to reflect the proportion of VEP in the population potentially eligible (percentage of the population registered in the party plus half of the unaffiliated, which is the denominator used by the board of elections). Finally, information about education and income levels in the precincts were calculated using Census 2000 data. This information is available at the block-group level, and block groups and precincts largely overlap. Proportional estimates of income and education were used when a single precinct covered portions of two or more block groups.[6]

Mobilization

Given the importance of mobilization, indicators of candidate activity are also needed. Therefore, I chose several candidates to approach for personal interviews. Candidates were chosen to maximize diversity of political party affiliation, gender, race, and municipal or state office. In these interviews, I asked questions about the candidate's campaign efforts in both primary and general elections, their personal route to political activity, and the nature of their personal and political social networks. On the basis of their recommendations, I also spoke with a few campaign managers and political activists about the campaign process. These interviews provide additional detail about candidate efforts, their own perceptions of the campaign process, and the extent to which they intentionally or unintentionally call on their friendship networks when campaigning. I intentionally reserved questions about friendships until the end of the interview, to see if candidates mentioned social networks without prompting. Combining previous research with information from these interviews, I constructed several measures of campaign activity and exposure to direct and indirect candidate mobilization.

---

[6] Proportions were obtained by disaggregating the population to the block level, then re-aggregating to reflect the actual number of people from each block group in the precinct.

It was extremely difficult to obtain direct measures of candidate activity. When I spoke with candidates, few remembered exactly what they had done in the way of campaigning in the election a mere three months prior to our discussion. Nonetheless, based on these conversations, as well as simple logic about the costs of various activities and availability of funding, it is possible to use the office at stake and competitiveness of the race as proxies for likely types of campaign activity. I also used results from candidate interviews to identify precincts that were likely to be mobilized, including the neighborhoods where candidates lived and additional neighborhoods that were often mentioned as politically or socially important to several candidates.

One familiar indicator of general campaign activity is the closeness of the election results. Also available from the county board of elections was additional information about the contours of each election: how many candidates entered, how much money was raised and spent, and how many votes each candidate received. I used this data to create variables indicating the seriousness of the campaign and the amount of related campaign activity. A contested election is a binary indicator of whether or not there are at least two candidates running for office. Election closeness is coded as a continuous variable indicating the margin between the highest vote getter and the closest competitor (Patterson and Caldeira 1983; Cox and Munger 1989). Any given precinct may be involved in multiple elections during the same cycle, and I control for this as best as possible with a simple dummy variable.

Because the social theory argues that proximity to candidates is a spur to voting, I gathered information about the candidates in the elections as well. Candidate home addresses are reported to the board of elections. I matched these candidate home addresses to voting precinct, census block group, and spatial coordinates using a similar procedure to the voter roll records. Candidates whose addresses were outside of the county were not considered. Most candidates for local office were from inside the county, with the relatively minor exception of the state and federal legislative districts that included only small portions of the county. Further inspection of candidates for these districts revealed that none had close political, social, or business ties to the county in consideration, and thus they could be safely discarded from consideration as an influence in low-salience elections.

Of course, candidates may have social ties to areas outside of their precincts, and may also reach out to organized groups outside of their precincts as part of their efforts to mobilize. In this Southern, urban

county (like many others with significant levels of residential segregation), it seems likely that the location of social connections might vary
systematically by race. In particular, black churches have been found to
be a potent force in encouraging African-American electoral participation
(Tate 1991; Calhoun-Brown 1996). If candidates draw on social ties and
organized groups outside of their own residential neighborhoods, using
candidates' own neighborhoods to represent the location of their social
ties would lead to underestimation of the impact of candidates' social
ties on turnout. Although precise measures of social ties were not available, candidate interviews were used to develop proxies for additional
sources of social ties outside of the residential context. These proxies are
described in more detail in the subsequent section.

Not surprisingly, I found that mobilization efforts are limited by
the funds available as well as campaign opportunities, both of which
are largely tied to the office(s) on the ballot in a given election. Many
elections, such as primaries, municipal races without accompanying
national races, and runoffs or special elections are very low-stimulus
affairs. There is variation even within these low-stimulus elections,
however. In some elections, candidates put little to no effort into the
campaign, at least in some neighborhoods. This often occurs during
a runoff election or other unscheduled special election for a relatively
low-profile office. It might also characterize races in which one candidate was not particularly serious and was not considered a legitimate
threat to the incumbent.

In more serious races – smaller races for city council, school board
or county commission that were expected to be close, or at-large city or
county races (all of which were quite close) – candidates went beyond
contacting regular voters via direct mail and the use of yard signs and
spent significant time trying to reach out via personal appearances to
organized groups or through canvassing. Candidates are also likely
to focus their personal appearances, either intentionally or accidently,
on one group that is easy to reach and very responsive: their personal
social networks (Rosenstone and Hansen 1993). Weak-tie social networks are easy for candidates to reach and likely to result in a large number of votes. Moreover, weak-tie networks are likely to play an important
role in the fund-raising efforts of many candidates and are likely to be
activated intentionally, even if not for the purposes of gaining votes.
Turnout among the population of people with direct or indirect social
ties to a candidate may be quite high, as high as in a very-high-profile
national race. This is because the effective reference group for friends of

the candidate is not of size zero, as it is for many citizens, but may include much of their extended friendship group.

CANDIDATES, CAMPAIGNING, AND SOCIAL TIES

Candidate interviews provided strong support for the claim that candidates campaign through weak social ties, particularly in low-salience elections. Moreover, interviews suggested that institutionalization of social ties varied between the black and white communities in the county, and also between the areas closer to the center of the city and further away. Thus, variations in the institutionalization of weak social ties play a major role in determining candidate campaign strategy, and turnout among the groups reached by the campaign. I will first summarize the major points gleaned from these interviews, and then explain in more detail how I translated interview data into an operationalization of which citizens were subject to what types of mobilization activity.

Candidate activity varies with importance of the race and funds available. Candidates clearly indicated a hierarchy of campaign activity pursued during an election cycle. They reported that their choice of mobilization activities depended on the closeness of the race and the money available to them (two very highly correlated factors, as they claimed it was easier to raise money when a race was expected to be close). At the lowest funding levels, candidates often sent the "obligatory" direct mail letters to regular voters in their own party. One candidate expressed some doubt in this activity, but all agreed it was standard procedure in a low-cost campaign. Appearances to groups were also common in low-cost campaigns, as was the use of yard signs. Slightly higher funding levels enabled the selective purchase of billboard space, and in countywide races with significant funding, other media purchases were also possible. Candidates indicated that in countywide races, it is also possible to use free media opportunities to their advantage, as the newspaper and radio outlets were all open to covering campaign events in these higher-profile races.

Candidates reach out to weak-tie friendships to raise funds. The candidates were all asked to describe campaigning and what sorts of activities were involved in campaigning. All mentioned fund-raising as one of the most important campaign activities. When asked to describe fund-raising, most mentioned personal phone calls and letters to acquaintances or indirect acquaintances. Moreover, the social world that connects the donors and candidates seems very small indeed. One candidate noted that some donors wait to be called, and fully expect to have candidates contact them and request donations, as they might have weak links to multiple candidates. Another mentioned that colleagues from his former workplace, as well as colleagues met in the course of doing business, provided significant financial support for his campaign.

Candidates use weak- and strong-tie friendships for campaign support. All candidates also mentioned the importance of social connections to their campaign work. Much of this support appeared without effort by the candidate: Many reported that friends and neighbors who just "wanted to help" contacted them spontaneously Sometimes these connections were weak ties mediated by organizational affiliations, some political (e.g., League of Women Voters) and some social (e.g., Country Club). Strong ties also proved important for direct campaign support; one candidate noted that his mother had gone door to door and that he won more than 90% of the vote in her precinct! Given that candidates must spend much of their campaign time on personal appearances and fund-raising, social connections are likely to be very important in generating spontaneous grassroots support. Candidates were especially likely to call on both strong and weak ties when recruiting volunteers to put yard signs out in their yards and neighborhoods.

Candidates reach regular voters, but on an individual basis. As previously mentioned, the candidates all claimed that direct mail to the most regular of voters was what you "have to do" to increase name recognition. Funds available limited how far down candidates could go on the rolls when sending out notices of the upcoming election.

Candidates go where the people are. All candidates try to make the most of their limited time during campaign season. For all the candidates, they noted that this meant that the top priority on their time was raising money. The next priority, however, was to go where there were large concentrations of people, particularly people to whom they had at least weak social connections as discussed earlier. The candidates mentioned neighborhood festivals, organizational meetings, church dinners, and other places where many people were gathered in one place.

Candidates go where the votes are. Few candidates evidenced a particularly nuanced understanding of voter turnout in the way that it is considered in the research literature, certainly not to the point where they could consciously focus on neighborhoods with very high levels of social capital, for example (Cox, Rosenbluth, and Thies 1998). Nonetheless, the candidates quite likely did reach out to the neighborhoods with the highest social capital, simply by focusing on the neighborhoods with consistently high turnout in previous elections. The candidates clearly knew which precincts had high turnout in previous elections and which ones did not. Some of this variation was surely the result of a self-fulfilling prophecy, where mobilization effort follows prior records of high turnout. But some of it was likely due to the existence of institutions such as churches, country clubs, local shops, restaurants, and barbershops that stimulated the formation and maintenance of social ties that encourage voter turnout.

Previous candidates are often weakly tied to current candidates, and help each other out. Not surprisingly, most candidates also mentioned their ties to other candidates, and the role that those previous or current candidates played in the campaign. One candidate was encouraged to enter the race by a current elected official, and was assisted in the race by multiple candidates and party leaders whom he knew through work. Another candidate had initially been reluctant to run for public office, and was encouraged by current officials and party leaders. All of the successful candidates had run for political office after receiving the encouragement or request of existing political leaders. Thus, social connections to existing political leaders, only some of which were a direct result of the initial involvement in nonelected political life, played an important role in the campaign. All candidates mentioned that the support of other officials and known political leaders was important in the campaign process, both in helping secure funds and in getting in front of the right groups and getting the best media coverage.

Institutionalized ties are drawn on more often than friendships or other informal ties. Interestingly, none of the candidates referred to their neighbors as important social connections, or as important in their campaigns. This was not surprising for African-American candidates from majority-white residential areas, as the data clearly showed that they were drawing political support from other neighborhoods with a higher concentration of African-American voters. However, I had expected white candidates to rely on their politically active and affluent neighbors. However, although many of those mentioned were neighbors (as revealed by follow-up questions), the majority of the friendships mentioned by candidates of both races were initially described as institutional in character: occupation, social club, church, political organizations, and family.

There was a slight variation in institutional emphasis based on the race of the candidate. Black candidates more often mentioned institutionalized political organizations, whereas the white candidates more often mentioned institutionalized social and economic organizations.

Meanwhile, for the white candidates, there was a strong overlap between their church, social clubs, occupation, and political contacts (typically unorganized, but drawn from these other institutions). Overwhelmingly, their contacts were drawn from the southeastern quadrant of the city, even if not in the immediate few blocks surrounding the candidate's home. The black candidates all mentioned reaching out to institutions outside of their neighborhoods: churches, political groups, formal service organizations such as the Rotary Club, and also informal social organizations like restaurants and other small businesses. This variation stems not from any inherently racial characteristics, but from the different social and political environments that create and maintain political power in a county marked by high levels of residential and economic segregation by race.

Based on my interview data, therefore, I realized that it was important to develop indicators of the location not simply of the where the candidate lived, but of both the institutionalized and informal ties that candidate was likely to draw on in the course of the campaign. For white candidates, geographic location was a reasonable proxy to the very local institutions often drawn on in campaigns: church and social club, as well as networks of previous political candidates. For black candidates, however, geographic proxies were very misleading. Therefore, it is necessary to take a closer look at the geographic indicators of social ties for black candidates in particular. In the next section, I will develop and discuss the indicators used to determine the degree and focus of candidate mobilization activity in the rest of this chapter.

Institutions and Social Ties: Measuring Campaign Activity

First, it helps get a sense of the racial distribution of the population in the county, given that interviews revealed that institutional ties varied with the race of the candidate. In what follows, I discuss how I identified the major institutions of each racial group[7] and how I translated this into indicators of mobilization activity.

The African-American community in this county has been strong and vibrant since the end of slavery, and the area has been consistently named as one of the top places for black families to live in America. In recent histories of African-American life in the area (Randolph 1992; Frye 1997),

---

[7] The Latino population in this county has been growing in recent years, but it is a quite new presence in the area and is not yet a significant political force.

a few relevant features stand out. First, numerous formal and informal institutions have a long history in the area. A college was founded in the area in the late nineteenth century, and it is still an important historically black university today. Numerous independent presses owned by local African Americans were founded in the late nineteenth century, one of which still publishes a weekly paper with a significant readership today. Primary education for African Americans was widespread from an early point. A private African-American social club founded in 1944 provided a physical location for socializing in a style similar to country clubs for white Southerners, and was the largest of its kind in the southeastern United States. Numerous restaurants, barbershops (Harris-Lacewell 2004), and other long-standing small businesses serve as local landmarks – physical locations that serve as informal sources of information and socializing for the community, and which were identified by name during candidate interviews. Churches have a long-standing and important presence in the community; a running joke among locals is that the first thing to ask a newcomer to the area (white or black) is "How ya'll doin' and have ya'll found a church yet?" All of these institutions are identified in Figure 8.1.

As shown on the map in Figure 8.1, black churches in particular are clustered along two major areas. There is little doubt that the church leaders play an active role in encouraging church members to vote in many cases. Early voting locations in the 2004 general election were open on Sunday, and church members went directly from services to the early voting location. Church leaders encouraged attendees to make it to the polls, and were a great aid to candidates according to the candidates themselves. However, it is important not to overstate the direct role of the churches and church leaders, because it is far from clear that churches play this same active role in the primaries. In many Democratic primaries, the black voters from these neighborhoods are choosing between two or more black candidates with similar backgrounds. I was told of cases where church leaders helped mobilize voters for general elections but not primary elections.

In the primaries, the key issue seemed instead to be the multiple social ties that candidates held to these neighborhoods, through various neighborhood institutions. All of the black candidates attended church in the northern neighborhoods, although none of them lived there. All of the candidates mentioned other ties to the neighborhood, some organizational, but many informal ties as well through restaurants, small business, and other institutions. "I eat [there] whenever I can," said one

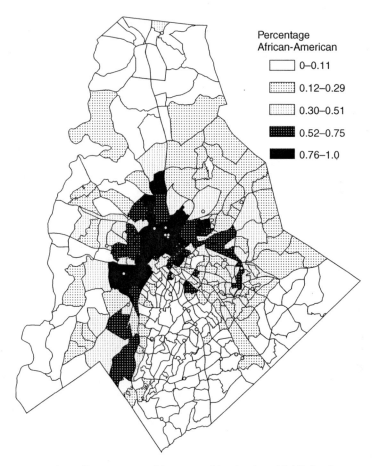

FIGURE 8.1. County map with race and institutions highlighted.

candidate, "and just ask people who look approachable to vote for me." The churches seemed to play a role in the general fabric of the society, but were mentioned in relation to personal campaign efforts about as often as it was mentioned by the white candidates, who also were frequent church attendees with plentiful social ties to their congregation.

It is worth noting that the institutional heart of both the black and white communities has changed little over the past century. Amazingly, most of the institutions forming the backbone of the African-American community actually predate urban renewal programs of the 1960s, somehow surviving the "root shock" (Fullilove 2004) of the experience. As part of "urban renewal," bulldozers came to wipe out most of the inner-city neighborhoods where poor and rich blacks lived, shopped, worshipped, and socialized, yet many of the institutions simply moved further north, relocating within precisely the area noteworthy for its high rates of voter turnout given the average income and education of the predominantly black citizens living there. Figure 8.1 shows a representative sample of institutional locations of both the black and white communities. Major African-American institutions (churches, college, and businesses) appear in the majority African American neighborhoods, whereas predominantly and historically white-dominated institutions appears in majority white neighborhoods.

Among whites, there is some evidence that younger institutions are starting to produce political leaders as well. Several people I spoke with observed that there has been political tension over the past few years between the oldest wealthy, and more liberal, neighborhoods closer to the city and the more conservative residents of the newer wealthy neighborhoods further south from the center of the city. The churches, country clubs, and other institutions associated with these two residential enclaves are largely nonoverlapping in terms of membership. These newer neighborhoods, however, have institutions whose members are now in their second or third generation of local residence. Candidates from the newer wealthy neighborhoods were therefore able to report drawing on people they had known during their childhoods to help with campaigning; primarily people affiliated with these now-mature institutions.

Length of residence could clearly confound the analysis. People who have lived at their current location for longer periods of time are more likely to vote (Squire, Wolfinger, and Glass 1987; Rosenstone and Hansen 1993) and presumably also have stronger ties to the local community. While some of the candidates with whom I spoke were not lifelong or even long-time residents of the community, all were affiliated with historically significant institutions whose members were traditionally long-time county residents. These institutions could absorb these new members and give them access to the important social ties without relying on the current candidates personal friendships. However, residents of the fast-growing new neighborhoods at the outskirts of the city did not have such a benefit. These neighborhoods may have the economic resources to build new country clubs, but these country clubs are not yet the types of institutions that produce political clout. Despite good reason to think that length of residence is yet another indicator of social location, I conducted all of the analyses in the latter half of the chapter with data only from citizens registered locally for at least six years, obtaining very similar results. This suggests that social ties matter for turnout, even when controlling for length of residence and biasing the results against the social theory's predictions.[8]

In summary, I use two different indicators of candidates' social ties. For white candidates, residential location is a very good proxy for the social institutions that are the source of their weak ties. Because this is not the case for black candidates, I use instead the two areas highlighted on the map, as well as any other precincts specifically mentioned by a particular candidate, as the area where direct and indirect mobilization through weak social ties takes place. Finally, using a combination of the closeness of the race and the geographic reach and importance of the race, it is possible to make a reasonably good guess about the funding available to the candidate, and thus of the campaign activities employed.

MOBILIZATION AND TURNOUT AT THE PRECINCT LEVEL

Now that we have better-informed indicators of mobilization activity and candidates' social ties, it is time to turn to an analysis of the turnout data. To control for the uneven distribution of party identification throughout the county, I focus on elections in which races were contested in both parties. I then compare turnout in precincts with and without mobilization activity and links to candidates, showing that turnout is higher in areas with mobilization. In fact, turnout variation is very close to point predictions based on simulations. Finally, I use a combination of geographical and quantitative analysis to show that social groups with links to candidates and candidate-initiated mobilization, rather than voters' demographic characteristics, are the primary determinants of systematic variation in turnout propensity in low-salience elections.

Although data from many elections was available, I will concentrate this analysis on the 2004 primary, an election that did not introduce any confounds with respect to partisan identification or national politics. In the 2004 primary election, there was no presidential primary, but two major offices on all county ballots (the governorship and the county commission at-large nominations) were contested in both parties. Therefore, variation in precinct turnout is unlikely to stem from partisan composition of the precinct. Similar analysis of other elections yielded similar results.[9]

---

[8] Date of registration was available from the local Board of Elections.
[9] More information on other elections, including maps of turnout, is available from the author.

TABLE 8.2. *Precinct-Level Turnout in the 2004 Primary*

Mobilization Level	Standard	Additional Close Election
None	8%	14%
Candidate	9%	18%
Local candidate in close election *or* active efforts	12%	19%
Local candidate *and* active efforts	25%	40%
Average	8%	16%

Source: Mecklenburg County voter roll data, geocoded using ArcGIS.

To remind the reader of the earlier predictions summarized in Table 8.1, we expect that in precincts where there is an election, but little or no campaign activity, voters should turn out at very low levels (less than 10% of the population). Table 8.2 gives a quick summary of turnout in the election, broken down further by the residence of the candidate and the level of effort put into mobilization activity in each precinct. Mobilization activity effort is an indicator capturing both institutionalized social ties to the candidate and self-reports of the candidates as to which precincts were the particular focus of campaigns.

In addition to the statewide and countywide races on all ballots, there were additional local races on the ballots of some precincts. In only one area (a county district), however, was there an additional high-profile race.[10] There is a clear split between those precincts where there was an additional high-profile race and those precincts where the additional races on the ballot were never seriously contested.[11] Nonetheless, some of this relationship may be attributable not to the efforts of the district candidates, but to another candidate mobilization factor: A candidate involved in an extremely close and high-profile race for the governorship also lived in this district. The overall pattern of turnout in this particular district versus the remainder of the county deserves further discussion, and will be postponed temporarily, to consider the difference within the two categories related to the presence of candidate mobilization efforts.

---

[10] The race was for a county district seat – usually not a particularly high-profile race. However, this particular race was very high-spending, as reported to me by a source near to one of the campaigns.

[11] Defined as precincts where the winning margin for the candidate exceeded 20 percentage points. The typical margin in such precincts was closer to 50% to 70% of the vote.

Looking first at the standard races where there is no candidate activity, the average turnout across precincts in this category is about 8% of the VEP. These elections all feature important elections on the ballot, but the precincts in this category did not receive any special efforts from the candidate. In these situations, mobilization theory would suggest that candidates might be able to reach first movers through a combination of campaign efforts and media coverage, but little additional discussion would be generated. As predicted by the social theory, turnout is approximately 8% to 10% of the population.

At the next level of activity, we can see that candidate residence in a given precinct did not appear to spur additional participation, as long as the additional local race was neither a close one nor one in which candidates devoted unusual efforts to reaching out to their neighbors. These precincts were generally where black candidates lived, and as previously discussed, these candidates rarely used their neighborhoods as a source of campaign support. However, in the precincts where an additional high-profile race was waged, even candidates who were not personally involved in a close race may have had a small affect on turnout, although the sample was so small that the difference is not statistically significant.

Taking this into account, a clear increase can be seen between precincts where little or no effort was directed and precincts where a candidate drew on institutionalized weak ties to campaign. Again, these are precincts where candidates either reported to me that mobilization activity took place (black candidates), or such activity was inferred through residential location (white candidates). Average turnout was about 12% of the population in standard precincts with additional effort and about 19% in precincts with additional effort and/or candidate presence in precincts with an additional close race. A combination of word of mouth, letters to regular voters, yard signs, and public appearances by the candidates lifted turnout about 5% points in a precinct, on average.

Finally, worthy of special mention are the two precincts with a candidate in residence and with active mobilization efforts. These precincts both had the highest turnout in their respective categories, 6% to 12% higher than any other precinct. One precinct was the home of the candidate for governor, a well-known candidate in a very tightly contested race (margin of less than 1% of the votes statewide.) The three precincts geographically and socially contiguous to this one all had exceptionally high turnout rates as well, but none matched the turnout in the home precinct of the gubernatorial candidate. Turnout in the precinct with active mobilization but without an additional race was also exceptionally high, although considerably less than the home precinct of the gubernatorial candidate. The candidate living in this precinct was not involved in a particularly close race, but the community was mentioned by several black candidates as an important source of social ties, as discussed earlier.

So far, we have seen that the point predictions of social turnout theory are again quite accurate. However, we have not yet directly compared the social turnout theory to the civic resources theory. The two models predict very different relative participation rates among different demographic groups, although only the social theory predicts actual levels of turnout. If resources such as income and education matter in and of themselves, the results we have seen so far could be misleading. It could be that candidates are drawn from demographic groups that are already predisposed to turn out at higher levels because of their socioeconomic status; candidates may live in precincts with higher incomes and educations than other precincts, and the correlation between living near a candidate and higher turnout may be spurious. As Table 8.2 shows, candidate's presence does not always increase turnout. Although I provide a more standard statistical treatment later, the most straightforward way to approach this problem initially is with a visual representation of the data.

Demographically, the county exhibits a relatively high level of segregation along racial, educational, and income-based lines. Figure 8.2 gives a broad overview the county's demographics, from 2000 Census data. The map in Figure 8.2(a) shows the percentage of the population that has a college degree. The map in Figure 8.2(b) shows the percentage with a household income of more than $100,000. For easy reference, candidates' home locations appear on the maps as well.

As is apparent from the maps, the vast majority of the candidates come from a single pie-piece-shaped region in the southeastern part of the county. Candidates in high-profile statewide or countywide races (denoted by dots) in particular are almost all drawn from this sector. Moreover, as can be seen from Figure 8.3, this area also held the additional tight race for county commissioner. Thus, three factors that would boost turnout – the presence of candidates in a high-profile race, a population with exceptionally high levels of civic resources, and an additional race that was invested in heavily by the candidate – seem hopelessly entangled. The combination of these factors did indeed push turnout to very high levels (at least for a primary) in these neighborhoods.

However, by looking outside of this pie-shaped area, it is possible to disentangle the relationships among candidate location, mobilization efforts, and civic resources. The civic resources model would be supported

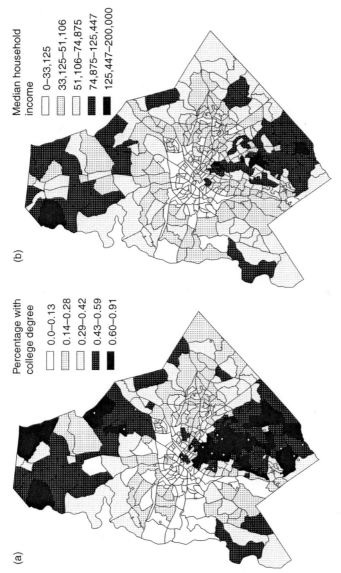

Percentage with
college degree
☐ 0.0–0.13
☐ 0.14–0.28
☐ 0.29–0.42
■ 0.43–0.59
■ 0.60–0.91

Median household
income
☐ 0–33,125
☐ 33,125–51,106
☐ 51,106–74,875
■ 74,875–125,447
■ 125,447–200,000

(a)

(b)

FIGURE 8.2. County map with education and income.

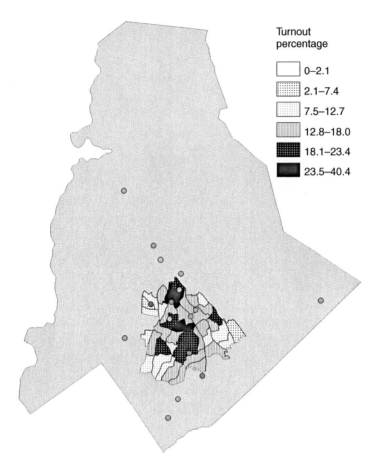

FIGURE 8.3. Map of district with additional high-profile campaign.

if turnout was particularly high in the other areas of the city with high
levels of education and income. These other areas are highlighted in
Figure 8.2(b) and consist of the northern part of the county, the north-
east edge, and the southwestern tip. Based purely on indicators of political resources (education and income), there is no reason to suspect that
turnout would vary across these areas, or that turnout would be very
different than in the southeastern pie piece. Recall that voters throughout the county had the opportunity to vote in at least two high-profile
and relatively close races regardless of whether they chose to vote in the
Republican or Democratic primary.

However, the map of turnout at the precinct level in the 2004 presidential primary in Figure 8.4, suggests that this is not the case. In fact,

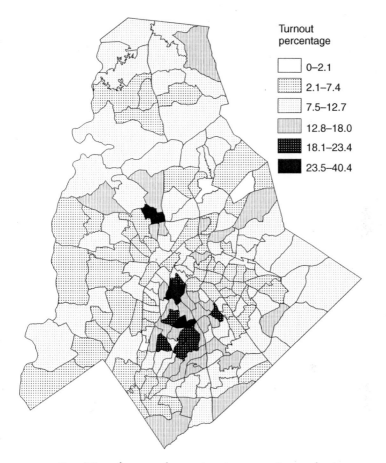

Turnout
percentage

- [ ] 0–2.1
- [ ] 2.1–7.4
- [ ] 7.5–12.7
- [ ] 12.8–18.0
- [ ] 18.1–23.4
- [ ] 23.5–40.4

FIGURE 8.4. Map of turnout by precinct in 2004 primary election.

across the entire range of primary elections, this same pattern repeats itself. Turnout is very high in the southeastern pie piece and in the predominantly African-American communities in the north and northwest indicated in Figure 8.1, but is rarely high in any other areas of the county, regardless of income or education.

An eyeball comparison of average education in Figure 8.2(a) and average turnout rate in Figure 8.4 seems to support strongly the claims of the social theory: outside of the highly mobilized neighborhoods, turnout in a low-salience election appears to be randomly distributed across precincts. Turnout is not higher in the higher-education precincts. To confirm that this is not an optical illusion, I regressed precinct level turnout rate on variables indicating candidate mobilization activity (measured from

TABLE 8.3. *Predicting Turnout Rates at the Precinct Level*

	Estimated Effect on Turnout Rate
Percentage with college degree (0 to 1)	0.0065 (0.0077)
Extra campaign (1 = yes)	0.026* (0.0053)
Mobilization level (0 to 3)	0.057* (0.0078)
Extra campaign × Mobilization	0.026 (0.016)
(Intercept)	0.060 (0.0060)
	$R^2 = .56$ $n = 190$

* indicates significance level of $p < 0.001$.
Source: Mecklenburg County voter roll data, geocoded using ArcGIS

0 to 3), percentage of the population with a college degree on turnout, and whether there were any additional races in the precinct. Estimates in Table 8.3 confirm the accuracy of the visual inspection. Each additional level of candidate activity translated into a significant increase in turnout of about 5 percentage points, but that percentage of the precinct population with a college education had no substantive or significant effect on turnout.

Education and income, then, may be related to turnout in low-salience elections, but only because it is an indicator of social proximity to candidates (and, to a lesser extent, exerts a continuing influence through social network size). If education and income provide civic resources that increase commitment to civic participation or enhance the ability to pay the costs of turning out to vote, then one would expect turnout in all neighborhoods to increase as the proportion of community members with a college degree or extremely high income increased. However, as can be seen by looking at candidate residential location in Figure 8.3, turnout in predominantly white areas seems to cluster around the residential neighborhoods of the candidates, almost all of whom reside in the southeastern quadrant close to the center city. Very high turnout rates among African Americans, meanwhile, do not appear to be related to the residential location of candidates, but are linked closely to the institutionalized weak ties discussed by candidates in personal interviews. Thus, the social theory provides a better explanation of variation in turnout for low-salience elections on several counts. First, it explains why an association between neighborhood socioeconomic status and turnout rate is present in some cases (although not in others). Second, it explains why the association between education and turnout does not hold across the board, and accurately predicts when the correlation will weaken or disappear.

In conclusion, then, this chapter has found no evidence that education or income subsidize the cost of turning out to vote in low-salience elections. Indeed, given the value of an hour or two for many of these extremely wealthy citizens, turnout is personally quite costly (Green and Shapiro 1994). Rather, in the county studied in the chapter, education and income appear to be decent but imperfect proxies for embeddedness in a long-standing white political elite, a social network that includes most of the people who control political and economic power in the city. Given the relationship between weak-tie network size and social position, it is not surprising to find that the impact of indirect mobilization spills over into the entire geographic area where much of this elite group resides, resulting in increased turnout in these neighborhoods, but not in other wealthy, white neighborhoods peripheral to the geographic center of political power. The only neighborhoods that vote at similarly high rates in low-salience elections are those at the social and geographic center of another local political elite: the African-American community built around historically black institutions and still frequented by prominent African-American leaders and political candidates.

9

Paradox Lost

The view of turnout presented in this work continues a transition begun by Rosenstone and Hansen and the strategic mobilization view, and advanced by the field experiments of Gerber, Green, and collaborators. We have moved from viewing the turnout decision as a product of atomistic individuals concerned primarily with individual or partisan gain to, now, seeing turnout as emerging from the interaction of strategic political actors and conditionally cooperative citizens embedded in social networks.

In this picture, the turnout story starts with politicians who want to win an election, and thus devote resources to mobilizing potential voters and to raising the salience of an upcoming election.[1] Campaign activity sets off a chain reaction among civic-minded citizens whose decisions are largely conditional on the decisions of those around them. Social interaction among potential voters spread the initial mobilizing impulse, with different structures varying in their effectiveness in doing so. Furthermore, citizens in different locations within a given structure vary in their likelihood of receiving the mobilization impulse directly or indirectly. Thus, the social theory of turnout predicts that variation in social network structure – both the stronger discussion ties that make up a potential voter's reference group and the weak ties that may link the potential voter to direct and indirect mobilization by candidates – is a primary source of variation in voter turnout.

---

[1] Of course, politicians will try to selectively mobilize likely supporters rather than to increase turnout in general – they may even act to demobilize their opponent's supporters through negative advertising (Iyengar and Ansolabehere 1995) or through a venerable tradition of dirty tricks.

The social theory of turnout thus provides a rather radical reinterpretation of our empirical understandings of voter turnout, according a newly significant role to social ties and social structure and diminishing the role of individual characteristics such as years of formal education. As demonstrated in the preceding two chapters, the relationship between turnout and socioeconomic status variables such as income and education is largely spurious, masking an underlying causal relationship between social network structure and social location on the one hand and turnout rates on the other. A conditional mobilization process is more likely to increase turnout among citizens who are: (1) located in close proximity, socially or geographically, to a candidate or to mobilization activities; or (2) embedded in large but loosely-knit social network contexts well suited to spreading low-cost cooperative behaviors such as voting. Wealthier and more educated citizens are more likely to enjoy these sorts of social locations and social contexts, but when SES and social structural variables diverge, social structure and location are linked much more closely to turnout than are income and education.

The social theory has been defended throughout this work in three distinct ways. First, the conditional decision-making model at the heart of the theory accurately represents the dynamics of decision making. Second, as highlighted in the second half of the book, the social theory's predictions fit very well with observed patterns of participation. Compared to the well-known civic-resources model, the social theory of voter turnout does as good or better of a job of accounting for empirical variation in turnout. Finally, the social theory of voter turnout accounts for empirical anomalies or paradoxes that other theories have been unable to explain without resorting to ad hoc modifications.

CONDITIONAL CHOICE AND THE CONDITIONAL DECISION-MAKING MODEL

First, the conditional-choice approach provides a generalizable mathematical model of conditional decision making, useful for voting as well as other social dilemmas. The framework sidesteps the seemingly endless debates inspired by rational choice and instead provides an account of individual decision making compatible with a large body of evidence on how real people make decisions. As discussed earlier, conditional choice is compatible with numerous findings in behavioral economic studies of decision making. Decision-making strategies such as satisficing, rules of thumb, and heuristic aids to decision making have been well documented in economics and psychology (see, e.g., Simon 1955, Kahneman 2002).

Further, although I have not explored this aspect in depth here, conditional choice is grounded in a microfoundational account of the mental processes of social cognition. Limits in cognitive capacity force people to rely most of the time on automatically activated scripts and schemas to navigate everyday social situations (see, e.g., Fiske and Taylor 1991). Individual variation in these scripts and schemas, acquired through interaction in a social context, is a potential source of individual heterogeneity in the use of conditional decision rules. The other likely sources of individual variation are consciously chosen social identities or impression management motives or goals (Goffman 1959). People might desire to present themselves in a variety of ways to others (e.g., unprejudiced, appropriately feminine, or conscientious) and may vary in the degree to which these motives are directed toward internal (i.e., self-impression) or external audiences.

At this point, however, I do not claim to provide a motivational story of voting turnout – and thus this account may fall short of what some people want from an explanation of voting. However, I do claim that the conditional decision-making model is at least as applicable (if not more so) to empirical social research than a context-free cost-benefit model. The model succeeds not only by being true to our current understanding of the individual psychological process, but also by better reflecting the underlying dynamics of social interaction. If rational choice can be viewed not as a description of the mental process of decision making, but instead as a model of actors who behave "as if" motivated by rational considerations (Friedman 1953), then my social decision-making model can be viewed in a similar "as if" fashion. On these terms, it outperforms prior rational-choice models in these terms by more accurately predicting patterns of political participation.

The representational accuracy of the conditional decision model is augmented by its generalizability to other situations. Whereas I have chosen parameters that reflect the situation in which potential voters find themselves, other situations might be modeled with conditional choice, but using different weights on the basic decision rules. For example, relative to voting, some decisions situations might put a damper on unconditional cooperation (for example, the costly decision to protest a repressive regime), or change the mix between mean- and median-matching behavior (perhaps by making behavior more or less visible to others), or even make unconditional noncooperation a relevant strategy (for example, for potential voters in post-war Iraq, who may have felt a duty to vote or a contrary duty to abstain in order to weaken the legitimacy of a disliked government). Whereas I focus solely on turnout in this book, using conditional choice to model different situations might offer a fertile area for future research.

The mathematical model of conditional decision making builds on earlier work on thresholds and collective dynamics as in the classic works of Schelling and Granovetter, but the basic mathematical approach is integrated into a larger framework for understanding the role of social interaction in decision making. Conditional decision makers do not merely mimic or conform to others; rather, they are more fully fleshed-out social actors who respond to both the meaning of the social situation and to their observations or expectations of what others around them will do. A simplification of social meaning down to two crucial components – who is involved and the relationship between them – provides a way to think systematically about how conditional decision rules are distributed in social situations, opening up the possibility for relatively unique empirical applications of the conditional decision-making model dynamics.

Crucially, assuming that people respond to the social meaning of the situation allows the use of empirical data to set the parameters of the simulation model (Law and Kelton 1982; Schreiber 2002). Unlike many engineers, however, I draw on data seemingly unrelated to voter turnout to set the parameters of the model. Instead, subject behavior in experimental public goods and bargaining games is used to estimate the distribution of decision rules in low-cost social dilemmas similar to voting turnout. One noteworthy aspect of this design is that the use of experiments at this key juncture in theoretical development (i.e., at the link between perceptions of the decision situation and observable behavior) may increase confidence in any "causal" predictions of the model, although such predictions still must be assessed against observational (or nonexperimental) data. When paired with experimental evidence, the conditional decision model makes quite specific predictions as to the scale and variability in voter turnout during later stages of theory testing.

The use of empirical data to calibrate a model of social dynamics is a heavily criticized and debated practice in the agent-based modeling community, and seemingly defies the advice to simplify all models (Axelrod 1984, 1997). However, basic threshold dynamics are now well understood (Rolfe 2009; Watts 2009), and thus there is no concern that the model used in this book is overly complex. The larger threat is that, as with all mathematical models, you get out what you put in. Mathematical models, like statistics, can be used to support almost any viewpoint; selecting the right model from among many can be a bigger challenge than analyzing the dynamics of a particular model. The engineering approach to simulations, adapted by this book, is designed to avoid such problems and could provide a useful template for incorporating empirical data into all stages of building and testing formal models.

EMPIRICAL SUPPORT FOR A NEW VIEW OF EDUCATION AND INCOME

The social theory of voter turnout can also be justified by its empirical performance. The second half of the book directly tests the empirical implications of the social theory of turnout against those of the civic-resources model in two different electoral situations. I focus in particular on individual education as a key dividing line between the two theories. The way that the two theories treat education encapsulates the key difference between them, although this key difference also colors the way that other demographic variables are interpreted within the social theory. Education is taken by the civic-resources model as a training ground for the sorts of civic skills and interests that are necessary to encourage voter turnout. Education makes it easier for people to register to vote and gather information about political candidates, and also increases engagement in, and thus the intrinsic benefit gained from involvement in, politics. In the social theory of turnout, education is an imperfect proxy for important differences in systematic patterns of strong and weak social network ties in the population, and does not represent either inherent or socialized differences between more and less educated citizens.

The dynamic impact of social structure on turnout propensity varies depending on the salience of the election (which in turn depends largely on the level of resources available for mobilizing campaign activities). In low-salience elections, social location emerges as the most important predictor of turnout. When candidates have relatively limited resources and are unable to generate widespread knowledge of and interest in their campaign, they rely heavily on weak ties and institutional affiliations to reach out to potential voters. This prediction was tested directly against the predictions of a civic-resources understanding of socioeconomic status in Chapter 8. There is a strong correlation between socioeconomic status and proximity to candidates, but at times they do diverge. I find that when SES and proximity to candidates do diverge, only proximity to candidates continues to predict higher turnout rates. In local elections, low-SES precincts can turn out at high rates if they are proximate to candidates and campaigns, whereas high-SES precincts show high turnout only if they too are located close to candidates and their mobilizing activities.

In elections with higher stakes than local elections, and thus with more intensive campaigning, the excitement and activity surrounding the election is likely to spread widely. This decreases the importance of proximity to candidates for generating knowledge of and interest in an upcoming election. In higher-stakes races, the social theory of turnout predicts that social structure will play a different but still vital role: Citizens embedded in large and relatively loosely structured networks of close social ties are more likely to vote than others.

As we saw in Chapter 7, most college-educated citizens (along with about a third of those without a college degree) are embedded in social networks that are more conducive to the spread of voting and similar sorts of (relatively undemanding and somewhat public) cooperative behavior than are the networks of the remainder of those without a college degree. Thus, the correlation between voting and education turns out to be spurious; more educated people do not vote at higher rates because they can overcome the costs of voting more easily, or because they get more of a thrill out of participating in the political process, or because they have learned about civics and politics in the classroom. The higher rates of turnout among the college-educated stems from variation in social network structure, not from any individual characteristics that more educated people are more likely to possess.

MAKING SENSE OF EXISTING RESEARCH

In addition to striking success in direct empirical tests, the social theory also gains support from the neat and parsimonious accounts it provides of other observed empirical patterns in voter turnout. Perhaps most obviously, the theory does not view as paradoxical the national decline in American voter turnout that has accompanied a sharp increase in the percentage of the population with a college degree (Miller 1992). Because education is not presumed to "do" anything to (or signal anything about) an individual, there is no expectation that an increase in education levels would herald an increase in voter turnout, leaving nothing paradoxical at all about the two concurrent trends. The decrease in turnout in the second half of the twentieth century is most likely attributable to the changes in mobilization activity across this time period (Rosenstone and Hansen 1993), although it may be that a change in organizational activity and social network structure may reinforce these trends (Putnam 2000; McPherson et al. 2006, although see Fischer 2009 for a contrasting view).

Another highlight of the social theory is that aggregate turnout variation fits neatly into the same theoretical framework used to address individual turnout variation. Aggregate changes in the costs of turnout, often associated with institutional voting and registration arrangements that vary across and within nations, are translated into a small shift in the likelihood of voting unconditionally. This modeling assumption is supported by experimental data and produces simulation results with a close resemblance to observable variation across various democratic nations and U.S. states.

Additionally, the social theory provides a formal, individual-level model to complement the strategic politician's theory of elections and mobilization (Rosenstone and Hansen 1993; Aldrich 1993; Cox 1999). Mobilization by political elites may account for aggregate variation in turnout rates across elections, even within the same political or geographic area; however, mobilization does not work to increase turnout solely through direct contact with a political activist. Instead, mobilization is translated into voting through discussion within friendship networks, and higher levels of electoral salience will produce more discussion within the latent social networks of voters. In low-salience elections, voters are assumed to look to few, if any, friends when making a turnout decision, whereas in a high-salience election, they will look to most or all of their regular contacts. This modeling assumption is supported by observed patterns of political discussion (Huckfeldt 1987; Klofstad, McClurg, and Rolfe 2009; Rolfe 2010), and again produces accurate variations in simulated turnout.

Finally, the theory does not view voting itself as paradoxical. I do not argue that people ignore costs and benefits, or even that conditional decisions are unrelated to personal goals or motives. However, I suggest (and evidence shows) that in social dilemmas in which people perceive a clash between self-interest and social norms, people are often willing to cooperate, conditional on the cooperation of others. Far from paradoxical, voting is simply a relatively common social interaction in which people – who are, after all, quite used to dealing with other people in their daily lives – adjust their behavior to the observed and expected behavior of others using probabilistic, and probably largely unconscious, rules of thumb for getting on in a complex world full of competing demands and expectations for their time and attention. People who vote may believe that voting is a civic duty (and that understanding of the social situation does matter for what they will ultimately do), but they do not vote simply because of a sense of civic duty, social pressure, or any other single, conscious motivation.

My argument, in short, is that a social theory of turnout simply works better than the prevalent economic and civic-resources-based view, at multiple levels. The underlying social decision model is a better "as if" representation of actual individual decision making than a cost-benefit model, and, unlike traditional approaches, it also accounts for the social dynamics that are an unavoidable aspect of all social interaction. When specific predictions of the social theory are compared to those of the civic-resources approach, particularly with regards to the effects of education in both high- and low-salience elections, the social theory benefits from substantial empirical support. Finally, a social theory of turnout can account for the existence of voting as well as other empirical regularities all in the same neat theoretical framework, while making only two assumptions of any significance, both of which receive substantial empirical support.

FURTHER IMPLICATIONS

Whereas this book has focused on explaining voter turnout, there are additional implications of its account of this phenomenon, as well as the more general conditional choice framework. I will conclude by putting forth the four areas to which I see this work as most relevant, moving from the most specific to the most general. First, the book offers several methodological contributions that might be incorporated into future research. Second, the argument here has a significant payoff in terms of our understanding and use of the "usual suspects" in survey research more broadly. Next, this work sheds new light on the basic questions of representational equality that undergird much of the work on political participation, and suggests new paths to pursue for those interested in greater equality. Finally, the work has a potential relevance to deeper questions about the nature of civic and social life and social capital, and the other sorts of social dilemmas that are so often at the basis of many of the topics of interest in the social sciences.

For researchers interested in the empirical applications of theoretical models, I adopt two relatively unique methodological techniques in my implementation of the computational model in this work.[2] For one, as highlighted earlier, I incorporate empirical data into the model in what I hope to be a persuasive manner. In addition, my focus on network structure led me to incorporate more realistic network structures into my simulations. The field of agent-based simulation is still in the early stages of incorporating realistic social network ties into simulation models. Watts and Strogatz (1998), among others, have clearly shown that the topology of agent relationships can significantly affect simulation results, but relatively little has been published on the subject. I used a model of network formation developed by Jin et al. (2001) for other purposes to first simulate realistic networks of relationships between my potential voters, and then ran the conditional decision model using those simulated networks of social ties. This was an integral methodological step, allowing for more precise claims about the effects of network size and structure.

Another large methodological hurdle to overcome was finding existing data sources suitable to testing predictions about social structure. Traces of the impact of social structure on social dynamics are exceedingly difficult to capture in survey data, and even moderately useful measures are rarely included in election surveys given the assumed necessity of extensive snowball sampling (Wasserman and Faust 1994) and poor response rates to difficult and time-consuming network batteries.[3] I addressed this problem in two ways. One was to simply call on as many different types of evidence as possible: Thus I use geospatial analysis of turnout data from voter rolls, in combination with qualitative data from interviews with candidates in Chapter 8, and pair it with the more traditional analysis of individual survey data seen in Chapter 7. Even in this more traditional context, I use a series of descriptive analyses of the relationship between education and social network composition to derive a novel indicator of social network context.

Next, for a broader subset of researchers concerned with political behavior and/or survey data, this work highlights the urgent need to rethink the treatment of education and other demographic usual suspects in survey work (Achen 1992). A host of these usual suspects, some theoretically motivated, others simply used as controls, are included in most estimates of individual opinions and behaviors based on surveys. I argue

---

[2] For other projects that also incorporate empirical data into the process of developing and testing computational models, see Bruch and Mare (2006) and Manzo (2009).

[3] See Rolfe (2010) for a project currently underway, designed to address these and other survey measurement issues associated with theories invoking social structure.

that this undertheorized approach to survey analysis is misguided, and that a full interpretation of the meaning of given variables depends on careful analysis of social context, particularly among subgroups defined by race, gender, age, residence, or any other pertinent demographic variable that affects the friendships people form and the social and institutional spaces they inhabit. Without proper attention to the social context of individual action, it is easy to gloss over important insights in the data and rely instead on implicit social stereotypes as a guide for interpreting empirical patterns.

The social theory of turnout offers a new and, I believe, persuasive account of how education captures an important but overlooked element of social context. The implications of this new interpretation go far beyond education and voter turnout; turnout is one of the most studied forms of political behavior, but it is only one of many social behaviors correlated with demographic variables such as education, race, and gender. Thus, even though the results here apply only narrowly to the phenomena of voter turnout, the possibility of reinterpreting existing findings extends beyond the realm of turnout to other social dilemmas, other demographic variables, and perhaps other social and political behaviors as well.

This enterprise of rethinking our understanding of the "usual suspects" is of particular importance when discussing social phenomena that have a clear moral dimension and interpretation. Education is of particular interest to me because of the widespread, explicit or implicit, assumption that formal education produces or enhances much of the moral fiber of democratic citizenship: the "cognitive capacity" to be an informed and thoughtful citizen, for example, or elevated levels of civic duty and tolerance supposedly acquired through education. My aim is not to call into question the benefits inherent in a liberal education or an advanced degree. (I certainly would not argue that my efforts are of no value to the students who sit in my classes!) However, I do want to call into question the easy assumption that higher education is responsible for so much of what is good and noble in a democratic citizen.

Ultimately, a revised understanding of the causal mechanisms that produce empirical variation in voter turnout may result in the development of more effective pragmatic interventions to increase the representational equality of the electorate. We already know that a general increase in college education in America has occurred concurrent with a decline in voter turnout (Miller 1992), and there is little reason to think that vocabulary lessons would actually increase turnout, no matter how strong its statistical association with turnout (Verba, Schlozman, and Brady 1995). To some extent, this change in pragmatic approach is already underway, thanks in large part to the research of Green, Gerber, and colleagues. Whereas the significant increase in door-to-door canvassing in the 2004 and 2008 presidential elections clearly had a substantial impact on turnout in those elections,[4] it is unclear how much a one-time mobilization contact of an individual is transformed into a habitual increase in turnout (see Arcenaux and Nickerson 2009). On the other hand, it is entirely reasonable to imagine that the introduction of institutions to encourage the formation and maintenance of strong and weak social ties among those at a natural structural disadvantage would increase turnout – particularly if such institutions encouraged the development and maintenance of political and social power at a more local level. Thus, better understandings of the roots of participation matter not only in an academic sense, but in a very pragmatic one as well, even if recommendations might be more difficult to implement than a simple change in registration deadlines.

At the pragmatic level, then, my findings suggest that to bring more people into the political process, we should not focus on encouraging additional years of schooling, but rather on the even more difficult task of integrating the less-educated into the rich, diverse, and potent social networks of the more-educated members of what has become a highly class-divided society. Education may be intrinsically and instrumentally valuable in many ways, but it does not have an independent role in encouraging voting, whether by making participation seem more desirable or less costly. Rather, education provides access to a world rich in social ties and the institutions that foster such ties. Such ties are expensive to create and maintain, in terms of money, time, and effort, and are geographically bounded; college education is, for many, a crucial point of access to this social world, and this accounts for its close and long-observed association with voter turnout.

Of course, the power of institutions to foster the creation of meaningful social ties may have real limits. The persistent influence of parental education on the behavior of their adult children seen in Chapter 7 suggests that childhood experiences may not be easily overcome, and that the full transition into a new social setting may take generations. In other words, there may be no quick solutions to many of the social problems rooted in systematically impoverished social relationships.

---

[4] Local experts describe face-to-face mobilization as a pivotal force in the 2004 and 2008 presidential races in the city and county (and ultimately state) featured in Chapter 8.

The suggestion that institutions might foster social ties also highlights the close relationship between the theory of social decision making and the original sociological conception of social capital as inhering in the ties between individuals (Coleman 1990). Indeed, this work is similar to Granovetter's (1985) work on weak ties in that it operationalizes exactly how ties might create social capital – whether through the spread of cooperation in my case or through the creation of occupational opportunity in Granovetter's. In both cases, people with large, diverse networks are uniquely advantaged by the existence of social ties, both direct and indirect. Whereas much research on social capital makes the mistake of treating it as an individual attitudinal variable (reducible to social trust), the structural components of social capital do matter for individual political and social behavior, and thus for political and social inequality, and the quality of American citizenship as well. If I am right, participatory democracy would benefit most not from increased formal education, civic education, or even canvassing campaigns, but from long-term changes to the structure of social networks that allow a greater number of social ties, especially nonoverlapping ties, to flourish.

Appendix A

Simulations of the Conditional Cooperation Model

Simulations are similar to mathematical deduction in that the outcomes of the simulation process follow necessarily, albeit probabilistically, from the formal mathematical description of the model. The primary difference is that simulations provide numerical estimates of solutions to nonlinear dynamical systems that are otherwise intractable using existing analytical methods. This section provides a brief introduction to the agent-based simulations used throughout the book. Table A.1, adapted from previous work (Rolfe 2009), gives a short overview of the simulated parameters. Additional parameter combinations were used to verify that the model worked as expected, some of which are reported in Chapters 5 and 6. All simulations were created and run using the Repast simulation language (Collier, Howe, and North 2003), including a special implementation of the network creation algorithm from Jin et al. (2001).

First, the simulation creates a population of agents or citizens and gives each agent a decision rule to follow and friends to refer to when making decision. Unless otherwise noted, all simulations model 1,000 potential voters. Each of these voters is allowed to interact with all other agents in the all-see-all condition, or with specified neighbors in the biased random network condition described later here. After friendship circles are created, agents are assigned a vector of weights for each decision rule. As discussed previously, these weights range between 0% and 100% reliance on each of the three decision rules: unconditional cooperation, mean-matching linear conditional cooperation, and median-matching focal point conditional cooperation. The unconditional decision rule weight is used to assign all agents probabilistically to an initial state of either voting ($d_i = 1$) or not voting ($d_i = 0$).

TABLE A.I. *Simulation Parameters*

Action	
Number of actions possible	One binary
Fixed action?	Yes
Decision Rule Distribution	
Initial activity	Unconditional rule
Unconditional rule mean	$\mu_\alpha \in [0.10, 0.20]$
Mean-matching linear rule mean	$\mu_\beta \in [0.375, 0.475]$
Median focal point rule mean	$\mu_\gamma \in [0.375, 0.475]$
Information	
Actor attributes	No
What is observed	Actions
Updating sequence	N/A
Memory of past observations	No
Who is observed?	
Interaction space	Global networks (All see all)
	Local: Von Neumann neighbors on 2-D torus
	Local: biased random networks
Active choice of interactions	No
Agents move in space?	No
Number of agents	1,000

One additional parameter is set during the initial model setup phase: Each agent is assigned a uniformly distributed threshold to compare to the outcome of that agent's individual decision rule during each time step of the dynamic simulation. If the probability of voting produced by the decision rule exceeds this threshold, the agent votes; otherwise, the agent abstains. This specification does not suggest that real voters are using thresholds; rather, it is meant to capture the impact of memories or common knowledge in a one-shot decision (Rolfe 2009). Voters do not simply sit at home and wait until they see a neighbor walk down the street before deciding whether or not to vote, but may well have a sense of how likely friends and family members are to participate on the basis of observed behavior during past social dilemmas, past elections, "cheap talk" prior to an election (Dawes, van de Kragt, and Orbell 1990; Kerr and Kaufman-Gilliland 1994), or a more systematic source of common knowledge (Chwe 1999). Thus, use of a fixed threshold in a conditional decision model simulates cooperation/turnout rates in a one-shot probabilistic decision or single election given estimated (not observed) level of participation among others.

At this point, the static stage of the initial setup of the simulation is complete, and the simulation now enters the dynamic phase. The dynamic phase of the simulation starts at the initial time point (t = 0), with every agent assigned to some initial state of activity. During the time step between t = 0 and t = 1, each agent has an opportunity to observe whether or not those around her voted in the prior time period (i.e., t = 0). She then uses her decision rule to update her decision of whether or not to vote, taking into account the actions of others (which was initially set at 0, but will now be updated on the basis of observed activity.) After all agents have had a chance to update their turnout decision, the model steps to the next time period (t = 2), and the updating process starts over again. The simulation goes through multiple time steps (anywhere from 10 to 100 or more) until it reaches the point where no more agents are willing to change their mind. At that point, this unique run of the simulation is complete, and final-round turnout is recorded. This two-stage simulation process of initial model setup followed by dynamic time-steps is repeated 100 times for each parameter combination.

VALIDATING THE PROGRAMMED MODEL

The details of programmed model validity are not discussed elsewhere in this book, but validation of the programmed model is an important, although sometimes overlooked, step in model development. The various model parameters given in Table A.1 describe a relatively generic mathematical model. This model must then be translated into a program or simulation using a programming language (in this case, Repast) to obtain computational results when the model is analytically intractable. The debugging or verification process will find many programming errors. Small mistakes made during the programming process might not show up as bugs, but will nonetheless produce unintended results. For example, suppose agents were accidentally assigned not a threshold that remained fixed throughout all time steps of the simulation, but one that was reassigned during each time step. This small difference would produce a substantially different set of results than those produced by the intended static threshold model. The programmed model used in this book was validated using results validation and sensitivity analysis (Law and Kelton 1982).

The programmed version of the conditional cooperation or turnout model used in this volume was first validated by comparing simulated cooperation to both existing analytical results (Dodds and Watts

2004; Granovetter 1978) and other simulations. First, simulations of the basic model dynamic were run using well-known parameter combinations such as those found in Granovetter's (1978) article on threshold models. Ironically, the initial results were not as expected. A small difference in the size of the simulated population (100 agents in the original article compared to 1,000 agents in my simulations) made a significant difference in average participation. In this case, a small mistake in the program actually produced a finding of substantive importance that merited further analysis and comment (see Rolfe 2009). In addition, simulated results were compared to projected analytical results, taking into account the specific initial conditions of each run of the simulation. Although agent-based modeling is best used to analyze systems that are analytically intractable, it is usually possible to verify at least the basic dynamic of the computational model by comparing simulation results with existing analytical results obtained from the same mathematical system.

Next, an extensive sensitivity analysis was conducted on the programmed conditional cooperation or turnout model. A sensitivity analysis requires extensive and time-consuming parameter sweeps: slowly changing the value of each parameter in the model by small increments while holding the other parameters constant. A researcher can also find out where the model "breaks" or produces degenerate or nonsensical results. A thorough sensitivity analysis provides substantial insight into the contingent impact of each of the model parameters. In addition, a complete analysis serves as a robustness check to ensure that the programmed model is robust to small (and presumably inconsequential) changes. The complete sensitivity analysis of the model in this book led to the systematic categorization of conditional decision model parameters as reported in Table A.1 and Rolfe (2009); although most results are not reported. Partial examples of parameter sweeps appear in Chapters 5 and 6.

MODEL EXTENSIONS: NETWORK CONSTRUCTION

In a global or all-see-all network, agents have information on, can respond to, and are affected by the actions of all other agents in a population. Global reference networks may be chosen to represent the influence of mass media or the behavior of crowds (Granovetter 1978). Global reference groups vary only in the size of the population being modeled. Larger crowds will typically produce higher rates of diffusion than smaller crowds, unless the behavior in question is not likely to diffuse at all. Therefore, if a global network topology is used when a local topology would be more appropriate, the ease with which behaviors will spread will likely be overestimated.

For the simulations in this book, the biased random network construction method is used to create local network topologies that reflect characteristics of actual social networks. Biased random net construction achieves this goal by faithfully replicating the process of actual friendship formation and the biases that typically affect that friendship process (Rapoport 1979; Skvoretz 1985; Skvoretz 1990; Skvoretz, Fararo, and Agneessens 2004). There are two sources of bias to consider in the creation of a network: structural bias and node or compositional biases (Skvoretz 1990). Structural bias is inherent in the structure of the network itself and includes processes such as reciprocity, or the trend toward mutual friendships, and triad closure, or the trend toward mutual friends of person i to become friends as well (Skvoretz 1985; Skvoretz 1990). Node bias is the bias in the network created by differences in agents and their attributes. Sources of node bias include agents who choose more friends than others do, or the tendency to choose friends with similar attributes (homophily) (Fararo 1981; Fararo and Skvoretz 1984).

Despite the potential importance of node or compositional biases, particularly homophily, to affect interactions in the real world, I use a biased net technique that works primarily through a triad closure bias to increase the density of personal networks above that typically found in random graphs. The method described by Jin et al. (2001) is employed, although approaches that focus on a more comprehensive account of network structure directly may be more accurate and/or flexible (Skvoretz 1990; Snijders 2002).

The basic logic of the Jin et al.'s (2001) method is that it proceeds in steps. During each step, a few pairs of actors are first selected to be friends, and the appropriate ties are added to the network. Then, mutual friends of these actors are selected to also be friends. This process is repeated until all actors have the maximum number of friends, although a third step could be added in whereby ties are removed, and thus the network is always gradually changing itself.

In the Jin et al.'s model, the average density of personal networks can be changed by altering the relative proportion of selections made in the first (random) and second (mutual friends) substeps of network creation. Table A.2 provides the combinations of parameter values used to produce the networks used in this book using the JinGir network construction method in Repast to create networks of approximately the desired average degree and density. Although the JinGir method does seem to

TABLE A.2. *Median Degree (and Density) of Simulated Networks*

Degree	Average Personal Network Density			
	0.003	0.001	0.0005	0.0001
4	3.5 (0.46)	4.3 (0.41)	4.4 (0.34)	4.4 (0.22)
8	4.1 (0.44)	7.9 (0.44)	8.3 (0.35)	8.4 (0.24)
12	9.9 (0.53)	12.1 (0.38)	12.4 (0.28)	12.4 (0.19)
16	13.0 (0.53)	16.1 (0.35)	16.3 (0.24)	16.4 (0.16)
20	8.1 (0.50)	19.0 (0.36)	20.0 (0.35)	20.4 (0.16)

replicate variation in personal network density, results suggest that there is still "additional social structure in the network that is not captured by the graph" (Jin et al. 2001, p. 1).

The process did produce networks with substantial variation, and I ran several iterations at the specified values of r_0 and degree to produce approximately 100 networks, each with the desired network properties (average degree and density). These networks were used for all simulations with biased networks. In all cases, I set the r_2 parameter at 2 and the remove parameter at 0.005. Variations in these two parameters can be used to further fine-tune the simulated networks. A stoptick of 20 was used for most simulations, although it is possible to increase the average degree of simulated networks in some cases by running simulations longer.

Appendix B

Methodological Notes on the General Social Survey

Analysis of the 1985 General Social Survey (GSS) data presents three distinct problems: sample selection, nonresponse to individual items, and misreporting of voter turnout. These three issues overlap, given that many of the key variables of concern – education, race, income, and voter turnout – are associated with at least two of three potential sources of bias. The issues of sample selection are especially damaging, given that current samples seem to be selected in part on the dependent variable of interest, voter turnout. Based on careful consideration, however, I believe that even though the estimates themselves are undoubtedly biased by these problems, better data or better statistical corrections would not change the substance of my findings.

Looking first at turnout overreport, there are two potential concerns: (1) are the less educated members of the multieducational world more likely to overreport turnout than the highly educated members, and (2) are the members of the multieducational world systematically more likely to overreport turnout than the members of the low-education world? The literature on overreport bias in the NES suggests that the systematic sources of bias run opposite to the direction of concern in the first case, and that any bias in the second case might actually provide evidence for a key assumption of my underlying individual decision model: that voting is a form of conditional cooperation.

Overreporting has been traced back to three primary causes, although only two are relevant here: undersampling of nonvoters and the claim of nonvoters to have voted (Traugott and Katosh 1979; Sigelman 1982; Anderson and Silver 1986; Silver, Abramson, and Anderson 1986; Silver, Anderson, and Abramson 1986; Burden 2000). Following on the work of Brehm (1993), Burden (2000) has found that difficult-to-reach or non-responsive survey subjects are generally less likely to be voters; these nonrespondents are also likely to contain more college-educated nonvoters than the pool of those who consent to be surveyed (Silver, Abramson, and Anderson 1986; Brehm 1993). Thus, adding these respondents would most likely decrease any remaining correlation between education and turnout, controlling for social location.

The second systematic source of overreporting is misreporting by people who did not vote but claim that they did. Are these respondents systematically different from either other nonvoters or from actual voters? One study finds that respondents with high educational attainment are more likely to claim that they voted when in fact they did not (Silver, Anderson, and Abramson 1986). Compensating for this bias would again work in favor of my hypotheses because the bias inflates the turnout rates of the more educated rather than the less educated. Correcting for the bias would, again, further diminish any individual-level effects of education.

On another note, misreports also bring to light the notion that whereas voting in a particular election is a one-time binary act (Almond and Verba 1963; Sigelman 1982), being a voter in general is more probabilistic. Rather than being strictly nonvoters or strictly voters, people seem to vote with something that appears to be a probabilistic function, particularly in national elections. Sigelman, Roeder, Jewell, and Baer (1985) find evidence of something resembling a core of consistent voters surrounded by a periphery of less involved, sometime voters.

Thus, self-reported turnout may pick up on individuals' general sense of being likely to vote (or having voted in the past) while failing to cue memories of not voting in a particular election for incidental reasons such as bad weather, a sick child, a busy day at work, and so on. Belli et al. (1999) are able to decrease overreporting by changing the wording of turnout questions to help respondents realize that they might be substituting general voting memories for those of a specific election.[1] This is especially true if considerable time has passed since an election and the tendency to report general memories for specific ones increases (as it is in the 1985 GSS, which is administered several months to a year after the actual election). The notion of a more generalized reporting of voting

[1] Belli and colleagues' study is also noteworthy in that it demonstrates that overgeneralization of past behaviors and memory failure, perhaps even more than social desirability, are likely to be at the root of misreports. While evidence shows that misreporting turnout would certainly not be at odds with a conditional decision-making model, their support of a more generalized turnout decision is more in keeping with the spirit of this work.

tendencies is also backed by evidence that nonvoters who report voting are likely to be more like voters than nonvoters (Sigelman 1982), and to be in the pool of occasional voters even if they were not among voters in any given election (Sigelman et al. 1985; Sigelman and Jewell 1986). In looking at ten elections (primary and general) that cover a span of five years, Sigelman and Jewell (1986) find that only 0.1% of voters who are registered for the entire five-year period fail to vote in at least one election during that time.

Even though this number does not include people who were not on the rolls at any point during that time (either because they were initially too young or unregistered, or because they moved during the period), the trend confirms Timpone's (1998) finding that education and other demographic variables primarily affect the likelihood of someone choosing to register, not to actually vote once registered.[2] Comparisons of pre-election intention to vote and post-election reported vote in the American National Election Study (ANES) find that misreports occur almost exclusively among those who professed that they intended to vote prior to the election – again suggestive of a generalized tendency to vote.[3]

In summary, there is ample evidence to suggest that a correction of the GSS data for overreport of turnout would strengthen, rather than weaken, my claim that individual education has little or no effect once social location is accounted for. To the extent that turnout might be more likely to have been overreported in the multieducational world than in the low-education world, this bias is not a cause for alarm.

First, it supports a modeling assumption: that voting is a probabilistic decision and that there are more people who consider themselves voters because they vote occasionally than are people who vote in any given election. Although it is likely that some of the difference in reported turnout in a given election between the multieducational and low-education world might be erased by using validated vote, it is highly unlikely that this difference would account for much more than a small percentage of the difference between the two populations. Misreporting would be found to some degree in both populations (even if it was found more often in the multieducational population), but it only accounts for about 12% of the total overreport found on the NES (Burden 2000). Taking misreports

---

[2] Education plays a greatly diminished role in Sigelman and Jewell's (1986) estimates of percentage of elections voted in, coming in well behind age and income.

[3] Although a person with a tendency to vote is obviously not the same as a habitual voter, the existence of both types of voters is predicted by the conditional cooperation function.

into account, then, would erase at most a few percentage points in the difference between the populations. Even this correction might be unnecessary, given good reason to think that this model is focused on explaining generalized voting tendency.

Overreporting is potentially more damaging to our uncertainty regarding the estimates of the influence of race and income on turnout. Race, household income, and marital status all play a substantial role in both selection into the sample and tendency to misreport turnout. A model is available that can be used to correct for the demographic correlates of misreporting (Katz and Katz 2010), but the lack of concern for differences in record-keeping across communities makes even this method questionable for Americans of color. Putting aside concerns about race for the time being, future work will address the issue of household income using nonsurvey data as a way of getting around the multiple sample problems.

The large number of nonresponses to the income question (about 7% of the sample) increased potential issues with the household income variable. In the original data, about 100 distinct cases were missing on the household income and parental education variables. Therefore, I ran the same models with both listwise deletion and multiple imputation. By and large, the estimates were relatively robust to the use of the two approaches, with a few important exceptions. Estimates of the effects of race, both direct and interactive, household income, marital status, and core network size decreased in the imputed data, whereas estimates of the influence of occupational prestige increased. None of the estimates changed significantly enough to be of concern, although a better model of refusal to provide household income may yield more stable estimates.

Ultimately, there is little doubt that the biggest problem faced when conducting survey analysis of voter turnout is that we are quite sure that in doing so, we are looking at cases that have been selected on the dependent variable of interest, and that the same process that generates turnout also seems to generate willingness to respond to surveys. This is not an insignificant problem, given falling response rates to national surveys. Pending further work to find sufficient exogenous information to sort out the various causal pathways that lead to survey nonresponse, item nonresponse, and vote misreport, it appears that the known sources of bias would not change the substantive results reported in this book.

References

Abelson, R. P. 1964. "Mathematical Models of the Distribution of Attitudes under Controversy." In *Contributions to Mathematical Psychology*, eds. N. Frederiksen and H. Gulliksen, pp. 42–160. New York: Holt, Rhinehart, and Winston.

Abelson, R. P., D. R. Kinder, M. D. Peters, and S. T. Fiske. 1982. "Affective and Semantic Components in Political Person Perception." *Journal of Personality and Social Psychology* 42: 619–630.

Abdelal, Rawi, Yoshiko M. Herrera, Alastair Iain Johnston, and Rose McDermott. 2006. "Identity as a Variable." *Perspectives on Politics* 4: 695–711.

Achen, Christopher H. 1992. "Social Psychology, Demographic Variables, and Linear Regression: Breaking the Iron Triangle in Voting Research." *Political Behavior* 14: 195–211.

Achen, Christopher H., and W. P. Shively. 1995. *Cross-Level Inference*. Chicago: University of Chicago Press.

Akerlof, George. 1980. "A Theory of Social Custom, of Which Unemployment May Be One Consequence." *Quarterly Journal of Economics* 94(4): 749–775.

1982. "Labor Contracts as Partial Gift Exchange." *Quarterly Journal of Economics* 97: 543–569.

Aldrich, John H. 1993. "Rational Choice and Turnout." *American Journal of Political Science* 37(1): 246–278.

Almond, Gabriel A., and Sidney Verba. 1963. *The Civic Culture*. Princeton, NJ: Princeton University Press.

Amaral, L. A. N., A. Scala, M. Barthelemy, and H. E. Stanley. 2000. "Classes of Small-World Networks." *Proceedings of the National Academy of Sciences of the United States of America* 97(21): 11149–11152.

Anderson, Barbara, and Brian Silver. 1986. "Measurement and Mismeasurement of the Validity of the Self-Reported Vote." *American Journal of Political Science* 80: 771–785.

Andreoni, James. 1988. "Why Free Ride?: Strategies and Learning in Public Goods Experiments." *Journal of Public Economics* 37: 291–304.

1995. "Warm-Glow Versus Cold-Prickle: The Effects of Positive and Negative Framing on Cooperation in Experiments." *Quarterly Journal of Economics* 110(1): 1–21.

Arceneaux, Kevin, and David W. Nickerson. 2009. "Who Is Mobilized to Vote? A Re-Analysis of Eleven Randomized Field Experiments." *American Journal of Political Science* 53(1): 1–16.

Artinger, Florian, F. Exadaktylos, H. Koppel, and L. Sääksvuori. 2009. "Unraveling Fairness: Do as Thou Expecteth Others to Do." Paper presented at "Behavioural Economics, Economic Psychology: Theory and Policy," Joint Conference, International Association for Research in Economic Psychology and Society for the Advancement of Behavioral Economics, Halifax, Nova Scotia, Canada, July.

Asch, Solomon E. 1955. "Opinions and Social Pressures." *Scientific American* 193(5): 31–35.

Ashenfelter, Orley, and Stanley Kelley. 1975. "Determinants of Participation in Presidential Elections." *Journal of Law and Economics* 18(3): 695–733.

Axelrod, Robert M. 1984. *The Evolution of Cooperation.* New York: Basic Books.

1997. *The Complexity of Cooperation.* Princeton, NJ: Princeton University Press.

Axtell, R., and J. Epstein. 1999. "Coordination in Transient Social Networks: An Agent-Based Computational Model of the Timing of Retirement." In *Behavioral Dimensions of Retirement Economics,* ed. H. J. Aaron, pp. 146–174. Washington, DC: Brookings Institution Press.

Bailey, Stefanie, and Peter V. Marsden. 1999. "Interpretation and Interview Context: Examining the General Social Survey Name Generator Using Cognitive Methods." *Social Networks* 21(3): 287–309.

Baldwin, M. W., and J. G. Holmes. 1987. "Salient Private Audiences and Awareness of the Self." *Journal of Personality and Social Psychology* 52: 1087–1098.

Bargh, John A., Mark Chen, and Lara Burrows. 1996. "Automaticity of Social Behavior: Direct Effects of Trait Construct and Stereotype Activation on Action." *Journal of Personality and Social Psychology* 71(2): 230–244.

Barkow, Jerome H., Leda Cosmides, and John Tooby. 1992. *The Adapted Mind: Evolutionary Psychology and the Generation of Culture.* Oxford: Oxford University Press.

Barzel, Yoram, and Eugene Silberberg. 1973. "Is the Act of Voting Rational?" *Public Choice* 16: 51–58.

Baybeck, Brady, and Scott D. McClurg. 2005. "What Do They Know and How Do They Know It? An Examination of Citizen Awareness of Context." *American Politics Research* 33(4): 492–520.

Bearman, Peter. 2005. *Doormen.* Chicago: University of Chicago Press.

Bearman, Peter, and P. Parigi. 2004. "Cloning Headless Frogs and Other Important Matters: Conversation Topics and Network Structure." *Social Forces* 83: 535.

Beck, Nathaniel. 1975. "The Paradox of Minimax Regret." *American Political Science Review* 69(3): 918.

Bednar, Jenna, and Scott Page. 2007. "Can Game(s) Theory Explain Culture?: The Emergence of Cultural Behavior Within Multiple Games." *Rationality and Society* 19: 65–97.

Belli, Robert F., Michael W. Traugott, Margaret Young, and Katherine A. McGonagle. 1999. "Reducing Vote Overreporting in Surveys: Social Desirability, Memory Failure, and Source Monitoring." *Public Opinion Quarterly* 63(1): 90–108.

Bendor, Jonathan, Daniel Diermeier, and Michael M. Ting. 2003. "A Behavioral Model of Turnout." *American Political Science Review* 97(2): 261–280.

2004. "The Empirical Content of Adaptive Models." Stanford GSB Working Paper No. 1877, Social Science Research Network Elibrary.

2007. "Comment: Adaptive Models in Sociology and the Problem of Empirical Content." *American Journal of Sociology* 112: 1534–1545.

Bendor, J., D. Mookherjee, and D. Ray. 2001. "Aspiration-Based Reinforcement Learning in Repeated Interaction Games: An Overview." *International Game Theory Review* 3: 159–174.

Bennett, Stephen Earl, and Linda L. M. Bennett. 1992. "From Traditional to Modern Conceptions of Gender Equality in Politics: Gradual Change and Lingering Doubts." *The Western Political Quarterly* 45(1): 93–111.

Berelson, Bernard, Paul Felix Lazarsfeld, and William N. McPhee. 1954. *Voting: A Study of Opinion Formation in a Presidential Campaign*. Chicago: University of Chicago Press.

Berinsky, Adam J. 2005. "The Perverse Consequences of Electoral Reform in the United States." *American Politics Research* 33: 471–491.

Bernard, H. Russell, Eugene C. Johnsen, Peter D. Killworth, Christopher McCarty, Gene A. Shelley, and Scott Robinson. 1990. "Comparing Four Different Methods for Measuring Personal Social Networks." *Social Networks* 12(3): 179–215.

Bernard, H. Russell, Gene Ann Shelley, and Peter Killworth. 1987. "How Much of a Network Does the GSS and RSW Dredge Up?" *Social Networks* 9(1): 49–61.

Bettinger, Eric, and Robert Slonim. 2006. "Using Experimental Economics to Measure the Effects of a Natural Educational Experiment on Altruism." *Journal of Public Economics* 90: 1625–1648.

Bicchieri, Cristina. 2002. "Covenants without Swords: Group Identity, Norms, and Communication in Social Dilemmas." *Rationality and Society* 14: 192–228.

Bicchieri, Cristina, and E. Xiao. 2009. "Do the Right Thing: But Only if Others Do So." *Journal of Behavioral Decision Making*.

Blais, André. 2006. "What Affects Voter Turnout?" *Annual Review of Political Science* 9: 111–125.

Blais, André, and R. Young. 1999. "Why Do People Vote? An Experiment in Rationality." *Public Choice* 99: 39–55.

Blau, Peter M. 1977. "A Macrosociological Theory of Social Structure." *American Journal of Sociology* 83(1): 26–54.

Blumer, Herbert. 1937. "Social Psychology." In *Man and Society: A Substantive Introduction to the Social Science*, ed. Emerson Peter Schmidt, pp. 144–198. New York: Prentice Hall.

Bobo, Lawrence, and Frederick C. Licari. 1989. "Education and Political Tolerance: Testing the Effects of Cognitive Sophistication and Target Group Affect." *Public Opinion Quarterly* 53: 285–308.

Bohnet, I., and Y. Baytelman. 2007. "Institutions and Trust: Implications for Preferences, Beliefs and Behavior." *Rationality and Society* 19: 99.

Bolton, G. E., and A. Ockenfels. 2000. "ERC: A Theory of Equity, Reciprocity, and Competition." *American Economic Review* 90(1): 166–193.

Bonacich, Philip. 1972. "Norms and Cohesion as Adaptive Responses to Potential Conflict: An Experimental Study." *Sociometry* 35: 357–375.

    1976. "Secrecy and Solidarity." *Sociometry* 39: 200–208.

Bond, R., and P. B. Smith. 1996. "Culture and Conformity: A Meta-Analysis of Studies Using Asch's (1952b, 1956) Line Judgement Task." *Psychological Bulletin* 119: 111–137.

Bosman, Ronald, Joep Sonnemans, and Marcel Zeelenberg. 2001. "Emotions, Rejections, and Cooling Off in the Ultimatum Game." University of Amsterdam Digital Academic Repository.

Brady, Henry E., and David Collier. 2004. *Rethinking Social Inquiry: Diverse Tools, Shared Standards*. Lanham, MD: Rowman & Littlefield.

Brañas-Garza, Pablo et al. 2010. "Altruism and Social Integration." *Games and Economic Behavior* 69(2): 249–257.

Brehm, John. 1993. *The Phantom Respondents: Opinion Surveys and Political Representation*. Ann Arbor: University of Michigan Press.

Brewer, M. B., and W. Gardner. 1996. "Who Is This "We"? Levels of Collective Identity and Self Representations." *Journal of Personality and Social Psychology* 71: 83–93.

Brody, Richard H. 1978. The Puzzle of Political Participation in America. In *The New American Political System*, ed. Anthony King, pp. 287–324. Washington, DC: American Enterprise Institute.

Bruch, E. E., and R. D. Mare. 2006. "Neighborhood Choice and Neighborhood Change." *American Journal of Sociology* 112: 667–709.

    2009. "Segregation Dynamics." In *Oxford Handbook of Analytical Sociology*, eds. P. Bearman and P. Hedström, 269–293. Oxford: Oxford University Press.

Bruggeman, Jeroen. 2008. *Social Networks*. London: Routledge.

Burden, Barry. 2000. "Voter Turnout and the National Election Studies." *Political Analysis* 8: 389–398.

Burkett, T. 1997. Cosponsorship in the United States Senate: A Network Analysis of Senate Communication and Leadership, 1973–1990. Unpublished Doctoral Dissertation, University of South Carolina.

Burt, Ronald S. 1980. "Innovation as a Structural Interest: Rethinking the Impact of Network Position on Innovation Adoption." *Social Networks* 2(4): 327–355.

    1984. "Network Items and the General Social Survey." *Social Networks* 6(4): 293–339.

Calhoun-Brown, Allison. 1996. "African American Churches and Political Mobilization: The Psychological Impact of Organizational Resources." *Journal of Politics* 58(4): 935–953.

Camerer, Colin. 2003. *Behavioral Game Theory: Experiments in Strategic Interaction*. Princeton, NJ: Princeton University Press.

Camerer, Colin, and Richard H. Thaler. 1995. "Anomalies: Ultimatums, Dictators and Manners." *Journal of Economic Perspectives* 9(2): 209–219.

Campbell, Angus, Philip E. Converse, Warren E. Miller, and Donald E. Stokes. 1960. The *American Voter*. New York: John Wiley and Sons.

Campbell, Angus, Gerald Gurin, and W. E. Miller. 1954. *The Voter Decides*. Oxford: Row, Peterson, and Co.

Campbell, David E. 2006. *Why We Vote: How Schools and Communities Shape Our Civic Life*. Princeton, NJ: Princeton University Press.

Campbell, Karen E., and Barrett A. Lee. 1991. "Name Generators in Surveys of Personal Networks." *Social Networks* 13(3): 203–221.

Campbell, Karen E., Peter V. Marsden, and Jeanne S. Hurlbert. 1986. "Social Resources and Socioeconomic Status." *Social Networks* 8(1): 97–117.

Carpenter, Jeffrey, S. Burks, and E. Verhoogen. 2005. "Comparing Students to Workers: The Effects of Social Framing on Behavior in Distribution Games." *Field Experiments in Economics* 10: 261–289.

Carpenter, Jeffrey, Cristina Connolly, and Caitlin Myers. 2008. "Altruistic Behavior in a Representative Dictator Experiment." *Experimental Economics* 11: 282–292.

Carpenter, Jeffrey, E. Verhoogen, and S. Burks. 2005. "The Effect of Stakes in Distribution Experiments." *Economics Letters* 86(3): 393–398.

Cassel, Carol A. 2004. "Voting Records and Validated Voting Studies." *The Public Opinion Quarterly* 68(1): 102–108.

Cederman, Lars-Erik. 1997. *Emergent Actors in World Politics: How States and Nations Develop and Dissolve*. Princeton, NJ: Princeton University Press.

Cesario, J., J. E. Plaks, and E. T. Higgins. 2006. "Automatic Social Behavior as Motivated Preparation to Interact." *Journal of Personality and Social Psychology* 90: 893–910.

Chartrand, T. L., Dalton, A. N., and Fitzsimons, G. J. 2007. "Nonconscious Relationship Reaction: When Significant Others Prime Opposing Goals." *Journal of Experimental Social Psychology* 43: 719–726.

Cho, Wendy. 2003. "Contagion Effects and Ethnic Contribution Networks." *American Journal of Political Science* 47(2): 368–387.

Chong, Dennis. 1991. *Collective Action and the Civil Rights Movement*. Chicago: University of Chicago Press.

1995. "Rational Choice Theory's Mysterious Rivals." *Critical Review* 9: 37.

Chuah, Swee-Hoon, Robert Hoffmann, Martin Jones, and Geoffrey Williams. 2007. "Do Cultures Clash? Evidence from Cross-National Ultimatum Game Experiments." *Journal of Economic Behavior & Organization* 64: 35–48.

Chwe, Michael Suk-Young. 1999. "Structure and Strategy in Collective Action." *American Journal of Sociology* 105(1): 128–156.

2001. *Rational Ritual: Culture, Coordination, and Common Knowledge*. Princeton, NJ: Princeton University Press.

2008. "Statistical Game Theory." Working paper.

Cialdini, R. B. 2001. *Influence: Science and Practice*. Boston: Allyn and Bacon.

2005. "Basic Social Influence Is Underestimated." *Psychological Inquiry* 16: 158–161.

2007. "Descriptive Social Norms as Underappreciated Sources of Social Control." *Psychometrika* 72: 263–268.

Cialdini, R. B., R. R. Reno, and C. A. Kallgren. 1990. "A Focus Theory of Normative Conduct: Recycling the Concept of Norms to Reduce Littering in Public Places." *Journal of Personality and Social Psychology* 58: 1015–1026.

Cialdini, R. B., and M. R. Trost. 1998. "Social Influence: Social Norms, Conformity, and Compliance." *The Handbook of Social Psychology*, ed. Daniel T. Gilbert, Susan T. Fiske, and Gardner Lindzey, pp. 151–192. New York: McGraw-Hill.

Clark, R. D., and A. Maass. 1988. "Social Categorization in Minority Influence: The Case of Homosexuality." *European Journal of Social Psychology* 18: 347–364.

Cochran, Moncrieff. 1990. *Extending Families: The Social Networks of Parents and Their Children*. Cambridge: Cambridge University Press.

Coleman, James S. 1990. *Foundations of Social Theory*. Cambridge, MA: Harvard University Press.

Coleman, James S., Elihu Katz, and Herbert Menzel. 1957. "The Diffusion of an Innovation among Physicians." *Sociometry* 20(4): 253–270.

1966. *Medical Innovation: A Diffusion Study*. Indianapolis, IN: Bobbs-Merrill Co.

Collier, Nick, Tom Howe, and Michael North. 2003. "Onward and Upward: The Transition to Repast 2.0." Proceedings of the First Annual North American Association for Computational Social and Organizational Science Conference, Electronic Proceedings, Pittsburgh, PA.

Cook, K. S., and K. A. Hegtvedt. 1983. "Distributive Justice, Equity, and Equality." *Annual Reviews in Sociology* 9: 217–241.

Cook, K. S., and J. M. Whitmeyer. 1992. "Two Approaches to Social Structure: Exchange Theory and Network Analysis." *Annual Review of Sociology* 18: 109–127.

Cox, Gary W. 1997. *Making Votes Count*. New York: Cambridge University Press.

1999. "Electoral Rules and the Calculus of Mobilization." *Legislative Studies Quarterly* 24(3): 387–419.

2005. "Electoral Institutions and Political Competition Coordination, Persuasion and Mobilization." In *Handbook of New Institutional Economics*, eds. Claude Ménard and Mary M. Shirley, pp. 69–90. Dordrecht: Springer.

Cox, Gary W., and Michael C. Munger. 1989. "Closeness, Expenditures, and Turnout in the 1982 U.S. House Elections." *American Political Science Review* 83(1): 217–231.

Cox, Gary W., Frances McCall Rosenbluth, and Michael F. Thies. 1998. "Mobilization, Social Networks, and Turnout: Evidence from Japan." *World Politics* 50(3): 447–474.

Cronin, Helena. 1991. The *Ant and the Peacock: Altruism and Sexual Selection from Darwin to Today*. Cambridge and New York: Cambridge University Press.

Croson, Rachel. 1996. "Partners and Strangers Revisisted." *Economic Letters* 53: 25–32.

Dawes, Robyn M. 1980. "Social Dilemmas." *Annual Reviews in Psychology* 31: 169–193.

Dawes, Robyn. M., J. McTavish, and H. Shaklee. 1977. "Behavior, Communication, and Assumptions about Other Peoples' Behavior in a Commons Dilemma Situation." *Journal of Personality and Social Psychology* 54: 811–819.

Dawes, Robyn M., and Richard H. Thaler. 1988. "Anomalies: Cooperation." *Journal of Economic Perspectives* 2(3): 187–197.

Dawes, Robyn, A. J. Van De Kragt, and J. M. Orbell. 1990. "Cooperation for the Benefit of Us-Not Me, Or My Conscience." In *Beyond Self-Interest*, ed. Jane Mansbridge, pp. 97–110. Chicago: University of Chicago Press.

De Sola Pool, Ithiel, and Manfred Kochen. 1978. "Contacts and Influence." *Social Networks* 1: 5–51.

Deutsch, M. 1975. "Equity, Equality, and Need: What Determines Which Value Will Be Used As the Basis of Distributive Justice." *Journal of Social Issues* 31: 137–149.

Dodds, Peter S., and Duncan J. Watts. 2004. "Universal Behavior in a Generalized Model of Contagion." *Physical Review Letters* 92: 218701.

Downs, Anthony. 1957. *An Economic Theory of Voting*. New York: Harper.

Dunbar, R. 1992. "Neocortex Size as a Constraint on Group Size in Primates." *Journal of Human Evolution* 22(6): 469–493.

1993. "Co-Evolution of Neocortex Size, Group Size and Language in Humans." *Behavioral and Brain Sciences* 16(4): 681–735.

1998. *Grooming, Gossip, and the Evolution of Language*. Cambridge, MA: Harvard University Press.

Dunning, D., C. Heath, and J. M. Suls. 2004. "Flawed Self-Assessment: Implications for Health, Education, and the Workplace." *Psychological Science in the Public Interest* 5: 69–106.

Eckhoff, T. E. 1974. *Justice: Its Determinants in Social Interaction*. Rotterdam: Rotterdam University Press.

Edlin, Aaron, Andrew Gelman, and Noah Kaplan. 2007. "Voting As a Rational Choice: Why and How People Vote to Improve the Well-Being of Others." *Rationality and Society* 19(3): 293.

Elster, Jon. 1989. The *Cement of Society*. Cambridge: Cambridge University Press.

Engelmann, Dirk, and Urs Fischbacher. 2002. "Indirect Reciprocity and Strategic Reputation Building in an Experimental Helping Game." Institute for Empirical Research in Economics University of Zurich Working Paper Series ISSN 1424–0459, Working Paper No. 132, November.

Falk, A., U. Fischbacher, and S. Gächter. 2011. "Living in Two Neighborhoods – Social Interaction Effects in the Laboratory." *Economic Inquiry*. Online.

Falkinger, J., E. Fehr, S. Gächter, and R. Winter-Ebmer. 2000. "A Simple Mechanism for the Efficient Provision of Public Goods: Experimental Evidence." *American Economic Review* 90(1): 247–264.

Fararo, Thomas J. 1981. "Biased Networks and Social Structure Theorems." *Social Networks* 3(2): 137–159.

Fararo, Thomas J., and John Skvoretz. 1984. "Biased Networks and Social Structure Theorems: Part II." *Social Networks* 6(3): 223–258.

Fehr, E., and U. Fischbacher. 2004. "Third-Party Punishment and Social Norms." *Evolution and Human Behavior* 25(2): 63–87.

Fehr, Ernst, and Ernst Schmidt. 1999. "A Theory of Fairness, Competition and Cooperation." *Quarterly Journal of Economics* 114(3): 817–868.

Fehr, Ernst, and Simon Gächter. 2000. "Cooperation and Punishment in Public Goods Experiments." *American Economic Review* 90(4): 981–994.

Feld, Scott L., and Bernard Grofman. 1989. Toward a Sociometric Theory of Representation: Representing Individuals Enmeshed in a Social Network. In *The Small World*, ed. Manfred Kochen, pp. 100–107. Norwood, NJ: Ablex Publishing.

Ferejohn, John, and Morris Fiorina. 1974. "The Paradox of Not Voting." *American Political Science Review* 68(2): 525–536.

1975. "Closeness Counts Only in Horseshoes and Dancing." *The American Political Science Review* 69(3): 920–925.

Ferejohn, J., and D. Satz. 1994. "Rational Choice Theory and Folk Psychology." Unpublished Typescript, Stanford University.

Finkel, Steven E., Edward N. Muller, and Karl-Dieter Opp. 1989. "Personal Influence, Collective Rationality, and Mass Political Action." *American Political Science Review* 83(3): 885–903.

Fischbacher, Urs, Simon Gächter, and Ernst Fehr. 2001. "Are People Conditionally Cooperative? Evidence from a Public Goods Experiment." *Economics Letters* 71(3): 397–404.

2009. "The 2004 GSS Finding of Shrunken Social Networks: An Artifact?" *American Sociological Review* 74: 657–669.

Fischer, Claude. 1982. *To Dwell among Friends: Personal Networks in Town and City*. Chicago: University of Chicago Press.

2009. "The 2004 GSS Finding of Shrunken Social Networks: An Artifact?" *American Sociological Review* 74(4): 657–669.

Fischer, Claude S., and Yossi Shavit. 1995. "National Differences in Network Density: Israel and the United States." *Social Networks* 17: 129–145.

Fiske, Alan P. 1992. "The Four Elementary Forms of Sociality: Framework for a Unified Theory of Social Relations." *Psychological Review* 99: 689–723.

Fiske, Alan P., and Susan T. Fiske. 2007. "Social Relations in our Species and Our Cultures." In *Handbook of Cultural Psychology*, eds. S. Kitayama and D. Cohen, pp. 283–306. New York: Guilford.

Fiske, Alan P., and Philip E. Tetlock. 1997. "Taboo Trade-Offs: Reactions to Transactions That Transgress the Spheres of Justice." *Political Psychology* 18: 255–297.

Fiske, Susan T., and S. L. Neuberg. 1990. "A Continuum Model of Impression Formation from Category-Based to Individuating Processes: Influences of Information and Motivation on Attention and Interpretation." *Advances in Experimental Social Psychology* 23: 1–74.

Fiske, Susan T., and Shelley E. Taylor. 1991. *Social Cognition*. New York: McGraw-Hill.

Fitzsimons, Gráinne M., and John A. Bargh. 2003. "Thinking of You: Nonconscious Pursuit of Interpersonal Goals Associated with Relationship Partners." *Journal of Personality and Social Psychology* 84(1): 148–164.

Forsythe, Robert, Joel Horowitz, N. E. Savin, and Martin Sefton. 1994. "Fairness in Simple Bargaining Experiments." *Games and Economic Behavior* 6: 347–369.

Fowler, James H. 2006. "Altruism and Turnout." *Journal of Politics* 68: 674–683.

Frank, R. H., T. Gilovich, and D. T. Regan. 1993. "Does Studying Economics Inhibit Cooperation?" *Journal of Economic Perspectives* 7: 159–171.

1996. "Do Economists Make Bad Citizens?" *Journal of Economic Perspectives* 10: 187–192.

Frank, Robert H. 1989. *Passions within Reason: The Strategic Role of the Emotions*. New York: W. W. Norton & Co.

Franklin, Mark N. 2004. *Voter Turnout and the Dynamics of Electoral Competition in Established Democracies since 1945*. Cambridge: Cambridge University Press.

Freeman, L. C., and C. R. Thompson. 1989. "Estimating Acquaintanceship Volume". In *The Small World*, ed. Manfred Kochen, pp. 147–158. Norwood, NJ: Ablex Publishing.

French, John. 1956. "A Formal Theory of Social Power." *The Psychological Review* 63: 181–194.

Frey, Bruno S. 1971. "Why Do High Income People Participate More in Politics?" *Public Choice* 11: 101–105.

Friedman, Milton. 1953. *Essays in Positive Economics*. Chicago: University of Chicago Press.

Frith, C. D., and U. Frith. 1999. "Interacting Minds – A Biological Basis." *Science* 286: 1692. Online at http://www.cmstory.org/aaa2/menu.htm

Frohlich, Norman, Joe Oppenheimer, Pat Bond, and Irvin Boschman. 1984. "Beyond Economic Man: Altruism, Egalitarianism, and Difference Maximizing." *Journal of Conflict Resolution* 28(1): 3–24.

Frye, Kathryn. 1997. "An African American Album, Volume II." Technical Report Charlotte Mecklenburg Public Library.

Fullilove, Mindy Thompson. 2004. *Root Shock: How Tearing Up City Neighborhoods Hurts America, and What We Can Do About It*. New York: One World/Ballantine Books.

Gamson, A., David Croteau, William Hoynes, and Theodore Sasson. 1992. "Media Images and the Social Construction of Reality." *Annual Review of Sociology* 18: 373.

Geertz, Clifford. 1973. The *Interpretation of Cultures*. New York: Basic Books.

Gelman, Andrew, and Gary King. 1993. "Why Are American Presidential Election Campaign Polls So Variable When Votes Are So Predictable?" *British Journal of Political Science* 23: 409–451.

Gerber, Alan S., and Donald P. Green. 2000. "The Effects of Canvassing, Telephone Calls, and Direct Mail on Voter Turnout: A Field Experiment." *American Political Science Review* 94(3): 653–663.

Gerber, Alan S., Donald P. Green, and Christopher W. Larimer. 2008. "Social Pressure and Voter Turnout: Evidence from a Large-Scale Field Experiment." *American Political Science Review* 102(1): 33–48.

Gerber, Alan S., and Todd Rogers. 2009. "Descriptive Social Norms and Motivation to Vote: Everybody's Voting and So Should You." *Journal of Politics* 71: 178–191.

Gilbert, D. T., and P. S. Malone. 1995. "The Correspondence Bias." *Psychological Bulletin* 117: 21–38.

Gimpel, James, J. Celeste Lay, and Jason E. Schuknecht. 2003. *Cultivating Democracy: Civic Environments and Political Socialization in America.* Washington, DC: Brookings Institution Press.

Goeree, J. K., M. A. McConnell, T. Mitchell, T. Tromp, and L. Yariv. 2008. "Linking and Giving among Teenage Girls." California Institute of Technology Working Paper.

Goffman, Erving. 1959. The *Presentation of Self in Everyday Life.* Garden City, NY: Doubleday.

Gosnell, Harold F. 1927. *Getting Out the Vote: An Experiment in the Stimulation of Voting.* Chicago: University of Chicago Press.

1930. *Why Europe Votes.* Chicago: University of Chicago Press.

Gould, Roger V. 1993. "Collective Action and Network Structure." *American Sociological Review* 58(2): 182–196.

2003. *Collision of Wills: How Ambiguity about Social Rank Breeds Conflict.* Chicago: University of Chicago Press.

Granovetter, Mark S. 1973. "The Strength of Weak Ties." *American Journal of Sociology* 78(6): 1360–1380.

1978. "Threshold Models of Collective Behavior." *American Journal of Sociology* 83(6): 1420–1443.

1985. "Economic Action and Social Structure: The Problem of Embeddedness." *American Journal of Sociology* 91(3): 481–510.

Green, Donald P., Alan S. Gerber, and David W. Nickerson. 2003. "Getting Out the Youth Vote in Local Elections: Results from Six Door-to-Door Canvassing Experiments." *Journal of Politics* 65(4): 1083–1096.

Green, Donald P., and Ian Shapiro. 1994. *Pathologies of Rational Choice Theory: A Critique of Applications in Political Science.* New Haven, CT: Yale University Press.

Greenwald, A. G., M. R. Banaji, L. A. Rudman, S. D. Farnham, B. A. Nosek, and D. S. Mellott. 2002. "A Unified Theory of Implicit Attitudes, Stereotypes, Self-Esteem, and Self-Concept." *Psychological Review* 109: 3–25.

Hammer, Muriel. 1980. "Predictability of Social Connections Over Time." *Social Networks* 2: 165–180.

Harary, Frank. 1959. "A Criterion for Unanimity in French's Theory of Social Power." In *Studies in Social Power*, ed. Dorwin Cartwright, pp. 168–182. Oxford/Ann Arbor: University of Michigan Press.

Harbaugh, W. T., and K. Krause. 2000. "Children's Contributions in Public Good Experiments: The Development of Altruistic and Free-Riding Behaviors." *Economic Inquiry* 38: 95–109.

Hardin, Russell. 1982. *Collective Action.* Baltimore: Johns Hopkins University Press.

Harris-Lacewell, Melissa Victoria. 2004. *Barbershops, Bibles, and BET: Everyday Talk and Black Political Thought.* Princeton, NJ: Princeton University Press.

Hedström, Peter. 2005. *Dissecting the Social.* New York: Cambridge University Press.

Heider, Fritz. 1944. "Social Perception and Phenomenal Causality." *Journal of Psychology* 51: 107–112.

Hempel, Carl Gustav. 1966. *Philosophy of Natural Science.* Prentice-Hall Foundations of Philosophy Series. Englewood Cliffs, NJ: Prentice-Hall.

Henrich, Joseph, Robert Boyd, Samuel Bowles, Ernst Fehr, Colin Camerer, and Herbert Gintis. 2004. *Foundations of Human Sociality: Economic Experiments and Ethnographic.* Oxford: Oxford University Press.

Highton, Benjamin. 1997. "Easy Registration and Voter Turnout." *Journal of Politics* 59(2): 565–575.

Hirschleifer, J. 1987. "On the Emotions as Guarantors of Threats and Promises." In *The Latest on the Best: Essays on Evolution and Optimality*, ed. J. Dupre, pp. 307–326. Cambridge, MA: MIT Press.

Hoffman, Elizabeth, Kevin McCabe, Keith Shachat, and Vernon Smith. 1994. "Preferences, Property Rights and Anonymity in Bargaining Games." *Games and Economic Behavior* 7: 346–380.

1996. "Social Distance and Other-Regarding Behavior in Dictator Games." *American Economic Review* 86: 653–660.

Hogg, M. A., and D. Abrams. 1988. *Social Identifications: A Social Psychology of Intergroup Relations and Group Processes.* London: Routledge.

Honaker, James, Anne Joseph, Gary King, Kenneth Scheve, and Naunihal Singh. 1998–2002. "AMELIA: A Program for Missing Data." Available at http://gking.harvard.edu/amelia

Hong, Ying-Yi, Veronica Benet-Martinez, Chi-Yue Chiu, and Michael W. Morris. 2003. "Boundaries of Cultural Influence: Construct Activation as a Mechanism for Cultural Differences in Social Perception." *Journal of Cross-Cultural Psychology* 34: 453–464.

Hong, Ying-Yi, Grace Ip, Chi-Yue Chiu, Michael W. Morris, and Tanya Menon. 2005. "Cultural Identity and Dynamic Construction of the Self: Collective Duties and Individual Rights in Chinese and American Cultures." *Social Cognition* 19(3): 251–268.

Huang, Gang, and Mark Tausig. 1990. "Network Range in Personal Networks." *Social Networks* 12(3): 261–268.

Huckfeldt, Robert. 1979. "Political Participation and the Neighborhood Social Context." *American Journal of Political Science* 23(3): 579–592.

1980. "Variable Responses to Neighborhood Social Contexts: Assimilation, Conflict, and Tipping Points." *Political Behavior* 2(3): 231–257.

2000. A Report on the Social Network Battery in the 1998 ANES Pilot Study. Technical Report, Indiana University.

Huckfeldt, Robert, Paul Allen Beck, Russell J. Dalton, and Jeffrey Levine. 1995. "Political Environments, Cohesive Social Groups, and the Communication of Public Opinion." *American Journal of Political Science* 39(4): 1025–1054.

Huckfeldt, R. Robert, P. E. Johnson, and John D. Sprague. 2004. *Political Disagreement: The Survival of Diverse Opinions within Communication Networks.* Cambridge: Cambridge University Press.

Huckfeldt, Robert, and John Sprague. 1992. "Political Parties and Electoral Mobilization: Political Structure, Social Structure, and the Party Canvass." *American Political Science Review* 86(1): 70–86.

Imai, Kosuke, Gary King, and Oliva Lau. 2007. "Probit: Probit Regression for Dichotomous Dependent Variables." In *Zelig: Everyone's Statistical Software*, Kosuke Imai, Gary King, and Olivia Lau. Available at http://gking.harvard.edu/zelig

International IDEA (Institute for Democracy and Electoral Assistance). 2005. *Voter Turnout: A Global Survey.* Technical Report.

Isaac, R. Mark, James M. Walker, and Arlington W. Williams. 1994. "Group Size and the Voluntary Provision of Public Goods: Experimental Evidence Utilizing Very Large Groups." *Journal of Public Economics* 54(May): 1–36.

Iyengar, Shanto. 1991. *Is Anyone Responsible? How Television Frames Political Issues.* Chicago: University of Chicago Press.

Iyengar, Shanto, and Stephen Ansolabehere. 1995. *Going Negative.* New York: The Free Press.

Jackman, Robert W. 1987. Political Institutions and Voter Turnout in the Industrial Democracies. *American Political Science Review,* 81: 405–423.

Jin, Emily, Michelle Girvan, and Mark Newman. 2001. "The Structure of Growing Social Networks." *Physical Review E* 64: 046132. Online at http://pre.aps.org

Johnston, R. J., and C. J. Pattie. 2006. *Putting Voters in Their Place: Geography and Elections in Great Britain.* Oxford: Oxford University Press.

Jones, E. E., and K. E. Davis. 1965. "From Acts to Dispositions: The Attribution Process in Person Perception." *Advances in Experimental Social Psychology* 2: 219–266.

Kahneman, Daniel. 2002. "Maps of Bounded Rationality: A Perspective on Intuitive Judgment and Choice." In *Les Prix Nobel: The Nobel Prizes 2002,* ed. T. Frangsmyr, pp. 449–489. Stockholm: Nobel Foundation.

Kahneman, Daniel, Jack Knetsch, and Richard Thaler. 1986. "Fairness as a Constraint on Profit Seeking." *American Economic Review* 76(4): 728–741.

Katosh, J. P. and M. W Traugott. 1982. "Costs and Values in the Calculus of Voting." *American Journal of Political Science* 26(2): 361–376.

Katz, Jonathan N., and Gabriel Katz. 2010. "Correcting for Survey Misreports Using Auxiliary Information with an Application to Estimating Turnout." *American Journal of Political Science* 54(3): 815–835.

Kelleher, C., and D. Lowery. 2004. "Political Participation and Metropolitan Institutional Contexts." *Urban Affairs Review* 39(6): 720–757.

Kelley, Stanley, Richard E. Ayres, and William G. Bowen. 1967. "Registration and Voting: Putting First Things First." *The American Political Science Review* 61(2): 359–379.

Kenny, Christopher B. 1992. "Political Participation and Effects from the Social Environment." *American Journal of Political Science* 36(1): 259–267.

Kerr, Norbert, and Cynthia M. Kaufman-Gilliland. 1994. "Communication, Commitment and Cooperatioin in Social Dilemmas." *Journal of Personality and Social Psychology* 66(3): 513–529.

Key, V. O. 1949. *Southern Politics in State and Nation.* New York: A. A. Knopf.

Killworth, Peter D., and H. Russell Bernard. 1978. "The Reversal Small-World Experiment." *Social Networks* 1(2): 159–192.

Killworth, Peter D., H. Russell Bernard, and Christopher McCarty. 1984. "Measuring Patterns of Acquaintanceship." *Current Anthropology* 25(4): 381–397.

Killworth, Peter D., H. Russell Bernard, Christopher McCarty, and Gene A. Shelley. 1990. "Estimating the Size of Personal Networks." *Social Networks* 12: 289–312.

Kim, Jae-on, John R. Petrocik, and Stephen N. Enokson. 1975. "Voter Turnout among the American States: Systemic and Individual Components." *American Political Science Review* 69(1): 107–123.

King, Desmond S. 2000. *Making Americans: Immigration, Race, and the Origins of the Diverse Democracy.* Cambridge, MA: Harvard University Press.

King, Desmond S., and Rogers M. Smith. 2005. "Racial Orders in American Political Development." *American Political Science Review* 99: 75–92.

Klofstad, Casey A. 2007. "Talk Leads to Recruitment." *Political Research Quarterly* 60(2): 180–191.

Klofstad, Casey A., Scott D. McClurg, and Meredith Rolfe. 2009. "Measurement of Political Discussion Networks: A Comparison of Two 'Name Generator' Procedures." *Public Opinion Quarterly* 73: 462–483.

Knack, Stephen. 1992. "Civic Norms, Social Sanctions and Voter Turnout." *Rationality and Society* 4: 135–156.

Knack, S., and J. White. 2000. "Election-Day Registration and Turnout Inequality." *Political Behavior* 22(1): 29–44.

Kovarik, J. 2008. "Belief Formation and Evolution in Public Good Games." Universidad De Alicante Mimeo.

Law, Averill M., and W. David Kelton. 1982. *Simulation Modeling and Analysis.* McGraw-Hill Series in Industrial Engineering and Management Science. New York: McGraw-Hill.

Lazarsfeld, Paul Felix, Bernard Berelson, and Hazel Gaudet. 1944. The *People's Choice: How the Voter Makes Up His Mind in a Presidential Campaign.* New York: Duell, Sloan and Pearce.

Ledyard, John. 1995. "Public Goods." In *Handbook of Experimental Economics,* eds. John Kagel and Alvin Roth, pp. 111–194. Princeton, NJ: Princeton University Press.

Leider, Stephen, M. M. Mobius, T. Rosenblat, and Q. A. Do. 2009. "Directed Altruism and Enforced Reciprocity in Social Networks." *Quarterly Journal of Economics* 124(4): 1815–1851.

2010. "What Do We Expect from Our Friends?" *Journal of the European Economic Association* 8(1): 120–138.

Leighley, J. E. 1990. "Social-Interaction and Contextual Influences on Political-Participation." *American Politics Quarterly* 18(4): 459–475.

Levi, M. 1988. *Of Rule and Revenue.* Berkeley: University of California Press.

Lichbach, Mark Irving. 2003. *Is Rational Choice Theory All of Social Science?* Ann Arbor: University of Michigan Press.

Liebrand, W. B. G. 1984. "The Effect of Social Motives, Communication and Group Sizes on Behavior in an N-Person Multi Stage Mixed Motive Game." *European Journal of Social Psychology* 14: 239–264.

Lijphart, Arend. 1997. "Unequal Participation: Democracy's Unresolved Dilemma." *The American Political Science Review* 91(1): 1–14.

López-Pintado, Dunia, and Duncan J. Watts. 2008. "Social Influence, Binary Decisions and Collective Dynamics." *Rationality and Society* 20: 399–443.

Lupia, Arthur. 2006. "How Elitism Undermines the Study of Voter Competence." *Critical Review* 18: 217.

Lynch, M. 2001. "Noise and Politics." *Social Studies of Science* 31: 446–454.

Lynn, M., and A. Grassman. 1990. "Restaurant Tipping: An Examination of Three 'Rational' Explanations." *Journal of Economic Psychology* 11(2): 169–181.

Maass, Anne, Russell D. Clark III, and Gerald Haberkorn. 1982. "The Effects of Differential Ascribed Category Membership and Norms on Minority Influence." *European Journal of Social Psychology* 12: 89–104.

Macy, Michael W. 1991. "Chains of Cooperation: Threshold Effects in Collective Action." *American Sociological Review* 56(6): 730–747.

Macy, Michael W., and Andreas Flache. 2002. "Learning Dynamics in Social Dilemmas." *Proceedings of the National Academy of Sciences of the United States of America* 99 (Suppl 3): 7229–7236.

Macy, Michael W., and John Skvoretz. 1998. "The Evolution of Trust and Cooperation between Strangers: A Computational Model." *American Sociological Review* 63(5): 638–660.

Manzo, Gianluca. 2009. *La Spirale des Inégalités: Choix Scolaires en France et en Italie au XXe Siècle*. Paris: Presses de l'Université Paris-Sorbonne.

Margolis, Howard. 1982. *Selfishness, Altruism, and Rationality*. Cambridge: Cambridge University Press.

Markus, H. R., and S. Kitayama. 1991. "Culture and the Self: Implications for Cognition, Emotion, and Motivation." *Psychological Review* 98: 224–253.

Marsden, Peter V. 1987. "Core Discussion Networks of Americans." *American Socioligical Review* 52: 122–131.

Marsden, Peter V., and Karen E. Campbell. 1984. "Measuring Tie Strength." *Social Forces* 63(2): 482–501.

Martin, Robin, and Miles Hewstone. 2003. "Majority Versus Minority Influence: When, Not Whether, Source Status Instigates Heuristic Or Systematic Processing." *European Journal of Social Psychology* 33: 313–330.

Marwell, Gerald, and Ruth E. Ames. 1979. "Experiments on the Provision of Public Goods I: Resources, Interest, Group Size and the Free Rider Problem." *American Journal of Sociology* 84: 1335–1360.

1980. "Experiments on the Provision of Public Goods II: Provision Points, Stakes, Experience, and the Free-Rider Problem." *American Journal of Sociology* 85(4): 926–937.

1981. "Economists Free Ride, Does Anyone Else? Experiments on the Provision of Public Goods, IV." *Journal of Public Economics* 15(3): 295.

Mauss, Marcel. 1954. *The Gift: Forms and Functions of Exchange in Archaic Societies*. Glencoe, IL: Free Press.

McCarty, Christopher. 2002. "Measuring Structure in Personal Networks." *Journal of Social Structure* 3(1): 1–11.

McCarty, Christopher, H. R. Bernard, P. D. Killworth, G. A. Shelley, and E. C. Johnsen. 1997. "Eliciting Representative Samples of Personal Networks." *Social Networks* 19(4): 303–323.

McClurg, Scott D. 2003. "Social Networks and Political Participation: The Role of Social Interaction in Explaining Political Participation." *Political Research Quarterly* 56(4): 449–464.

2004. "Indirect Mobilization – the Social Consequences of Party Contacts in an Election Campaign." *American Politics Research* 32(4): 406–443.

McDonald, Michael P. 2002. *US State Turnout Rates for Eligible Voters, 1980–2000.* Interunity Consortium for Political and Social Research (ICPSR) Study 1248.

McDonald, Michael P., and Samuel L. Popkin. 2001. "The Myth of the Vanishing Voter." *American Political Science Review* 95(4): 963–974.

McGraw, A. P., and P. E. Tetlock. 2005. "Taboo Trade-Offs, Relational Framing, and the Acceptability of Exchanges." *Journal of Consumer Psychology* 15: 2–15.

McPherson, M., L. Smith-Lovin, and M. E. Brashears. 2006. "Social Isolation in America: Changes in Core Discussion Networks Over Two Decades." *American Sociological Review* 71: 353–375.

McPherson, M., L. Smith-Lovin, and J. M. Cook. 2001. "Birds of a Feather: Homophily in Social Networks." *Annual Review of Sociology* 27: 415–444.

Mendelberg, Tali, and J. Oleske. 2000. "Race and Public Deliberation." *Political Communication* 17: 169–191.

Merriam, Charles E., and Harold F. Gosnell. 1924. *Non-Voting: Causes and Methods of Control.* Chicago: The University of Chicago Press.

Messick, D. M. 1993. "Equality as a Decision Heuristic." In *Psychological Perspectives on Justice: Theory and Applications*, eds. Barbara A. Mellers and Jonathan Baron, pp. 11–31. Cambridge: Cambridge University Press.

Milgram, Stanley. 1967. "The Small World Problem." *Psychology Today* 1: 61–67.

Miller, J. H. and S. E Page. 2004. "The Standing Ovation Problem." *Complexity* 9(5): 8–16.

Miller, Warren E. 1992. "The Puzzle Transformed: Explaining Declining Turnout." *Political Behavior* 14(1): 1–43.

Mintrom, Michael. 1997. "Policy Entrepreneurs and the Diffusion of Innovation." *American Journal of Political Science* 41: 738–770.

Mischel, W. 1968. *Personality and Assessment.* New York: Wiley.

Monroe, Kristen Renwick. 1994. "A Fat Lady in a Corset: Altruism and Social Theory." *American Journal of Political Science* 38(4): 861–893.

Moreira, André A., Daniel Diermeier, Abhishek Mathur, and Luis A. N. Amaral. 2004. "Efficient System-Wide Coordination in Noisy Environments Using Heuristic Methods." *Proceedings of the National Academy of Sciences* 101(33): 12085–12090.

Morton, Rebecca. 1991. "Groups in Rational Turnout Models." *American Journal of Political Science* 35(3): 758.

Moscovici, S., and B. Personnaz. 1980. "Studies in Social Influence: Minority Influence and Conversion Behavior in a Perceptual Task." *Journal of Experimental Social Psychology* 16: 270–282.

Moscovici, S., and M. Zavalloni. 1969. "The Group as a Polarizer of Attitudes." *Journal of Personality and Social Psychology* 12: 125–135.

Moskowitz, Gordon B., P. M. Gollwitze, W. Wasel, and B. Schall. 1999. "Preconscious Control of Stereotype Activation Through Chronic Egalitarian Goals." *Journal of Personality and Social Psychology* 77(1): 167–184.

Mugny, G., and S. Papastamou. 1982. The *Power of Minorities.* London: Academic Press.

Murnighan, J. Keith, and Michael Saxon. 1998. "Ultimatum Bargaining by Children and Adults." *Journal of Economic Psychology* 19: 415–455.

Neugebauer, T., J. Perote, U. Schmidt, and M. Loos. 2009. "Selfish-Biased Conditional Cooperation: On the Decline of Contributions in Repeated Public Goods Experiments." *Journal of Economic Psychology* 30(1): 52–60.

Newman, M. E. J. 2001. "The Structure of Scientific Collaboration Networks." *Proceedings of the National Academy of Sciences of the United States of America* 98(2): 404–409.

Nicholson, Stephen P., and Ross A. Miller. 1997. "Prior Beliefs and Voter Turnout in the 1986 and 1988 Congressional Elections." *Political Research Quarterly* 50(1): 199–213.

Nickerson, David W. 2008. "Is Voting Contagious? Evidence from Two Field Experiments." *American Political Science Review* 102: 49–57.

Nie, Norman H., Jane Junn, and Kenneth Stehlik-Barry. 1996. *Education and Democratic Citizenship in America.* Chicago: University of Chicago Press.

Niemi, Richard G. 1976. "Costs of Voting and Nonvoting." *Public Choice* 27(1): 115–119.

Nisbett, R., and T. Wilson. 1977. "Telling More Than We Can Know: Verbal Reports on Mental Processes." *Psychological Review* 84: 231–259.

Niven, D. 2004. "The Mobilization Solution? Face-to-Face Contact and Voter Turnout in a Municipal Election." *Journal of Politics* 66(3): 868–884.

Offerman, Theo, Joep Sonnemans, and Arthur Schram. 1996. "Value Orientations, Expectations and Voluntary Contributions in Public Goods." *The Economic Journal* 106(437): 817–845.

——— 2001. "Expectation Formation in Step-Level Public Good Games." *Economic Inquiry* 39(2): 250–269.

Oliner, Pearl, and Samual Oliner. 1988. The *Altruistic Personality: Rescuers of Jews in Nazi Europe.* New York: The Free Press.

Oliver, J. Eric. 2000. "City Size and Civic Involvement in Metropolitan America." *American Political Science Review* 94(2): 361–373.

Oliver, Pamela. 1980. "Rewards and Punishments as Selective Incentives for Collective Action: Theoretical Investigations." *American Journal of Sociology* 85(6): 1356–1375.

Oliver, Pamela E., and Gerald Marwell. 1988. "The Paradox of Group Size in Collective Action: A Theory of the Critical Mass. II." *American Sociological Review* 53(1): 1–8.

Olson, Mancur. 1965. The *Logic of Collective Action.* Cambridge, MA: Harvard University Press.

Ostrom, Elinor, James Walker, and Roy Gardner. 1992. "Covenants with and without a Sword." *American Political Science Review* 86: 404–417.

Padgett, John F., and Christopher K. Ansell. 1993. "Robust Action and the Rise of the Medici, 1400–1434." *American Journal of Sociology* 98(6): 1259–1319.

Palfrey, T., and H. Rosenthal. 1985. "Voter Participation and Strategic Uncertainty." *American Political Science Review* 79(1): 62–78.

Patterson, Samuel C., and Gregory A. Caldeira. 1983. "Getting Out the Vote: Participation in Gubernatorial Elections." *American Political Science Review* 77(3): 675–689.

Pattie, Charles, and Ron Johnston. 1998. "Voter Turnout at the British General Election of 1992: Rational Choice, Social Standing or Political Efficacy?" *European Journal of Political Research* 33: 263–283.

Pillutla, Madan, and J. Keith Murnighan. 1995. "Being Fair or Appearing Fair: Strategic Behavior in Ultimatum Bargaining." *Academy of Management Journal* 38(5): 1408–1426.

Plant, E. Ashby, and Patricia G. Devine. 1998. "Internal and External Motivation to Respond Without Prejudice." *Journal of Personality and Social Psychology* 75: 811–832.

Podolny, Joel M. 2001. "Networks as the Pipes and Prisms of the Market." *The American Journal of Sociology* 107(1): 33–60.

Popper, Karl R. 1968. The *Logic of Scientific Discovery*. 2nd ed. New York: Harper & Row.

Posner, E. A. 1998. "Symbols, Signals, and Social Norms in Politics and the Law." *Journal of Legal Studies* 27(2): 765–798.

Powell, G. Bingham, Jr. 1986. "American Voter Turnout in Comparative Perspective." *American Political Science Review* 80(1): 17–43.

Powell, G. Bingham, Jr., and Guy D. Whitten. 1993. "A Cross-National Analysis of Economic Voting: Taking Account of the Political Context." *American Journal of Political Science* 37(2): 391–414.

Putnam, Robert D. 2000. *Bowling Alone: The Collapse and Revival of American Community*. New York: Simon and Schuster.

Putnam, Robert D., Robert Leonardi, and Raffaella Nanetti. 1993. *Making Democracy Work: Civic Traditions in Modern Italy*. Princeton, NJ: Princeton University Press.

Rabin, Matthew. 1993. "Incorporating Fairness into Game Theory." *American Economic Review* 83(5): 1281–1302.

Randolph, Elizabeth S. 1992. *An African American Album: The Black Experience in Charlotte and Mecklenburg County*. Charlotte, NC: Public Library of Charlotte and Mecklenburg County.

Rapoport, Anatol. 1979. "A Probabilistic Approach to Networks." *Social Networks* 2: 1–18.

Reno, R. R., R. B. Cialdini and C. A. Kallgren. 1993. "The Transsituational Influence of Social Norms." *Journal of Personality and Social Psychology* 64: 104–112.

Reuben, Ernesto, and Frans Van Winden. 2006. "Reciprocity and Emotions When Reciprocators Know Each Other." Cesifo Working Paper Series No. 1674, Tinbergen Institute Discussion Paper No. TI 04–098/1, Social Science Research Network Elibrary.

Riker, William H., and Peter C. Ordeshook. 1968. "A Theory of the Calculus of Voting." *American Political Science Review* 62(1): 25–42.

Rogers, Everett M. 2003. *Diffusion of Innovations*. 5th ed. New York: Free Press.

Rolfe, Meredith. 2004. Social Networks and Simulations. In *Proceedings of the Agent 2004, Conference on Social Dynamics: Interaction, Reflexivity and Emergence*, University of Chicago and Argonne National Laboratory, Chicago, IL.

2009. "Conditional Choice." In *Oxford Handbook of Analytical Sociology*, eds. Peter Bearman and Peter Hedström, pp. 419–466. Oxford: Oxford University Press.

2010. "Sample Survey Measurement of Social Networks in Theory and in Practice." Paper presented at the American Political Science Association Annual Meeting, Washington, DC, September.

Rosenstone, Steven, and Mark Hansen. 1993. *Mobilization, Participation and Democracy in America*. New York: Macmillan Publishing Company.

Ross, Lee, D. Greene, and P. House. 1977. "The 'False Consensus Effect': An Egocentric Bias in Social Perception and Attribution Processes." *Journal of Experimental Social Psychology* 13: 279–301.

Roth, Alvin. 1995. "Bargaining Experiments." In *Handbook of Experimental Economics*, eds. John Kagel and Alvin Roth, pp. 854–863. Princeton, NJ: Princeton University Press.

Roth, Alvin, V. Prasnikar, M. Okunofujiwara, and S. Zamir. 1991. "Bargaining and Market Behavior in Jerusalem, Ljubljana, Pittsburgh, and Tokyo – An Experimental Study." *American Economic Review* 81(5): 1068–1095.

Rozin, P., L. Lowery, S. Imada, and J. Haidt. 1999. "The CAD Triad Hypothesis: A Mapping between Three Moral Emotions (Contempt, Anger, Disgust) and Three Moral Codes (Community, Autonomy, Divinity)." *Journal of Personality and Social Psychology* 76: 574–586.

Sanders, Elizabeth. 1980. "On the Costs, Utilities, and Simple Joys of Voting." *Journal of Politics* 42(3): 854–863.

Sanders, Lynn M. 1997. "Against Deliberation." *Political Theory* 25: 347–376.

Sanfey, Alan G., James K. Rilling, Jessica A. Aronson, Leigh E. Nystrom, and Jonathan D. Cohen. 2003. "The Neural Basis of Economic Decision-Making in the Ultimatum Game." *Science* 300: 1755–1758.

Schelling, Thomas C. 1973. "Hockey Helmets, Concealed Weapons, and Daylight Saving: A Study of Binary Choices with Externalities." *Journal of Conflict Resolution* 17(3): 381–428.

Scholz, J. T. and M. Lubell. 1998a. "Adaptive Political Attitudes: Duty, Trust, and Fear as Monitors of Tax Policy." *American Journal of Political Science* 42(3): 903–920.

1998b. "Trust and Taxpaying: Testing the Heuristic Approach to Collective Action." *American Journal of Political Science* 42(2): 398–417.

Scholz, J. T., and N. Pinney. 1995. "Duty, Fear, and Tax Compliance: The Heuristic Basis of Citizenship Behavior." *American Journal of Political Science* 39(2): 490–512.

Schotter, A., A. Weiss, and I. Zapater. 1996. "Fairness and Survival in Ultimatum and Dictatorship Games." *Journal of Economic Behavior and Organization* 31: 37–56.

Schram, Arthur, and Frans Van Winden. 1991. "Free Riding and the Production and Consumption of Social Pressure." *Journal of Economic Psychology* 12: 575–620.

Schreiber, Darren. 2002. "Validating Agent-Based Models: From Metaphysics to Applications." Working paper presented at the Midwest Political Science Association.

Schudson, M. 1999. The *Good Citizen*. New York: Martin Kessler Books.

Schuessler, Alexander A. 2000. *A Logic of Expressive Choice*. Princeton, NJ: Princeton University Press.

Schuman, Howard, Charlotte Steeh, Lawrence Bobo, and Maria Krysan. 1997. *Racial Attitudes in America: Trends and Interpretations*. Cambridge, MA: Harvard University Press.

Sen, Amartya. 1977. "Rational Fools: A Critique of the Behavioral Foundations of Economic Theory." *Philosophy and Public Affairs* 6(4): 317–344.

Settle, Russel F., and Buron A. Abrams. 1976. "The Determinants of Voter Participation: A More General Model. *Public Choice* 27: 81–89.

Sigelman, Lee. 1982. "The Nonvoting Voter in Voting Research." *American Journal of Political Science* 26(1): 47–56

Sigelman, Lee, and William D. Berry. 1982. "Cost and the Calculus of Voting." *Political Behavior* 4(4): 419–428.

Sigelman, Lee, and Malcolm E. Jewell. 1986. "From Core to Periphery: A Note on the Imagery of Concentric Electorates." *Journal of Politics* 48(2): 440–449.

Sigelman, Lee, Philip W. Roeder, Malcolm E. Jewell, and Michael A. Baer. 1985. "Voting and Nonvoting: A Multi-Election Perspective." *American Journal of Political Science* 29(4): 749–765.

Silver, Brian D., Paul R. Abramson, and Barbara A. Anderson. 1986. "Presence of Others and Overreporting Voting in American National Elections." *Public Opinion Quarterly* 50: 228–239.

Silver, Brian D., Barbara A. Anderson, and Paul R. Abramson. 1986. "Who Overreports Voting?" *American Political Science Review* 80: 613–624.

Simon, Herbert A. 1955. "A Behavioral Model of Rational Choice." *Quarterly Journal of Economics* 69: 99–118.

Sinclair, Betsy, Margaret McConnell, Melissa Michelson, and Lisa Garcia Bedolla. 2007. "Strangers Vs. Neighbors: The Efficacy of Grassroots Voter Mobilization." Paper Presented At the American Political Science Association Annual Meeting, Chicago, IL, September.

Skvoretz, John. 1985. "Random and Biased Networks: Simulations and Approximations." *Social Networks* 7: 225–261.

1990. "Biased Net Theory: Simulations, Approximations and Observations." *Social Networks* 12: 217–238.

2002. "Complexity Theory and Models for Social Networks." *Complexity* 8: 47–55.

Skvoretz, John, T. J. Fararo, and F. Agneessens. 2004. "Advances in Biased Net Theory: Definitions, Derivations, and Estimations." *Social Networks* 26: 113–139.

Smith, Rogers M. 1993. "Beyond Tocqueville, Myrdal, and Hartz: The Multiple Traditions in America." *American Political Science Review* 87: 549–566.

Snijders, Tom A. B. 2002. "Markov Chain Monte Carlo Estimation of Exponential Random Graph Models." *Journal of Social Structure* 3: 1–40.

Solnick, S. J. 2001. "Gender Differences in the Ultimatum Game." *Economic Inquiry* 39: 189–200.

Sondheimer, R. M., and D. P. Green. 2010. "Using Experiments to Estimate the Effects of Education on Voter Turnout." *American Journal of Political Science* 54(1): 174–189.

Squire, Peverill, Raymond E. Wolfinger, and David P. Glass. 1987. "Residential Mobility and Voter Turnout." *American Political Science Review* 81(1): 45–66.

Srull, T. K., and R. S. Wyer, Jr. 1989. "Person Memory and Judgment." *Psychological Review* 96: 58–83.

Stenner, Karen. 2005. The *Authoritarian Dynamic*. Cambridge: Cambridge University Press.

Stephens, Stephen V. 1975. "The Paradox of Not Voting: Comment." *American Political Science Review* 69(3): 914–915.

Stouffer, S. A. 1955. *Communism, Conformity, and Civil Liberties: A Cross-Section of the Nation Speaks Its Mind*. Garden City, NY: Doubleday.

Stouten, J., D. De Cremer, and E. Van Dijk. 2006. "Violating Equality in Social Dilemmas: Emotional and Retributive Reactions as a Function of Trust, Attribution, and Honesty." *Personality and Social Psychology Bulletin* 32: 894.

Straits, Bruce C. 1996. "Ego-Net Diversity: Same- and Cross-Sex Coworker Ties." *Social Networks* 18(1): 29–45.

Sugden, Robert. 1984. "Reciprocity: The Supply of Public Goods through Voluntary Contributions." *The Economic Journal* 94(376): 772–787.

Tabibnia, Golnaz, and Matthew D. Lieberman. 2007. "Fairness and Cooperation Are Rewarding: Evidence from Social Cognitive Neuroscience." *Annals of the New York Academy of Sciences* 1118: 90–101.

Tajfel, H., and J. C. Turner. 1979. "An Integrative Theory of Intergroup Conflict." In *The Social Psychology of Intergroup Relations*, eds. W. G. Austin and S. Worchel. Monterey, CA: Brooks-Cole.

Tate, Katherine. 1991. "Black Political Participation in the 1984 and 1988 Presidential Elections." *American Political Science Review* 85(4): 1159–1176.

Taylor, Michael. 1987. The *Possibility of Cooperation*. New York: Cambridge University Press.

Tenbrunsel, A. E., and D. M. Messick. 1999. "Sanctioning Systems, Decision Frames, and Cooperation." *Administrative Science Quarterly* 44(4): 684–707.

Tenn, Steven. 2007. "The Effect of Education on Voter Turnout." *Political Analysis* 15(4): 446–464.

Timpone, Richard J. 1998. "Structure, Behavior, and Voter Turnout in the United States." *American Political Science Review* 92(1): 145–158.

Tollison, R. D., and T. D. Willett. 1973. "Some Simple Economics of Voting and Not Voting." *Public Choice* 16: 59–71.

Traugott, Michael W., and John P. Katosh. 1979. "Response Validity in Surveys of Voting Behavior." *Public Opinion Quarterly* 43(3): 359–377.

Travers, Jeffrey, and Stanley Milgram. 1969. "An Experimental Study of the Small World Problem." *Sociometry* 32(4): 425–443.

Tullock, Gordon. 1967. *Toward a Mathematics of Politics*. Ann Arbor: University of Michigan Press.

1975. "The Paradox of Not Voting for Oneself." *American Political Science Review* 69(3): 919.

Uhlaner, Carol. 1989. "Relational Goods and Participation: Incorporating Sociability into a Theory of Rational Action." *Public Choice* 62: 253–285.

Vanberg, C. 2008. "Why Do People Keep Their Promises? An Experimental Test of Two Explanations." *Econometrica* 76(6): 1467–1480.

Van Dijk, E. and H. Wilke. 1994. "Asymmetry of Wealth and Public Good Provision." *Social Psychology Quarterly* 57: 352–359.

Van 't Wout, Mascha, René Kahn, Alan Sanfey, and André Aleman. 2006. "Affective State and Decision-Making in the Ultimatum Game." *Experimental Brain Research* 169: 564–568.

Van Winden, Frans. 2007. "Affect and Fairness in Economics." *Social Justice Research* 20: 35–52.

Verba, Sidney, and Norman H. Nie. 1972. *Participation in America*. New York: Harper and Row.

Verba, Sidney, Kay Schlozman, and Henry Brady. 1995. *Civic Participation*. Cambridge, MA: Harvard University Press.

Walsh, Katherine Cramer. 2004. *Talking About Politics: Informal Groups and Social Identity in American Life*. Chicago: University of Chicago Press.

Walter, Henrik, Birgit Abler, Angela Ciaramidaro, and Susanne Erk. 2005. "Motivating Forces of Human Actions: Neuroimaging Reward and Social Interaction." *Brain Research Bulletin* 67: 368–381.

Wasserman, Stanley, and Katherine Faust. 1994. *Social Network Analysis*. New York: Cambridge University Press.

Watts, Duncan J. 2003. *Six Degrees: The Science of a Connected Age*. New York: Norton.

Watts, Duncan J., and Peter S. Dodds. 2009. "Threshold Models of Social Influence." In *Oxford Handbook of Analytical Sociology*, eds. Peter Bearman and Peter Hedström. Oxford: Oxford University Press.

Watts, Duncan J., and Steven H. Strogatz. 1998. "Collective Dynamics of Small World Networks." *Nature* 393.

Wedeen, Lisa. 2002. "Conceptualizing Culture: Possibilities for Political Science." *American Political Science Review* 96: 16.

Wellman, Barry. 1979. "The Community Question: The Intimate Networks of East Yorkers." *American Journal of Sociology* 84(5): 1201–1231.

White, Harrison C. 1992. *Identity and Control: A Structural Theory of Social Action*. Princeton, NJ: Princeton University Press.

Willmott, Peter, and Michael Young. 1967. *Family and Class in a London Suburb*. London: New English Library.

Wolfinger, Raymond E., and Steven J. Rosenstone. 1980. *Who Votes?* New Haven, CT: Yale University Press.

Wood, Wendy. 2000. "Attitude Change: Persuasion and Social Influence." *Annual Review of Psychology* 50: 539–570.

Young, H. Peyton. 2009. "Innovation Diffusion in Heterogeneous Populations: Contagion, Social Influence, and Social Learning." *The American Economic Review* 99: 1899–1924.

Zajonc, R. B. 1980. "Feeling and Thinking – Preferences Need No Inferences." *American Psychologist* 35(2): 151–175.

Zheng, Tian, Matthew J. Salganik, and Andrew Gelman. 2006. "How Many People Do You Know in Prison? Using Overdispersion in Count Data to Estimate Social Structure in Networks." *Journal of the American Statistical Association* 101: 15.

Zuckerman, Alan. 2005. "Introduction." In *Social Logic of Politics*, ed. Alan Zuckerman. Philadelphia: Temple University Press.

Newspaper Articles

Dinan, J. 2004, November 1. "Why Every American's Voice Should Be Heard" [Letter to the Editor]. *New York Times*, p. A24.

Evans, B. 2004, October 27. "Failed Foreign and Domestic Policies [Letter to the Editor]. Chicago Daily Herald, p. 17 [late edition].

Krugman, Paul. 2004, November 2. "Faith in America." *New York Times*, p. A27.

Hart, Deanna. 2004, November 2. "Worth the Wait and Worth Improvement" [Letter to the Editor]. *Atlanta Journal-Constitution*, p. A15.

"Make Your Voice Heard," editorial. 2004, November 2. *Atlanta Journal-Constitution*, p. A14.

"Take Advantage of a Good Day Tuesday," editorial. 2004, November 1. *Chicago Daily Herald*, p. 14.

Tierney, John. 2004, October 24. "A Secret Weapon for Bush?" *New York Times*, p. N22.

Stastny, M. 2004, October 31. "Each of Us Has an Obligation to Vote" [Letter to the Editor]. Chicago *Daily Herald*, p. 19.

Wooten, Jim. 2004, October 26. "Voter Fraud Ought to Be Atop Hit List." *Atlanta Journal-Constitution*, p. A17.

"Vote, No Matter What," editorial. 2004, November 2. *New York Times*, p. A26.

"Voting Rights for Ex-Felons," editorial. 2004, October 27, p. A24.

Index

acquaintance networks, 88–90
African Americans, views on importance of
    voting, 55
age, and political activity, 139–140
alters, 16
Altgeld, John P., 59
altruism, as unconditional
    decision-making, 31
American National Election Study
    (ANES), 9, 48, 54
Ames, Ruth E., 66, 72
anonymous dictator games, 74
Asch, Solomon E., 23, 25
Atlanta Journal-Constitution, 47, 48, 50, 60
attractor states, 37
authority relationships, 45
automatic voter registration, 11

bargaining games
    standard example, 65
Bearman, Peter, 46
behavioral economics, 6
biased random network simulation, 86
Black Female indicator, 136–137
Black Southerner indicator, 136–137
Blais, André, 12
bounded rationality, 3, 4
Brady, Henry, 98, 137–138, 147
Burks, S., 76
business acumen, in social dilemmas, 66

campaigns
    choice of target groups, 101

conditional decision-making,
    100–101
expenditures and turnout, 13
and mobilization, 15
salience, 108–109
    as network size, 109–111
strategic mobilization perspective,
    99–100
Campbell, Karen E., 91
candidate presence, 171
candidate residence, 171, 176
canvassing, and mobilization, 14–16
Carpenter, Jeffrey, 76
Charlotte, North Carolina, municipal
    elections, 110
Cialdini, Robert, 21–22, 24
citizen competence, and voting,
    60–61
citizenship, in social dilemmas, 65–67
City Size variable, 136–137
civic duty
    promotion in media, 61
civic voluntarism model, 140
Civic Voluntarism study
    (1989–1990), 137
closeness of election outcome,
    and turnout, 13
cobweb method, 80
colored squares experiment, 24
Columbia School, 16
commodification of labor, 45
communal relationships, 45
compulsory voting, 11

conditional choice, 4–5
  applicability to voting, 180
  generalizability to other situations,
      180–181
  mathematical approach, 181
  overview, 17–18, 22
  and perception of reality, 63
  and social context, 17
  sources of individual variation, 180
conditional cooperation, 64
  in local social networks, 84–85
  simulations, 191–193
    validation of the programmed model,
      193–194
conditional decision-making, 5–7
  evidence for, 22–25
  involving complex heuristics, 26
  involving political attitudes, 26–27
  mathematical models, 28
    constructing, 39–41, 78–79
    dynamics, 36–39
    reasonableness checks, 82
    robustness checks, 82–84
  overview, 27–28
  social dilemmas, 6
  when others not present, 25–26
conditional decision rules, 28, 36
  basic rules, 5–6
  composite weighted rule, 34–35
  terminology, 35–36
contagion dynamics, 79–82,
contextual explanations of voter turnout,
      10–11
core personal networks, 90
cost-benefit logic
  empirical problems with, 9–10
  inadequacies of, 2, 7–9
  theoretical problems with, 7–9, 107–108
Cox, Gary W., 14, 99, 120, 137
critical mass level of cooperation, 33
Current Population Study series, 12

Daily Herald (Chicago), 47, 50, 51, 57, 61
descriptive norms, 24
dictator bargaining games, 65
diffusion dynamics, 79–82
direct mobilization, individual turnout,
      118–121
distribution of decision rules, 6, 38–39
doormen, and tenants, 46
Downs, Anthony, *An Economic Theory of
      Democracy* (1957), 8, 62

D-term, 8, 10
dynamics, in conditional decision models,
      36–39

Economic Theory of Democracy, An
      (Downs 1957), 8, 62
education
  and distribution of decision rules,
      117–118
  and high-salience elections, 125–126
  and political interest, 114–117
    comparison of social cooperation and
      civic voluntarism, 141
  and propensity to vote, 2
    comparison of social cooperation and
      civic voluntarism, 2, 10, 182
    linkage mechanism, 2, 10, 182
  as proxy for social network status, 17–18
  and unconditional cooperation,
      114–115
  data sources, 129–130
  fall in turnout with rise in college
      degrees, 183–184, 187–188
  homophily in U.S. society, 132–134
  social theory model implications,
      126–129
  study results, 177
educational social worlds, 134–135
egos, 16
election closeness, coding, 160
election day holidays, 101–102
electoral institutions, 12–13
Elster, Jon, 76
Engelmann, Dirk, 75
equality-based interactions, 45
equity relationships, 45

fairness
  appearance of, 69
  beliefs of economists, 67
  social dilemmas, 66
first movers, 19
  social theory of voter turnout, 102–103
Fischbacher, Urs, 75

Geertz, Clifford, 42
gender, as predictor of turnout
      probability, 138
general friendship networks, 90
General Social Survey (GSS), 48, 50, 116,
      130, 137
  methodological notes, 199–200

Gerber, Alan S., 27, 178, 188
Girvan, Michelle, 86
Gosnell, Harold Foote, *Non-Voting* (1924), 2, 7–8, 10, 54
Gould, Roger. V., 33
Granovetter, Mark S., 29, 84, 181, 189, 194
graphical method, 80
Green, Donald P., 178, 188
grid-based network simulations, 86
group exchanges, 67

Hansen, Mark, 15, 99, 120, 178
heuristics, 3, 5. *See also* rule of thumb
Huckfeldt, Robert, 126

identity content, 44
income, and turnout, 177
indirect mobilization, 14–15
initial activity, 37, 38–39
initial propensity to vote, and mobilization, 15
institutions
  as context, 11
  costs, 11–12

Jin, Emily, 86, 186, 191, 195–196
JinGir network construction method, 195–196
Junn, Jane, 17–18

Lazarsfeld, Paul Felix, 10
Ledyard, John, 70
Lee, Barrett A., 91
line length experiments, 22–24
litter collecting, 31–33
littering, 24
local social networks
  conditional cooperation in, 84–85
  simulating turnout on, 92–96
  simulation of, 85–88
  types of friendship ties, 88
Low Education World indicator, 134–136, 146

Macy, Michael W., 86
Marital Status variable, 140
Marwell, Gerald, 66, 72, 96
McDonald, Michael P., 158
mean-matching conditional decision rule, 31–33
  social dilemma studies, 72–73

median-matching conditional decision rule 33–34
  social dilemma studies, 73
Merriam, Charles Edward, *Non-Voting* (1924), 2, 7–8, 10, 54
Messick, D. M., 66
microfoundation for social cognition, 12, 180
minimax regret decision-making, 9
mobilization
  and canvassing, 14–16
  by strategic politicians, 14
  data sources, 159–162
motivational stories, discontinuity with evidence, 23, 25
motivations, and social theory of turnout, 7

name generators, 88
network centrality, 87
network position, 87
network size, 38–39, 86
networks, survey data available, 87
New York Times, 47, 50, 58–59, 62
Newman, Mark, 86
Nie, Norman H., 17–18
Non-Voting (Merriam and Gosnell), 2, 7–8, 10, 54

O'Connor, Justice, 60
Occupational Prestige variable, 146, 147
Oliver, Pamela, 96
Olson, Mancur, 96
Ordeshook, Peter C., 8
outcome state, 37

paradox of voter turnout, 8
  and conditional choice, 3
  partisanship, 9
  social theory of turnout, 178, 184–185
Parental Education variable, 140, 147–148
Partisan Strength variable, 140
partisanship, attempts to resolve paradox of voter turnout, 9
party mobilization, 13
personal networks
  data collection, 88
  degree, 86
    empirical estimates, 91–92
  density, 86–87
    empirical estimates, 91–92
  types, 91
Political Discussion frequency variable, 140

political interest
    as D-term, 10
    distribution in population, 114–117
Popkin, Samuel L., 158
PR (proportional representation), 12–13
presidential elections, closeness of election
        outcome, 13
previous election turnout, and turnout
        decision, 15
public goods games 24–25
    standard example, 65

quality of contact, and mobilization,
        15–16

Rabin, Matthew, 69
racial segregation, as conditional
        responsiveness, 29
real-world social networks, simulation, 86
Rehnquist, Justice, 60
relationships, social meanings, 44–45
religious attendance, as predictor of
        political activity, 138–139
Religious Liberalism indicator, 136–137
repeated public goods games, 74
resistance to influence, 38–39
resource-based theory of voter turnout,
        98–99
reverse-small world experiments, 88
Riker, William H., 8
Rogers, Todd, 27
Rosenbluth, Frances McCall, 120, 137
Rosenstone, Steven, 15, 99, 120, 178
rules of thumb, 5
rural location, and voter turnout, 10

Sanders, Elizabeth, 10
scale-free networks, 89
Schelling, Thomas C., 29, 181
Schlozman, Kay, 98, 137–138, 147
Schudson, M., 47, 49, 59–60
self-reports, value of, 25
situational parameter, 43
small-world experiments, 88
snowball samples, 90
social cleavages, 38–39
social context tradition, 16–18
social dilemmas
    citizenship, 65–67
    communality, 69
    conditional decisions, 6
    distribution of decision rules, 69–70
        costs, 75–77

experimental manipulations, 73–75
    self-reports, 72–73
equality, 67–68
similarity to voting, 66–67, 77
social identity, 52, 66, 67
social influence models, 126
Social Isolation variable, 136, 146
social location, 38–39
social meaning, as people and
        relationships, 43–46
social networks
    context, 122–123
    shape, 17
    size, 130
social pressure to vote, 7
social roles, 67
social situations, 29–30, 36, 43
under social theory of voter turnout
    campaigns, 100–101
    *comparison with civic resources
        perspective for low salience
        elections,* 151
    campaign use of social ties, 162
    data sources, 156
        mobilization, 159–162
        socioeconomic status, 157
        turnout rates, 157–159
        *activity correlation to salience and
            funds,* 162
        campaign support, 163
        fundraising, 162–163
        previous candidates, 164
        reaching voters, 163–164
    level of turnout, 155–156
    rationale for low turnout, 152–153
    who will turnout, 153–155
comparison with civic voluntarism, 141
    education and political interest, 141
    education and turnout, 141–144
    multivariate analysis, 144–148
cross-national turnout variation,
        101–106
    education, 131–136, 148–150
    first movers, 102–103
    individual variation in turnout, 113
        direct mobilization, 118–121
        indirect mobilization, 121–124
        individual tendencies to use decision
            rules, 113–118
    intranational turnout variation,
        106–109
    likelihood of political mobilization,
        136–137

low salience elections, 151
  turnout patterns, 152–156
overview, 98
salience and costs, 111–113
salience as network size, 109–111
variables utilized, 137–140
social theory of voter turnout, 3–4
  calibration using empirical data,
    181–182
  comparison with civic resources
      perspective for low salience
      elections
    campaign use of institutional ties,
      164–165
      African American community,
        165–168
      racial variations, 165
    campaign use of social ties
      neighbors, 164
    precinct level analysis, 169–176
  comparison with civic voluntarism
    education and turnout, 182
  implications, 185–189
  justification by empirical performance,
    182–183
  making sense of existing research,
    183–185
  overview, 178–179
  use of conditional choice, 179–182
social worlds indicator, 124
standing ovation, as conditional
    responsiveness, 28–30
Stehlik-Barry, Kenneth, 17–18
strategic mobilization perspective, on
    campaigns, 99–100
strategic politicians, mobilization
    by, 14
street musician experiment, 21–22
Strogatz, Steven H., 186

taboo tradeoffs, 45
Tenbrunsel, A. E., 66
Thies, Michael F., 120, 137
threshold dynamics, 80
Tit-for-Tat strategy, 33
trajectory of changes, 37
turnout decision
  as conditional response to decisions
    of social network, 4
  model, 96–97

U.S. Presidential elections, social theory
    of voter turnout simulations,
    102–103
unconditional actors, 5
unconditional decision-making rule, 31
  experimental isolation of, 74–75
  social dilemma studies, 72
unfairness, punishment of, 67

Van Dijk, E., 67–68
Verba, Sidney, 98, 114, 137–138, 147
Verhoogen, E., 76
voter registration
  as barrier to voting, 3, 11
  as cost, 102
  in social theory of voter turnout, 102
voter turnout, questions posed by, 1–3
voting
  as act fundamental to American
    citizenship, 48–50, 62–63
    dissenting views, 51
    non-voter views, 53–56
    partisan views, 51–53
  as act of American communality, 58–59
  as act of democratic equality, 57–58
  market pricing, 61–62
  as normatively desirable, 7–8
  as part of authority relationship,
    59–61
  relevance of social dilemmas,
    66–67, 77
  social meaning of, 19, 42–43
    data and methods used, 46–48
voting reforms, 2
  absentee voting, 2
  Motor Voter, 2
Voting Rights Act (1965), and voter
    turnout, 10
voting-eligible population estimations,
    158–159

Washington Post, 47, 49–50
Watts, Duncan J., 186
wealth, and propensity to vote, 2
weekend elections, 11
Wilke, H., 67–68
Work for the Government indicator,
    136–137

yard signs, 100–101

Other books in the series (continued from page iii)

Gary W. Cox, *Making Votes Count: Strategic Coordination in the World's Electoral System*

Gary W. Cox, *The Efficient Secret: The Cabinet and the Development of Political Parties in Victorian England*

Gary W. Cox and Jonathan N. Katz, *Elbridge Gerry's Salamander: The Electoral Consequences of the Reapportionment Revolution*

Raymond M. Duch and Randolph T. Stevenson, *The Economic Vote: How Political and Economic Institutions Condition Election Results*

Jean Ensminger, *Making a Market: The Institutional Transformation of an African Society*

David Epstein and Sharyn O'Halloran, *Delegating Powers: A Transaction Cost Politics Approach to Policy Making under Separate Powers*

Kathryn Firmin-Sellers, *The Transformation of Property Rights in the Gold Coast: An Empirical Study Applying Rational Choice Theory*

Clark C. Gibson, *Politicians and Poachers: The Political Economy of Wildlife Policy in Africa*

Avner Greif, *Institutions and the Path to the Modern Economy: Lessons from Medieval Trade*

Stephen Haber, Armando Razo, and Noel Maurer, *The Politics of Property Rights: Political Instability, Credible Commitments, and Economic Growth in Mexico, 1876–1929*

Ron Harris, *Industrializing English Law: Entrepreneurship and Business Organization, 1720–1844*

Anna L. Harvey, *Votes Without Leverage: Women in American Electoral Politics, 1920–1970*

Murray Horn, *The Political Economy of Public Administration: Institutional Choice in the Public Sector*

John D. Huber, *Rationalizing Parliament: Legislative Institutions and Party Politics in France Jack Knight, Institutions and Social Conflict*

John E. Jackson, Jacek Klich, and Krystyna Poznanska, *The Political Economy of Poland's Transition: New Firms and Reform Governments*

Jack Knight, *Institutions and Social Conflict*

Michael Laver and Kenneth Shepsle, eds., *Cabinet Ministers and Parliamentary Government*

Michael Laver and Kenneth Shepsle, eds., *Making and Breaking Governments: Cabinets and Legislatures in Parliamentary Democracies*

Margaret Levi, *Consent, Dissent, and Patriotism*

Brian Levy and Pablo T. Spiller, eds., *Regulations, Institutions, and Commitment: Comparative Studies of Telecommunications*

Leif Lewin, *Ideology and Strategy: A Century of Swedish Politics,* English ed.

Gary Libecap, *Contracting for Property Rights*

John Londregan, *Legislative Institutions and Ideology in Chile*

Arthur Lupia and Mathew D. McCubbins, *The Democratic Dilemma: Can Citizens Learn What They Need to Know?*

C. Mantzavinos, *Individuals, Institutions, and Markets*

Mathew D. McCubbins and Terry Sullivan, eds., *Congress: Structure and Policy*

Gary J. Miller, *Managerial Dilemmas: The Political Economy of Hierarchy*

Douglass C. North, *Institutions, Institutional Change, and Economic Performance*

Elinor Ostrom, *Governing the Commons: The Evolution of Institutions for Collective Action*

Daniel N. Posner, *Institutions and Ethnic Politics in Africa*

J. Mark Ramseyer, *Odd Markets in Japanese History: Law and Economic Growth*

J. Mark Ramseyer and Frances Rosenbluth, *The Politics of Oligarchy: Institutional Choice in Imperial Japan*

Jean-Laurent Rosenthal, *The Fruits of Revolution: Property Rights, Litigation, and French Agriculture, 1700–1860*

Michael L. Ross, *Timber Booms and Institutional Breakdown in Southeast Asia*

Shanker Satyanath, *Globalization, Politics, and Financial Turmoil: Asia's Banking Crisis*

Norman Schofield, *Architects of Political Change: Constitutional Quandaries and Social Choice Theory*

Norman Schofield and Itai Sened, *Multiparty Democracy: Elections and Legislative Politics*

Alastair Smith, *Election Timing*

Pablo T. Spiller and Mariano Tommasi, *The Instituional Foundations of Public Policy in Argentina: A Transactions Cost Approach*

David Stasavage, *Public Debt and the Birth of the Democratic State: France and Great Britain, 1688–1789*

Charles Stewart III, *Budget Reform Politics: The Design of the Appropriations Process in the House of Representatives, 1865–1921*

George Tsebelis and Jeannette Money, *Bicameralism*

Georg Vanberg, *The Politics of Constitutional Review in Germany*

Nicolas van de Walle, *African Economies and the Politics of Permanent Crisis, 1979–1999*

John Waterbury, *Exposed to Innumerable Delusions: Public Enterprise and State Power in Egypt, India, Mexico, and Turkey*

David L. Weimer, ed., *The Political Economy of Property Rights Institutional Change and Credibility in the Reform of Centrally Planned Economies*